D0912846

You Can't Make This Up!

Educational Leadership and Leaders in Contexts

Founding Editors

Tony Townsend (*Florida Atlantic University, Boca Raton, Florida, USA*)
Ira Bogotch (*Florida Atlantic University, Boca Raton, Florida, USA*)

VOLUME 5

The titles published in this series are listed at *brill.com/ellc*

You Can't Make This Up!

Stories from the Field – Resolving Educational Leadership Dilemmas

By

Linda Rae Markert

BRILL

SENSE

LEIDEN | BOSTON

All chapters in this book have undergone peer review.

The Library of Congress Cataloging-in-Publication Data is available online at http://catalog.loc.gov

Typeface for the Latin, Greek, and Cyrillic scripts: "Brill". See and download: brill.com/brill-typeface.

ISSN 2666-7746
ISBN 978-90-04-43491-2 (paperback)
ISBN 978-90-04-43492-9 (hardback)
ISBN 978-90-04-43686-2 (e-book)

This book is printed on acid-free paper and produced in a sustainable manner.

Advance Praise for
You Can't Make This Up!

"Professor Markert has created an outstanding collection of real-life professional experiences that can serve as actual simulations for both prospective and current school administrators. Such diversified, descriptive testimonials shared by school leaders gives resonance to the challenges and variety of leadership skills needed in today's educational environments. Just to have the chance to view a multitude of dilemmas touching so many different competencies is an excellent leadership training tool that truly encompasses reflective practice."
– **Cheryl A. McElhany, President, Extended Day Child Care Center, Dublin, CA**

"The case studies in this well-written book provide the perfect foundation for fruitful consideration of complex situations that face building leaders every day. It is one thing to be able to name the standards of professional leadership but quite another to be able to apply them from day to day. These case studies will inspire deep and authentic discussions about what did and what could have happened in each case presented. Emerging leaders will find this book a valuable resource for preparing themselves to respond to challenging situations. Current leaders will want to use the case studies as a way to explore with colleagues situations similar to those they have faced, thinking about what they did right and what they might want to change in their future responses."
– **Susan Coultrap-McQuin, Ph.D., Professor Emeritus & Former Provost, State University of New York at Oswego**

"In my years as an education attorney, many school leaders have stated they eventually wanted to write a book about their many *you can't make this up* experiences, and now Linda Rae Markert has done it! These multinational tales from the field provoke informed inquiry, critical analysis, and self-assessment, all in the format of a really good read."
– **Donald E. Budmen, Esq., Education Law Attorney, Ferrara Fiorenza PC, East Syracuse, NY**

"Gather a group of school principals together and you will hear a common refrain; you can't make this up! Ethical decision making, crucial conversations, and dealing with challenging situations are simply part of the job. Where this book really shines is in Markert's deft storytelling and thought-provoking

questions to ponder. Veteran and novice school leaders alike will see their own experiences come alive in the cases making self-reflection possible. Readers will gain new perspectives as they lead in these unique times."
– Beth Anne Lozier, Principal, Camillus Middle School, West Genesee Central School District

Contents

About the Author

Linda Rae Markert
earned her Ed.D. from the University of the Pacific; an M.S. from Illinois State University, and a B.S. from SUNY Oswego. She served more than thirteen years as Dean of SUNY Oswego's School of Education before returning to her full professor position in the Department of Educational Administration in 2011. She currently instructs graduate candidates in the Certificate of Advanced Study program in Educational Leadership. As Dean, she led SUNY Oswego's School of Education (SOE) to receive initial accreditation of its educator certification programs by the National Council for Accreditation of Teacher Education

(NCATE). She provided guidance & oversight for the establishment of many exemplary professional development partnerships with P–12 schools throughout Central New York, and in New York City. She is responsible for bringing over $3 million in external grant funds to SUNY Oswego. One of these funded initiatives is Project BLEND (Building Leadership Excellence for Needs-based Districts), for which she was the Principal Investigator and Director.

Linda received a Visiting Scholar appointment at the Massachusetts Institute of Technology, and completed a leadership symposium at the Harvard Graduate School of Education. In 2019 she completed a sabbatical research project titled "Educational Leadership for Tomorrow: Ethics, Standards & Global Engagement." She has published many refereed articles, several book chapters, and a university level textbook titled *Contemporary Technology: Innovations, Issues & Perspectives* (5th ed., Goodheart-Willcox, 2010).

She is married to William R. Hayes, has a son Alan, and a step-daughter Kathryn.

CHAPTER 1

Overview of This Conversation

Let me tell you a quick story!

This reminds me of that time when a bunch of us got together and .... Boy, did we all learn a valuable lesson!

I hear what you are saying, but tell me what your ideas look like in real life!

Undoubtedly, each of these quirky phrases has been used by all of us, at one time or another, to introduce or spark a lively conversation about an incident or series of incidents that occurred in the recent, or perhaps distant past. Those among us who are gifted with the venerable art of storytelling may arguably, at the same time, be the best teachers, doctors, lawyers, professors, financial advisors, or even school leaders with whom we want to be associated. Why is this? In educational settings, and during our life experiences in the medical, legal or economic professions, the power of storytelling should never be underestimated.

In a similar way, experts who work in the technical, scientific and engineering fields, generally find it necessary to explain complicated formulas and functions in everyday language. They manage this by drawing connections between their research in the laboratory or workshop, and the many ways the results of their labors will be applicable in our daily lives. Although we depend heavily on the expertise of scientists, technicians, and engineers, a significant portion of their collective work is anonymous. Few of us truly understand how or why various machines, tools and devices work the way they do, but we still use them routinely, and with confidence each day. Moreover, we probably purchased them in the first place after listening to a story, in the form of a skillful marketing advertisement, about how they can or will make our lives easier, healthier or happier.

While most of us might not enjoy reading technical manuals, we all take pleasure in hearing authentic tales about the many ways the devices being described can be used in our own homes, offices or workshops. Simply stated, stories serve to simplify complex or difficult subject matter.

Let's shift over to the field of education, and there is no question the vast array of responsibilities, challenges and expectations is becoming more complicated for today's school building leaders. This book focuses on the many

© KONINKLIJKE BRILL NV, LEIDEN, 2020 | DOI: 10.1163/9789004436862_001

competencies women and men need to effectively navigate this ever-chang-ing landscape that is transforming the educational profession. Aspiring educational administrators are expected to grapple with many leadership theories, legislative mandates, school report cards, and government regula-tions as they prepare to move out of their classrooms into leadership posi-tions. In each of these challenging areas of study, personal stories can bring written words, lengthy data charts, and complicated theoretical constructs to life, and thus aid these dedicated scholars in their long-term retention of new knowledge.

1   Beginning an International Conversation among School Leaders

The initial ideas for this book emerged more than a decade before these first conversations with school principals and vice principals began in the early months of 2019. While still holding a position as an academic dean in higher education administration, I spent time in dozens of public schools across the United States, and within my geographic region of residence. These visits afforded numerous opportunities for me to observe students, teachers, staff members, leaders and education candidates navigate their unique journeys vis-à-vis learning and practice. As I gradually began to make the somewhat daunting transition out of administration, to take the step back *up* to a teach-ing position, countless memories of past experiences flooded my head. Since I had been formally away from the classroom for more than thirteen years, the question that haunted me most was this: How will I ever be able to inspire prospective educational leaders as they enter and persist through a rigorous graduate program in order to earn certification in school building leadership? The most comforting response I conceptualized for myself was this: Tell them your own authentic stories!

Along the way I also took note of the many stories practicing school build-ing leaders shared about the unbelievable problems they had been expected to handle. Incredulously, I often wondered – did those things really happen? More often than not, they responded quite simply with these five words – *You can't make this up!* It was then I began to wonder if it might be possible to con-struct a national conversation among school building leaders – one that could highlight a variety of educational leadership dilemmas they had confronted, grappled with, and ultimately resolved.

In the fall of 2018, seventy-five building principals, randomly selected from two dozen school districts dispersed across the United States, were invited to join in this conversation. The number of administrators who agreed to partic-ipate was disappointingly low, and those who responded affirmatively were included. The next effort taken to facilitate the project was to reach out to my vast network of professional colleagues, and ask for their nominations of building principals and vice principals who they believed might be interested in making a contribution to this conversation. All of those individuals were then contacted, and most agreed to set up a meeting with me.

Serendipitously, one of my colleagues, Frederik Ahlgrimm, was then a Research Professor at Universität Potsdam in Germany. When he first learned about the design of this study, he enthusiastically offered to identify a number of school administrators in Germany who might be willing to offer their *Geschichten*. Thus, albeit modest, the conversation had been elevated to an international level. During my time interviewing school leaders in Germany, I had the unexpected good fortune to meet another of Professor Ahlgrimm's research associates who was then the Director of Operations for a K–13 school in Cyprus. He provided me with contact information for the head of the operation, and that school administrator also agreed to contribute her compelling story.

The ultimate goal was to collect a suitable number of stories such that each of the ten *Professional Standards for Educational Leaders* (PSEL) would be addressed minimally twice, and ideally three times (NPBEA, 2015). Ultimately, all but four of the thirty-five stories were recounted by school leaders who are employed in the United States. A combination of face-to-face and synchronous virtual interviews were conducted with school principals and vice principals to gather their stories about critical challenges they had confronted and resolved. The sensitive nature of the incidents described demanded all participants be guaranteed anonymity. Therefore, pseudonyms have been used in every story presented in the succeeding chapters. Resultantly, this book represents the commencement of an international dialog among school building leaders. It is written to allow both emerging educational leaders and practicing school administrators to read a series of short stories recounted by individuals employed in schools across the United States, in Germany and Cyprus.

2 A Context for Using Case Studies

Case studies provide an authentic avenue for leadership candidates to visualize themselves dealing with difficult, often controversial or ethical, issues as they consider various options for solving them (Beckner, 2004; Hayes, 2007; Hoy & Miskell, 2013; Kowalski, 2011; Midlock, 2011; Northouse & Lee, 2015; Reid, 2014; Shapiro & Stefkovich, 2016). In an effort to explain the essence of the case study method in pedagogical terms, a team of public policy researchers offered these ideas:

> The teaching case is a story, a narrative if you will, usually based on actual events and told with a definite teaching purpose. It does not have a correct answer or obvious solution, relying instead on the nature of the real world where answers are difficult to come by and solutions are always contested. [Readers] are introduced to the need to think carefully, to listen to the points made by others and to evaluate those arguments, to review alternative courses of action and their efficacy, and to interpret real-world experience. (Foster, McBeth, & Clemons, 2010, p. 523)

The anthology of present-day stories included in this book highlights the types of challenges school leaders encounter on a daily basis. All of these dilemmas demand informed decisions, and few are ever easily resolved (e.g., social media policies, heightened building security, academic dishonesty within online platforms, verbal/physical abuse and bullying, culturally inclusive school climate, incompetent teachers and/or leaders, etc.). Handwritten notes taken during my conversations with building administrators were transcribed, augmented, converted to a case study format, and aligned with selected elements within one of the ten PSEL. Drafts of the resultant narratives were sent back for review and approval by those educational leaders who "owned" them, and editorial revisions were made as they suggested. The titles of the case studies were initially scripted in my interview notes, and eventually derived from a statement made by one or more of the players in the scenario. They are printed in bold, small caps within each case study.

Perhaps the most significant feature of using case studies, either in teaching or within professional development sessions, is the discussants are essentially called upon to play the role of a decision-maker who is grappling with a situation where some type of immediate action is necessary. The action(s) being considered generally take many forms, a few of which include: examining additional data or evidence, seeking legal counsel, intervening in a crisis to protect someone's safety, or simply listening respectfully to an angry student, parent, or employee. Toward that end in this book, for each of the stories recapped, a number of "questions to ponder" are presented at a critical juncture in the case, providing an authentic avenue for either leadership candidates or leadership teams to visualize themselves dealing with difficult ethical considerations or legal issues as they examine various options for resolving them. Several examples of both ethical leadership options and legislative guidelines are provided in Chapter 12 to give readers a general idea of how they might begin their discourse.

Readers of this collection are encouraged to practice decision-making skills, and coping with ambiguities, before reading the summary statement titled "What Actually Occurred" which accompanies each of the thirty-five cases. Since each case is aligned with selected elements within one of the PSEL, emerging leaders will also become familiar with the competencies they will be expected to demonstrate as school building administrators, upon completion of their graduate programs. Currently employed school leaders will also find this book useful as a professional development reference when they ask their own leadership teams to ponder serious educational dilemmas they may be facing in their own school districts. Another innovative, albeit time consuming, approach to reviewing or examining these cases, entails asking individuals to role-play the parts of the person(s) portrayed in the stories.

3   Ethical Decision-Making & Interview Template

In late August of 2014, the educational community lost a dearly beloved person who had served many years as an effective, and highly compassionate school district superintendent. A copy of the tribute made to Jeanne, who was my colleague and friend, at her funeral service remains in my briefcase to this day, mainly because of this statement: *As a leader, whether the decision was made in a public forum or in the privacy of those closest to her, the questions she asked herself were always the same – Is it ethical? Was the process followed? Was it in the best interest of the kids?*

The fact that the first question this superintendent routinely asked herself centered on ethics resonates with me, since all decisions we make as school leaders must first and foremost be ethical. One might argue that some of the decisions leaders make are straightforward and purely technical (e.g., into which database should a report be filed?), and others might fall into the realm of personal preference (e.g., what color paint should be used in the newly renovated career services center?). For the most part however, educational leaders must make decisions where the well-being of many stakeholders is prominent. As noted above, the most important of these are the students for whom they are first and foremost responsible. And in these instances, it is rare for the decision-maker's options to be cut-and-dried, and easily predicted. In a majority of instances, educational leaders find themselves operating in gray areas where there is more than one solution up for consideration. And, more often than not, the dilemmas they confront are lacking one perfect or "right" solution, but rather pose two or more conflicting "rights."

Gilmour and Kinsella (2009) presented the following nine elements they believe school district administrators should include in their ethical decision-making processes:

- Values and beliefs that are in conflict in this dilemma;
- The individuals who are affected by the decision;
- What is best for the individuals involved;
- What is best for the institution;
- The possible side effects for the decision maker him/herself;
- Future ramifications of this decision;
- Legality of the solution;
- Fairness of the solution; and
- Demonstration of respect and caring for all those involved by the decision-maker. (pp. 122–123)

In many of the cases featured in the forthcoming chapters, one of the "questions to ponder" invites readers to identify any ethical considerations the school leader(s) portrayed should be taking into account. The *Online Cambridge Dictionary*[1] defines *ethics* as the "study of what is morally right and wrong, or a set of beliefs about what is morally right and wrong," and *morally* as being "based on principles that you or people in general consider to be right, honest, or acceptable."

Gilmour and Kinsella's (2009) list of nine elements therefore provides an excellent starting point for readers to use as a tool as they brainstorm ideas regarding a wide variety of leadership dilemmas, and several were included in the interview guidelines described below. Collectively, their inventory encourages educational leaders to determine precisely what additional information or data is needed before they take any action. Readers will notice this exact inquiry often appears in the list of questions included both within, and following the cases presented.

The school building leaders who participated in this international conversation were given a brief interview protocol several weeks in advance of my scheduled meetings with them. Displayed in the chart below, the guidelines were intended to prompt them to recall one or more stories they believed were both educational, and worth sharing with others. The template itself was not used during the interview, which allowed the dialog to move in whatever direction was necessary to get all of the critical facts on the table within a short period of time (i.e., most discussions were completed within 40–45 minutes, several in as few as 20 minutes).

Ethical Dilemmas in Education: Interviews with School Building Leaders

1. Here are several prevailing themes to consider as you recall challenging incidents/events:
   – Equity, Diversity & Cultural Responsiveness
   – Professional Development of Personnel
   – Leadership Capacity & Effectiveness
   – Academic/Curricular Systems
   – School Operations & Management
   – Relationships with Families & Community Members

2. The overarching theme for all should be:
   – Ethical Leadership & Professional Norms

3. Can you describe an incident or series of events that occurred, and subsequently resulted in an ethical dilemma requiring your attention as a school building leader?

4. What values, morals, or beliefs were in conflict for you as you considered the options you might choose to resolve the situation?[2]

5. How did you determine which course of action was best for[3]:
   – The individuals involved?
   – The institution as a whole?

6. Were there any legal issues you needed to consider? If yes, what were they?[4]

7. How did persons react to the decision(s) you made, or action(s) you took as a leader in response to this challenging situation?

8. What other reflections might you want to share regarding this leadership experience?
   – For example, what might you have done differently in the situation you described?

4   Alignment of Case Studies with Professional Standards for
       Educational Leaders

In 2015, following an in-depth, collaborative, and far-reaching review process, the National Policy Board for Educational Administration (NPBEA) endorsed a new set of Professional Standards for Educational Leaders (PSEL). These ten PSEL supplant and expand the previously approved six Interstate Leaders Licensure Consortium (ISLLC) standards, most recently revised in 2008 (American Institutes for Research, 2016). Since the late 1990s, school districts across the United States have used the ISLLC standards to guide the performance review and evaluation process for their building principals and middle level district leaders. As school districts have transitioned from ISLLC standards to the PSEL, three significant differences are being noticed by end users, including: (1) a clearer picture of what leadership practice should look like; (2) an explanation of why specific leadership actions are expected; and (3) a more refined/granular examination of ethical behaviors, and leadership responsibilities regarding cultural competencies.

The case studies you are about to read have been organized into ten chapters, each of which highlights one of the ten PSEL. These standards are foundational to all levels of educational leadership, but "the specific leadership activities [listed as elements] that follow each standard are cast more toward school-level leadership than district-level leadership" (NPBEA, 2015, p. 2). It is for this reason the stories have been aligned to selected elements within one of the ten standards that appeared most predominant in the focal school building leader's actions. In reality, most of the decision-making and problem-solving activities today's educational leaders undertake actually span many elements across more than one standard simultaneously. Therefore, while readers are asked, in the "follow-up questions" after each case, to ascertain the extent to which the principal or vice principal did (or did not) demonstrate the selected competencies within one specific standard, it also makes sense to examine other standards where her/his leadership skills were apparent. This exercise will provide an opportunity for readers to gain a deeper understanding of the PSEL, and acquire a broader view of our educational leadership landscape replete with its many interconnected challenges and complexities.[5]

The current Professional Standards for Educational Leaders (PSEL) are as follows:

1.   *Mission, Vision, and Core Values:* Effective educational leaders develop, advocate, and enact a shared mission, vision, and core values of high-quality education and academic success and well-being of each student.

2. *Ethics and Professional Norms*: Effective educational leaders act ethically and according to professional norms to promote each student's academic success and well-being.

3. *Equity and Cultural Responsiveness*: Effective educational leaders strive for equity of educational opportunity and culturally responsive practices to promote each student's academic success and well-being.

4. *Curriculum, Instruction, and Assessment*: Effective educational leaders develop and support intellectually rigorous and coherent systems of curriculum, instruction, and assessment to promote each student's academic success and well-being.

5. *Community of Care and Support for Students*: Effective educational leaders cultivate an inclusive, caring, and supportive school community that promotes the academic success and well-being of each student.

6. *Professional Capacity of School Personnel*: Effective educational leaders develop the professional capacity and practice of school personnel to promote each student's academic success and well-being.

7. *Professional Community for Teachers and Staff*: Effective educational leaders foster a professional community of teachers and other professional staff to promote each student's academic success and well-being.

8. *Meaningful Engagement of Families and Community*: Effective educational leaders engage families and the community in meaningful, reciprocal, and mutually beneficial ways to promote each student's academic success and well-being.

9. *Operations and Management*: Effective educational leaders manage school operations and resources to promote each student's academic success and well-being.

10. *School Improvement*: Effective educational leaders act as agents of continuous improvement to promote each student's academic success and well-being.

With these national standards in mind, let me tell you some stories! If at some level, they remind you of your own experiences in leadership, it is conceivable you might want to share them with us to include in a future version of this book!

Notes

1 See https://dictionary.cambridge.org/us/
2 Questions adapted from Gilmour and Kinsella's (2009) nine elements for ethical decision-making.

3   Questions adapted from Gilmour and Kinsella's (2009) nine elements for ethical deci-
    sion-making.
4   Questions adapted from Gilmour and Kinsella's (2009) nine elements for ethical deci-
    sion-making.
5   A download (PDF) of the standards can be found at: http://npbea.org/psel/

References

American Institutes for Research. (2016). *The Professional Standards for Educational
    Leaders (PSEL) 2015 and the Interstate Leaders Licensure Consortium (ISLLC) stan-
    dards 2008: A crosswalk.* Washington, DC: Center on Great Teachers and Leaders.
Beckner, W. (2004). *Ethics for educational leaders.* Boston, MA: Allyn and Bacon.
Foster, R. H., McBeth, M. K., & Clemons, R. S. (2010). Public policy pedagogy: Mixing
    methodologies using case studies. *Journal of Public Affairs Education, 16*(4), 517–540.
Gilmour, S. L., & Kinsella, M. P. (2009). *Succeeding as a female superintendent: How to
    get there and stay there.* Lanham, MD: Rowman & Littlefield Education.
Hayes, W. (2007). *All new real-life case studies for school administrators.* Lanham, MD:
    Rowman & Littlefield Education.
Hoy, W. K., & Miskel, C. G. (2013). *Educational administration: Theory, research and
    practice* (9th ed.). New York, NY: McGraw-Hill.
Kowalski, T. J. (2011). *Case studies on educational administration* (6th ed.). Boston, MA:
    Allyn and Bacon.
Midlock, S. F. (2011). *Case studies for educational leadership: Solving administrative
    dilemmas.* Upper Saddle River, NJ: Pearson Education Inc.
National Policy Board for Educational Administration (NPBEA). (2015). *Professional
    standards for educational leaders 2015.* Reston, VA: Author. Retrieved from
    http://npbea.org/psel/
Northouse, P. G., & Lee, M. E. (2015). *Leadership case studies in education.* Thousand
    Oaks, CA: Sage Publications, Inc.
Online Cambridge Dictionary. (2020, March 22). Retrieved from
    https://dictionary.cambridge.org/us/
Reid, D. J. (2014). *Dilemmas in educational leadership: The facilitator's book of cases.*
    New York, NY: Teachers College Press.
Shapiro, J. P., & Stefkovich, J. A. (2016). *Ethical leadership and decision making in educa-
    tion* (4th ed.). New York, NY: Routledge.

CHAPTER 2

Mission, Vision and Core Values

1 Are We Doing Enough?

PSEL – **Standard 1:** Effective educational leaders develop, advocate, and enact a shared mission, vision, and core values of high-quality education and academic success and well-being of each student

Selected Elements:
1b – In collaboration with members of the school and the community and using relevant data, develop and promote a vision for the school on the successful learning and development of each child and on instructional and organizational practices that promote such success.
1c – Articulate, advocate, and cultivate core values that define the school's culture and stress the imperative of child-centered education.
1e – Review the school's mission and vision and adjust them to changing expectations and opportunities for the school, and changing needs and situations of students.
1f – Develop shared understanding of and commitment to mission, vision, and core values within the school and the community.

1.1 *The Story*

When Mr. Terrence Fairbrother was appointed principal of Aspirational High School (AHS), his faculty members had seen two other principals come and go within the previous four years. The public's perceptions of the school were extremely low, and Mr. Fairbrother was determined to turn things around in that regard. He was convinced members of the community were only seeing negative things about the high school, and were unaware of the many exceptional programs being offered. The school, located in a large city, enrolled approximately 300 students in grades 9–12 and employed 56 teachers, all but 4 of whom had been hired before Principal Fairbrother's arrival. Two assistant principals also reported to him

The school's vision statement included phrasing that highlighted global citizenship, social competencies, academic skills, perseverance, and the desire to thrive as college/career ready graduates. As he began to make connections with members of the local neighborhoods where his students resided, Terrence Fairbrother repeatedly articulated these core values, thus describing what he believed to be true about Aspirational High School's high quality educational programs and opportunities. His personal vision involved a concerted effort to focus on restorative practices and trauma-informed instruction. Principal Fairbrother also knew it was critical to re-build bridges with members of his school community, and therefore used an event he called enrollment cookouts as one way to achieve this goal.

On numerous occasions, through front porch chats, he encouraged parents, family members and community representatives to help him re-brand Aspirational High School. The principal provided them with various positive messages about the school, and suggested they use them to counter the negative stories others might be espousing around the region. Terrence Fairbrother envisioned himself to be a principal both inside and outside of his school building, and continually asked teachers and members of his leadership team "ARE WE DOING ENOUGH?" Specifically, are we doing enough to make our high school a place where students want to be, where they like to be, and where they feel safe? Are we doing enough to help these kids be successful, both here and when they leave us?

During the first months of his tenure as principal, as Terrence Fairbrother actively championed initiatives to achieve the school's vision, a number of unfortunate events unfolded in the immediate vicinity of the building. On one occasion, two of his school's students attempted to rob an older woman who was walking to her vehicle. They hit her with a pole and then proceeded to break into her car. They were arrested and did not return to this high school.

It was not uncommon for Aspirational High School's students to make ill-advised decisions, and when they were found breaking the law, community members and the media routinely identified them as AHS kids. In one tragic incident, a member of the student body was killed which sent ripples of despondency throughout the school and local neighborhood.

A large majority of the teachers and professional staff at Aspirational High School admitted to feeling extremely demoralized. They expressed themselves during faculty meetings, making statements like: "I'm feeling so defeated! No matter what I do in class to help them make better choices, the kids continually manage to get themselves into trouble." Similarly, "I thought I'd finally gotten through to Mariella, and now we find out she was caught trying to steal a tube of lipstick from the convenience store." Principal Fairbrother listened to these and many other sentiments, and reflected on how he envisioned the future of Aspirational High School might evolve during his tenure.

1.2   *Questions to Ponder*

1.   If you were Terrence Fairbrother, what actions might you take at this point?
2.   Can you identify any ethical considerations he should be taking into account while attempting to resolve this case?
3.   How do you anticipate his ultimate decisions will impact the persons involved (e.g. students, teachers, staff members, families, community-at-large, etc.)?

1.3   *What Actually Occurred?*

Over the course of several months, beginning in mid-October, Principal Fairbrother spearheaded a multi-faceted approach to respond to the diverse needs of the students, teachers, professional staff members, administrators and families to whom he felt responsible. He assembled smaller teams of teachers and staff personnel to assess their levels of awareness about how restorative practices were being used in other schools across the region, and in school districts in neighboring states. Through this needs assessment he was able to work with district office leaders to design a series of targeted professional development sessions for his staff in an effort to help them develop new instructional strategies.

All teachers were shown ways to ensure they being were intentional as they created new lessons to meet the needs of every student in their classrooms. Teachers were encouraged to work together each morning to collaboratively develop engaging activities for their students. Principal Fairbrother was able to hire an external consultant who introduced his staff to issues related to trauma, providing evidence-based best practices for them to consider. Through sensitivity training, they were taught what actually happens to the brain when students are routinely exposed to traumatic incidents in their lives.

The school psychologist, who had expertise in group therapy, psychological assessment, and student counseling, facilitated a series of gender-specific assemblies for all students in the building. On a monthly basis, the boys were brought together to discuss and practice ways to avoid behaviors that might be labeled "toxic masculinity." Guest speakers, coupled with contemporary films, introduced them to a wide variety of ways they could begin to earn their own money while still attending high school. The girls convened separately and participated in activities where they discussed positive self-image, confidence, resilience, and collaborative problem-solving.

By late January, Terrence Fairbrother had started to see some positive shifts in two data points. Overall, daily attendance had increased from 63% (same time previous year) to 67%. And, when polled about their sense of belonging in Aspirational High School, the number of students who felt positive about their school had increased from 43% (same time previous year) to 51%. While proud of these improvements, the principal knew AHS had not yet become a comprehensive restorative justice school. Viewing the entire educational community as a work in progress, Terrence envisioned the establishment of a "peace room" in the building, combined with "peace centers" to be created by the teachers in all classrooms.

Mr. Fairbrother, together with his leadership team, continued to support teachers and staff members, and continually reminded them that their students wanted to please them. His constant refrain was this: "Keep building positive relationships with your kids every day, and they will want to be here learning with you every day! Keep asking yourselves, are we doing enough?"

1.4   *Follow-up Questions*

1. To what extent did Principal Terrence Fairbrother demonstrate (or fail to demonstrate) the selected leadership competencies identified above for PSEL #1 – *Mission, Vision and Core Values?*

2. What other strategies might this principal employ to improve the public's general perceptions regarding the mission, vision and core values of Aspirational High School?

2   I Am Your Child's Advocate

PSEL – **Standard 1:** Effective educational leaders develop, advocate, and enact a shared mission, vision, and core values of high-quality education and academic success and well-being of each student.

Selected Elements:
1a – Develop an educational mission for the school to promote the academic success and well-being of each student.

1b – In collaboration with members of the school and the community and using relevant data, develop and promote a vision for the school on the successful learning and development of each child and on instructional and organizational practices that promote such success.

1c – Articulate, advocate, and cultivate core values that define the school's culture and stress the imperative of child-centered education.

1e – Review the school's mission and vision and adjust them to changing expectations and opportunities for the school, and changing needs and situations of students.

1g – Model and pursue the school's mission, vision, and core values in all aspects of leadership.

2.1   *The Story*

Ms. Diana Vernon-Clarke is principal of a large, relatively new, elementary school located in a suburban neighborhood. The school enrolls 925 students in grades K–5. Twenty-seven of these students have IEPs and receive special education services through the school's resource program. One vice principal, a psychologist, and 45 teachers are employed in the school. At the time when the events in this story occurred, Diana Vernon-Clarke was in her fourth year as principal. Prior to receiving this appointment, she had served as vice principal for six years, and had been a special education teacher for three years in another elementary school in the same district.

The District Office has placed three full-day special education classrooms (K–1, 2–3 & 4–5) for students who have moderate-to-severe disabilities in Principal Vernon-Clarke's building. Approximately 26 children receive their academic programs in these self-contained facilities. Most teachers take part in the school's reverse mainstreaming program where, on a weekly basis, their students are given opportunities to share in the classroom activities within one of these three specialized learning environments.

Since her initial appointment as the building's leader, Diana has fostered a vibrant creative and inclusive culture among all teachers, professional staff members, and students. The school's slogan – *Create ~ Learn ~ Inspire* – is featured throughout the building. In establishing the reverse mainstreaming program, Diana knew all students would become more aware of differing abilities, and would learn about the true meaning of unity, kindness and compassion in their lives.

The school district's vision and mission statements were Board Approved at the start of Ms. Vernon-Clarke's second year as principal. These statements include words that emphasize the importance of lifelong learning, resilience, and success in a global society. The district's entire leadership team embraces the following core values: maximizing learning; building professional learning communities; nurturing supportive relationships; and respecting the skills, knowledge and experience all stakeholders bring to the district's educational community.

Jade and Stanley Nguyen relocated from a large urban center to this suburban school district when their son Robbie was about to enter the 1st grade, which was coincidentally the same year Ms. Vernon-Clarke became principal. Two years earlier, they had suffered the tragic loss of their eleven year old daughter, who was hit and killed by a drunk driver while she was riding her bicycle. The Nguyens were admittedly quite protective of Robbie who was autistic, and unfailingly attended all of the meetings regarding the development and approval of his IEP. Principal Vernon-Clarke had therefore gotten to know both of Robbie's parents quite well during her tenure as the building leader.

Having earned her teaching certification in Special Education, Diana was fully aware of the fact that parents, who had children with special needs, generally had a clear assessment of their daughter's or son's abilities. The parents accepted the fact Robbie required a one-on-one aid to support him in the blended general education classroom, with the additional assistance of a resource teacher. That said, they remained optimistic he would ultimately attend a prestigious university to earn a degree in civil engineering. Toward that end, Mr. and Dr. Nguyen went to many extremes to ensure Robbie received a well-rounded, fully inclusive general education.

By way of example, Stanley Nguyen brought in a preferred coach to work with Robbie during recess, assisting him with basketball skills. This intervention enabled Robbie, then in 3rd grade, to feel like a star player, and his classmates enjoyed the personalized coaching as well. An uninformed observer would simply see all of the kids playing together, and not notice anyone had special needs of any type.

Similarly, Dr. Jade Nguyen located a preferred science text, and asked Principal Vernon-Clarke to direct Robbie's teachers to incorporate this resource in their instruction for him. The textbook presented the more complex 4th grade scientific concepts, and was written at a simplified reading level. Diana respectfully received Robbie's mom's request, and his teachers dutifully added the book to the other classroom supports they had created for him.

Over the years, Robbie's teachers had all contributed to his IEP meetings, and had conscientiously reported on his progress within each grade level. As they worked tirelessly with the school psychologist, resource teacher, vice principal and principal to develop an IEP in response to the ever-widening gap Robbie's teachers were noting, everyone made these two comments: (1) "He always tries really hard!" And (2) "We are consistently taking extreme measures to provide additional instructional supports for him." Now as a 4th grade student, Robbie is still working at a 1st grade level in most classroom activities. And, the team found that his academic growth was evident primarily during the class times when he received resource services, using curricula taught at his own developmental level.

Principal Vernon-Clarke subsequently contacted Robbie's parents and requested they meet with her, and the team, to discuss recommendations regarding their son's placement for the following year. When they arrived for the discussion the next morning, Ms. Vernon-Clarke opened by saying,

> First and foremost, I AM YOUR CHILD'S ADVOCATE. I have taken a personal interest in Robbie, and have routinely visited him in his classrooms at

every grade level. Our recommendations at this point are based soundly on the results of the many different grade-specific assessments your son has completed.

The Nguyens were tremendously disappointed to hear Diana and her team surmise their only child needed a smaller, more specialized classroom environment. Their response to the principal's suggestion was immediate and quite emphatic – Dr. Jade Nguyen said

> There's no way we will allow you to transfer our Robbie to another school! He belongs here, and has every right to be in a *normal* 5th grade classroom next year, along with the same classmates he has been with since we registered him in this school four years ago. And, you can be sure we will take you to court if it's necessary to keep him here.

2.2   *Questions to Ponder*

1. If you were Diana Vernon-Clarke, what actions might you take at this point?
2. Can you identify any ethical considerations she should be taking into account while attempting to resolve this case?
3. How do you anticipate her ultimate decisions will impact the persons involved (e.g. Robbie, Jade and Stanley Nguyen, other students, teachers, staff members, families, community-at-large, etc.)?

2.3   *What Actually Occurred?*

Diana Vernon-Clarke was no stranger to difficult conversations with family members, so she graciously stood up as Dr. Nguyen ended her statement, and thanked them for coming in to discuss Robbie's learning needs. The principal promised the boy's parents she would review her notes, and convene another IEP meeting to which they would be invited. She then proceeded to escort the disgruntled couple through the Main Office complex, and out to the building's single point of entry.

As she watched them walk to their car, Diana reflected on the many meetings she had had with the Nguyens throughout Robbie's young life as a student in her building. It seemed to her they had made specialized requests on his behalf, on an almost monthly basis, since the middle of his 2nd grade placement. Ms. Vernon-Clarke knew it was critically important to create and sustain collaborative relationships with families for the benefit of all students, and she had worked hard to do just that.

Diana was delighted when family members became engaged partners in their children's education, but wondered aloud if Robbie's mom and dad had become overly optimistic about their son's academic abilities, and his social and emotional well-being in school. She recalled the IEP meeting the Nguyens had attended the previous year in preparation for their son's 4th grade placement.

During that session, the team reviewed Robbie's cumulative progress, and noted he had failed to make eight out of the ten goals written in his IEP. Most notably, Robbie was found lacking the language skills to stay on pace with his classmates, which was significantly impacting his ability to show growth in all subject areas, and further widening his learning gap. His teachers affirmed Robbie was a member of their class, but his presence occasionally proved disruptive for other students in the room. Regardless, the Nguyens refused to sign the IEP specifying a specialized classroom, and insisted Robbie be advanced, and be placed in the regular education 4th grade classroom. The District Office subsequently approved this placement.

Ms. Vernon-Clarke sat in her office and thoroughly reviewed the assessment scores, grade level reports, and handwritten notes that had accumulated in Robbie Nguyen's folder over four years. She knew the boy had intelligence, and had the capacity to learn – however, it remained apparent he was learning differently and more slowly than his grade level peers. He had performed well in 1st grade, and just slightly below grade level in 2nd grade. As the instructional pace accelerated in the 3rd, and now 4th grades, Robbie had fallen further and further behind.

While Diana fully sympathized with Dr. and Mr. Nguyen's convictions their son was ready to be promoted to the 5th grade, she knew this decision was both unethical, and would not be in Robbie's best interests overall. She held these beliefs in her mind as she scheduled a follow-up IEP meeting for Robbie Nguyen to take place the following week.

There were 18 persons in the room for this IEP discussion, including: five of Robbie's teachers, one resource teacher, Director of Special Education Programming, school psychologist, principal, vice principal, reading specialist, speech therapist, Dr. & Mr. Nguyen, the Nguyen's attorney, and three educational consultants the Nguyens had hired to review their son's academic records. At the end of several hours wherein all stakeholders' voices were heard, Principal Vernon-Clarke had *successfully* facilitated the development of a new IEP for 5th grade that specified a series of new learning goals for Robbie.

Regardless, as the meeting disbanded, Ms. Vernon-Clarke struggled to pronounce the meeting *successful* since Robbie's parents remained dissatisfied with the team's recommendations regarding an alternate placement for their son in a mild-to-moderate specialized classroom located in another of the district's elementary schools. Diana knew in her heart the Nguyens would reject the new IEP, and its prescribed alternate educational setting. The principal also believed this would prove disastrous for the young boy as he labored unnecessarily in an unsuitable learning environment.

Robbie's case was in fact reviewed several more times by the District Office's administration throughout the summer, and he was ultimately assigned to return to attend 5th grade in Principal Vernon-Clarke's elementary school. Diana could not help but question the extent to which this decision accommodated the parents' wishes, at the expense of meeting one of the school district's core values – maximizing learning for Robbie Nguyen.

2.4 *Follow-up Questions*

1. To what extent did Principal Diana Vernon-Clarke demonstrate (or fail to demonstrate) the selected leadership competencies identified above for PSEL #1 – *Mission, Vision and Core Values?*
2. What additional strategies might Ms. Vernon-Clarke have tried to best meet the special learning needs of Robbie Nguyen?
3. Can you identify any ethical considerations she should be taking into account while attempting to resolve this case?

3 #Enough

PSEL – Standard 1: Effective educational leaders develop, advocate, and enact a shared mission, vision, and core values of high-quality education and academic success and well-being of each student.

Selected Elements:
1b – In collaboration with members of the school and the community and using relevant data, develop and promote a vision for the school on the successful learning and development of each child and on instructional and organizational practices that promote such success.
1c – Articulate, advocate, and cultivate core values that define the school's culture and stress the imperative of child-centered education.
1d – Strategically develop, implement, and evaluate actions to achieve the vision for the school.
1e – Review the school's mission and vision and adjust them to changing expectations and opportunities for the school, and changing needs and situations of students.
1f – Develop shared understanding of and commitment to mission, vision, and core values within the school and the community.

3.1   *The Story*

At the time when the events in this story unfolded, Christa Zaner was in her tenth year as principal of a middle school where she had also served four years as vice principal. Located in a suburban neighborhood, the school enrolls 650 students in grades 5–8, and employs 55 full-time teachers, approximately 50% of whom were hired by Ms. Zaner. An additional 12 part-time teachers share their time between this school and the other middle school in the district. One vice principal reports to Principal Zaner.

The school's vision and mission statements were recently revised when the district hired its new superintendent, Dr. Owen Rausch. Following a series of leadership team sessions and community forums facilitated by Dr. Rausch, the resultant statements were collaboratively written to include phrasing that highlights authentic learning, civic duty, wellness, inspiration, personal success and innovative programming. The district now lists its priorities in four areas – teaching and learning, positive and safe school environment, community partnerships, and fiscal accountability. A new slogan is featured alongside the school district's logo – *Enter to Learn ~ Leave to Achieve!*

In the days following the horrific mass shooting at Marjory Stoneman Douglas High School in Parkland, Florida, thousands of students across the nation found ways to speak out about gun violence, school safety, and senseless bullying. Amidst intense media coverage, anxiety levels among students and teachers at all grade levels intensified, and the number of school absences rose significantly.

Principal Zaner, who herself is the mother of four school-aged children, observed these realities firsthand in her middle school. She and her vice principal found themselves taking a significantly greater number of phone calls, and email messages from concerned family members, who all wanted to know what precautions were being taken to ensure the safety and well-being of their children.

While Ms. Zaner had always made a point of visiting her teachers' classrooms on a regular basis, she felt compelled to be even more vigilant and visible throughout the day in an effort to calm everyone's nervous fears. It was during one of her drop-in visits to a 7th grade Study Hall that she discovered three students working together to create a colorful poster containing these words: #ENOUGH: *Protect Kids Not Guns – We Want to LIVE to Achieve!*

Christa couldn't help but notice the students' intentional play on the words of the school district's slogan, and decided to question them about the purpose of their poster. They respectfully shared the details of several Social Studies classes focused on civic engagement and responsibility, to which they had contributed. It was during one of those discussions they had learned about the forthcoming National Walkout Day planned to take place exactly one month following the date of the tragedy in Parkland, Florida.

The students candidly informed Principal Zaner they intended to rally their classmates to participate in this walkout, and their poster would be one of many to be carried during this important event. Ms. Zaner thanked the students for their honesty, and also reminded them about the Student Code of Conduct which describes the consequences for unexcused absences.

When she returned to her office, Christa called Superintendent Rausch's Administrative Assistant and requested a return phone call at his earliest convenience. Later that afternoon, Dr. Rausch showed up at the middle school to meet with her in person.

In the hours prior to the superintendent's unexpected arrival, Principal Zaner had received anxious messages from a dozen or so of her 7th and 8th grade teachers asking what they were supposed to do if their kids walked out of class as planned on March 14th the following week. The principal's administrative assistant also informed her about several parents who had called to say "under no circumstances should the school try to prohibit my son or daughter from walking out of school as planned, and their rights to freedom of expression should be protected." An equal number of family members left emphatic messages to imply they wanted their sons and daughters "to be kept safe and secure in their classrooms during the possible walkout." Apparently the small, and very vocal group of 7th grade students had already begun to recruit their classmates to join their peers across the country in speaking out against needless, and seemingly endless school violence.

Dr. Rausch listened intently as Ms. Zaner recounted these stories told to her by zealous students, concerned family members, anxious teachers, and inquisitive staff members. He knew intuitively that similar stories would likely be reported to him by the leaders in the other middle school and high school in the district. Prior to assembling his leadership team to discuss a plan of action, and knowing Christa Zaner was one of the district's more experienced school administrators, he solicited her thoughts regarding the impending situation that threatened to jeopardize one of the district's highest priorities.

3.2   *Questions to Ponder*

1.   What insights and recommendations should Principal Zaner offer to Superintendent Rausch?

2.   Can you identify any ethical considerations she should be taking into account while attempting to resolve this case?

3.   How do you anticipate her suggestions will impact the ultimate plan of action agreed upon by the district, and the persons involved (e.g. students, teachers, staff members, families, community-at-large, etc.)?

4.   To what extent is she demonstrating (or neglecting to demonstrate) the competencies identified above for PSEL #1 – *Mission, Vision and Core Values?*

3.3   *What Actually Occurred?*

Christa Zaner immediately reminded Superintendent Rausch that they did not have the luxury of time on their side. And, while it might be judicious to solicit input from all invested stakeholders, many of the 7th and 8th grade students in her building seemed intent on joining the national movement to participate in the walkout in exactly one week. Family and community members had lots of questions, and they expected to receive answers. The bottom line was this – it was imperative to get all members of the school district's leadership team on the same page, and have them be prepared to deliver a consistent message.

Dr. Rausch subsequently instructed each of the two middle school principals and the high school principal to "hit the pause button and do nothing for a couple of days." He decided to wait and see how superintendents in other school districts around the State and in neighboring States were planning to handle the situation in their school buildings. Needless to say, this brief waiting period caused a fair amount of confusion as Christa and her leadership colleagues continued to deal with the onslaught of telephone calls and email messages from concerned parents and family members.

Principal Zaner was relieved to ultimately receive news on Friday that her school district would follow suit with others in the region. Specifically, students were told definitively there would be consequences if they chose to leave the school building to participate in the walkout on Wednesday, March 14th the following week. In the dual interest of safety and honoring the civic engagement the students were demonstrating, Superintendent Rausch also allowed the building principals to create an alternative location inside their buildings for students to gather instead of leaving the premises. Christa couldn't help feeling like the plan of action felt somewhat rushed, and worried that everyone might not be fully on board, and knowledgeable about what they were supposed to do.

On the Monday prior to the National Walkout Day, Principal Zaner held a series of private meetings with the small group of 7th and 8th grade students who appeared to be leading the cause among their peers. They were informed about the transformation of the Large Group Instruction Room to be the internal walkout space. She tried to convince them to take their posters and march to this alternative interior location vs. departing from the building. Ms. Zaner explained the consequences for students leaving their classrooms at all would be greater for those who left the building, so it would be wise for them to stay inside. Principal Zaner also convened a brief faculty meeting at the end of the day on Monday to debrief with the teachers and staff members, a majority of whom had expressed support for the students who planned to participate in the walkout.

Teachers were told to stay in their classrooms, and continue to provide instruction for all students who remained. The principal surveyed all teachers who were free during the planned timeframe for the walkout to see who might be: either willing to supervise the students in the alternative interior space; or agreeable to be stationed at an exit door, and ready to accompany any students who chose to leave the building.

The superintendent made contact with members of the local fire and police departments to solicit additional support. He also described all aspects of the action plan to the district's two School Resource Officers (SRO).

As fate would have it, inclement weather caused the district to close all schools on Wednesday, and the school building principals breathed a collective sigh of relief. Ms. Zaner believed that fully 50% of the 7th and 8th grade students would have walked out of their classrooms to participate in the national event.

Very soon thereafter, the Superintendent held several community forums to allow students, families, and community members to share their ideas regarding school safety, security, and acts of violence/bullying. Some expressed a desire for metal detectors to be installed, and many others stated they didn't want their kids to attend a school that felt like a prison. The need for additional mental health counseling support was clearly articulated, and students themselves noted they felt safer when an SRO was present in their building.

The students in Ms. Zaner's middle school let her know they felt, as a result of the unexpected snow day, they had lost their chance to vocalize their views regarding the critical need for social change. The principal used this opportunity to facilitate a planned session as a substitute for the national walkout event. Three teachers agreed to work with her to organize a viewing of a brief *Rachel's Challenge* informational video on April 20th, the anniversary of the Columbine High School mass shooting in 1999. Approximately thirty 7th grade students attended the lunchtime event during which they were allowed to openly express their concerns and fears related to violence in schools. Those who attended seemed disappointed that so few of their peers, who most likely would have walked out of class on March 14th, actually showed up to participate on April 20th.

The school district has since hired an additional SRO, so each of the district's school buildings has immediate protection when necessary. Principal Zaner, like many others in her position, continues to support and work closely with her teachers in an ongoing effort to ensure students feel safe, and also empowered to articulate their diverse points of view in a respectful manner. Christa Zaner also wrote a proposal that convinced Superintendent Rausch to allocate funds in the budget that brings *Rachel's Challenge*[1] into their schools on an annual basis.

3.4   *Follow-up Questions*

1. To what extent did Christa Zaner demonstrate (or fail to demonstrate) the selected leadership competencies identified above for PSEL #1 – *Mission, Vision and Core Values?*
2. What could Ms. Zaner have done differently to ensure the middle school students in her building were kept safe, and also allowed to express their viewpoints regarding school violence?

Note

1   *Rachel's Challenge* is a bullying and school violence abatement program founded by Darrell Scott. He is the father of Rachel Scott who was the first student killed in the Columbine High School mass shooting in 1999. The programs exist to equip and inspire individuals to replace acts of violence, bullying, and negativity with acts of respect, kindness, and compassion. See https://rachelschallenge.org

CHAPTER 3

Ethics and Professional Norms

1   Do I Blow the Whistle?

PSEL – Standard 2 – Ethics & Professional Norms: Effective educational leaders act ethically and according to professional norms to promote each student's academic success and well-being.

Selected Elements:
2a – Act ethically and professionally in personal conduct, relationships with others, decision-making, stewardship of the school's resources, and all aspects of school leadership.
2c – Place children at the center of education and accept responsibility for each student's academic success and well-being.
2d – Safeguard and promote the values of democracy, individual freedom and responsibility, equity, social justice, community and diversity.
2e – Lead with interpersonal and communication skill, social-emotional insight, and understanding of all students' and staff members' backgrounds and cultures.

1.1   *The Story*

Dr. Rhonda Taft had been principal of her school in a large suburban district for more than a decade when a series of personnel-related events unfolded. Her high school was one of three in the district and enrolled approximately 1800 students in grades 9–12. Approximately 150 teachers were employed at the school, many of whom Dr. Taft had hired during her tenure. Three assistant principals also reported to her.

Over the years Principal Taft discerned the district's upper administrative team was overly obsessed with test scores and their schools' publicly available report cards. Several superintendents were hired and then left during her tenure, but each seemed to display a similar leadership style making constant demands of the district's team of dedicated school building leaders. In some cases, Dr. Taft received instructions from the District Office she felt she couldn't ethically abide by or respect.

By way of example, years earlier, and shortly after Dr. Taft assumed the principal's position at the school, she became aware of several practices that

© KONINKLIJKE BRILL NV, LEIDEN, 2020 | DOI: 10.1163/9789004436862_003

concerned her. A brief description of three such instances will provide context for her story.

One state exam a significant percentage of students had difficulty passing was Algebra I. In an effort to reduce the number of students who might officially fail this standardized assessment, AVID (Advancement Via Individual Determination) Math classes were established in the high school schedules. At a specific point in the year, students who were "on the bubble" for being able to pass Algebra I were transferred into the AVID course. They were still allowed to take the Algebra I exam, and, if they did well enough, the name of the course on their transcript was revised to show they had actually completed Algebra I. If they did poorly, as AVID students their scores didn't affect the overall Algebra I pass rate for the school.

Second, Principal Taft also learned the school had a practice of double blocking its Advance Placement courses in several disciplines including United States History and Physics. This scheduling strategy allowed students to get credit twice for essentially completing one class, which Rhonda knew was not legal.

Finally, the high school had a highly regarded "powerhouse" athletics program. Star athletes often received special dispensations when it came to the school's Code of Conduct. Stated differently, they were not always held to the same standards with regard to course grades and attendance as other students. Specifically, at the end of the first quarter marking period, the football team's star wide receiver was allowed to play in a game against a rival team despite the fact he had earned a D- in two of his junior level courses.

Dr. Taft made it a point to meet regularly with her leadership team to be certain they fully understood and complied with the published policies and procedures found in both the Students' and Teachers' Codes of Conduct. She provided support and guidance for her school counselors in a swift effort to rectify each of the above described improper practices.

As appropriate, Rhonda also found time to meet with teachers, staff members and families to keep communication channels open as various changes were implemented. In her heart she knew she had been hired to turn things around in this high school. Dr. Taft was fully confident she had the collaborative ability, social-emotional insight and moral obligation to safeguard the values of democracy, individual freedom and responsibility, equity, social justice, community and diversity. Ultimately she and her team members did just that, and the students in her building won several prestigious awards.

Even still, as time passed it was difficult for her to sit in district-led leadership meetings knowing these (and other) nefarious habits were still ongoing in the other schools. She wondered if their higher test scores were in fact earned by students in an honest and principled manner. More than once she found herself looking into the rearview mirror on her drive home asking "**DO I BLOW THE WHISTLE?** Or, do I keep my mouth shut – knowing full well things are being run ethically in my own building?"

During the final quarter of the year being highlighted in this case, Interim Superintendent Frederick Newley contacted Dr. Taft to let her know he was placing an Assistant Principal (AP) in her building to serve out the remainder term. This not yet tenured AP was apparently having some difficulty in the elementary school where he had been hired two years previously, and the building principal had requested he be removed. Mr. Newley also informed Principal Taft she would not be expected to submit a formal evaluation of Maxwell "Max" Buchanan's performance as her new AP since it was so late in the year. Dr. Taft was happy to have the extra administrator in her building and made it a point to provide Mr. Buchanan with a thorough orientation as he joined her team. Remarkably, Max Buchanan quickly developed a rapport with the 10th grade students assigned to him, and was well liked by the other three APS.

As the year drew to a close, Dr. Taft received an email message from Interim Superintendent Newley requiring her to complete a written evaluation of AP Buchanan. Rhonda made a call to Mr. Newley to remind him about the initial agreement he had made with her when Mr. Buchanan was placed in her building only five weeks earlier. He held firm regardless and informed her that the written evaluation had to be uploaded into the Human Resource (HR) portal by the end of the week! Having only seen Max's performance in her building, Dr. Taft completed the rubric honestly giving him scores of "Effective," or even "Highly Effective" in a couple cases, for nearly all indicators. She kept a copy of her report before filing it, well in advance of the Interim Superintendent's stated deadline.

Ten days later Mr. Buchanan showed up in Dr. Taft's office to say he had received her evaluation from HR, and learned he had been scored as either "Developing" or "Ineffective" across the board. The Interim Superintendent had therefore determined he should be dismissed from his position. Max asked Principal Taft if she might be willing to discuss this with him.

1.2   *Questions to Ponder*

1.   What series of actions should Principal Rhonda Taft take at this point?
2.   Can you identify any ethical considerations she should be taking into account while attempting to resolve this case? (See Chapter 12, Section 1)
3.   What do you expect she might say right away to Max Buchanan?
4.   How do you anticipate her actions and/or decisions will impact the persons involved (e.g. Max, other APS, students, HR Administration, Interim Superintendent, community-at-large, etc.)?

1.3   *What Actually Occurred?*

While it was definitely a challenge to not reveal her shock/disbelief upon hearing the news from Max Buchanan, Rhonda maintained her calm demeanor as she reviewed his copy of the evaluation report she had ostensibly submitted. All the while knowing her actual document had been altered, she adeptly proceeded to guide Max through the steps he needed to take to file an appeal. She encouraged him to meet with his union representative, and procure evidence (such as statements from the other Assistant Principals, and student class officers for the 10th grade) to support his appeal of the ruling for termination.

Immediately after Max left her office, Dr. Taft called the District Office to let them know she had urgent business to discuss with the Assistant Superintendent for Human Resources (ASHR). Within the hour she had her meeting with the assistant superintendent who resolutely compared the two evaluation documents Rhonda presented – her original report and the altered report. Dr. Taft further informed the ASHR that Max Buchanan would most likely be filing an appeal to the Interim Superintendent's ruling for termination. At no point during this discussion did Principal Taft indicate her suspicions about who might have altered her evaluation of the AP. Ultimately, the APHR recommended to the Interim Superintendent that Maxwell Buchanan be permitted to retain his AP position, and be transferred to another school building beginning that summer.

Interim Superintendent Newley reluctantly accepted this recommendation, but proceeded to make Principal Taft's life miserable for the following school year during which he routinely made remarks to besmirch her reputation in the district. In the face of these groundless comments, Dr. Taft acted ethically and professionally and maintained credibility with her leadership peers and the members of the administrative team in her own building.

During this stressful period in the year following the Max Buchanan incident, one of Dr. Taft's close friends, who was a middle school principal in the district, experienced a difficult incident during a planned fundraising event. A few of the 8th grade students had apparently broken some bottles in the parking lot, and the police were called by a family member who happened to be arriving to pick up her daughter. Although no one was hurt and no arrests were made, the middle school principal was accused of being negligent, and notified he needed to meet with Interim Superintendent Newley the following Monday. Over the weekend he contacted Rhonda to seek her advice. She reassured him things would eventually work out well, noting he might be reprimanded and possibly suspended for a brief period, but his job was not likely on the line.

On the contrary, the middle school principal learned during his meeting with the Interim Superintendent that he was to be terminated at the end of the school year. When Dr. Taft heard this news, she tried without success to be in touch with her friend. Two days later she learned he had committed suicide – a tragic incident the district did not handle well at all. In fact, Mr. Newley left the district unexpectedly to pursue another opportunity, and the remaining District Office administration distanced itself from the event entirely.

Feeling demoralized, Dr. Rhonda Taft submitted her resignation and moved out of the region. A year later she landed a position as an executive principal at another large urban combined middle-high school.

1.4   *Follow-up Questions*

1. To what extent did Principal Rhonda Taft demonstrate (or fail to demonstrate) the selected leadership competencies identified above for PSEL #2 – Ethics and Professional Norms? [Be sure to cite specific examples.]

2. What other actions might Dr. Taft have taken to provide assistance to Max Buchanan.

3. What other legal issues needed to be addressed by the district-level administrators to whom Dr. Taft reported as a school building leader?

2   He Just Showed up Unexpectedly[1]

PSEL – **Standard 2:** Effective educational leaders act ethically and according to professional norms to promote each student's academic success and well-being.

Selected Elements:
2b – Act according to and promote the professional norms of integrity, fairness, transparency, trust, collaboration, perseverance, learning, and continuous improvement.

2c – Place children at the center of education and accept responsibility for each student's academic success and well-being.

2d – Safeguard and promote the values of democracy, individual freedom and responsibility, equity, social justice, community and diversity.

2e – Lead with interpersonal and communication skill, social-emotional insight, and understanding of all students' and staff members' backgrounds and cultures.

2.1   *The Story*

Prior to becoming principal of a medium-size secondary school in wealthy part of a large metropolitan center in Germany, Dr. Renata Mueller had been a science teacher in the school for thirty years. At the time the episodes in this story occurred, Dr. Mueller had been principal for nearly a decade. This 'Gymnasium' enrolled approximately 820 students in grades 7–12, and employed 85 teachers, at least 50 of whom had been hired by Renata Mueller. Throughout her tenure, the ratio of girls to boys (2:1) had remained fairly constant, and there was very little cultural diversity among either the student or teacher population.

The school hosts an "Open Day" each year in January, during which family members and prospective students are invited to visit the school, review curricular offerings and meet with the teachers, professional staff, and the principal. Being a reputable school with a hundred years of tradition, the school attracts parents and students mainly for its artistic profile, and its music tradition with outstanding choirs, orchestras and bands.

Over the years Dr. Mueller had earned the respect of her peers as a skillful teacher, and many of the students she had taught earlier in her career now had sons and daughters who attended the same school. As alumni, these parents were very eager to participate in school functions, and always attended their children's teacher conferences. They also had fond memories of their classes with Renata Mueller, and were delighted to learn she had been appointed principal of their alma mater. They trusted her to place their children at the center of all educational decisions. Until recently, teachers rarely reported having to deal with disciplinary matters or attendance issues.

With the increased availability of access to social media platforms, female students had begun reporting incidents of cyberbullying to their teachers, who then recounted their stories to Principal Mueller. On several occasions, male students had posted derogatory statements about, along with offensive photographs and videos of the girls in their classes. Upon seeing these disgusting Facebook images, more than one of the female students reported to Dr. Mueller they did not want to come to school for fear of being physically mistreated by these boys in person.

In an effort to promote fairness and transparency, Renata first scheduled a series of meetings with smaller groups of the male students in her building. She worked collaboratively with their teachers to remind them about the school's Code of Conduct policies. Dr. Mueller further described examples of what should be construed as inappropriate behavior, both inside and outside the walls of the school. She repeatedly reinforced her expectations that they would always treat one another, and their female classmates with respect.

Following these sessions, Principal Mueller scheduled a similar series of small assemblies with the female students. A half dozen teachers, who the students had elected to fulfill the role of school counselor when necessary, were present at all of these meetings to assist the principal as she addressed the many questions and concerns the students put forward. For the most part, the female students were very familiar (and also compliant) with the school's policies and procedures. Therefore the discussions in Dr. Mueller's meetings with them tended to include a variety of strategies for building self-esteem, coping behaviors, and resilience. The principal also reminded them the school partnered with an external agency, so they had access to school social workers whenever it might be necessary.

By virtue of these meetings and several others she had with the students' family members, Dr. Mueller eventually discovered the identities of the male students who seemed to be demonstrating the most bothersome behaviors. She made it her business to visit their classrooms often to check in on them, and routinely let them know she wanted them to be successful both academically and socially. One 10th grade student, whose name had been mentioned by several females, was a boy named Luis who was visiting from Brazil. His father Antonio Lopez was an adjunct professor at a nearby university, and Luis had been placed in Renata's school right after the "Open Day" in January. For reasons that were not entirely clear to Renata, Luis apparently felt the "rules" in her school did not apply to him.

Luis seemed to be jovial and most outgoing when he was showing off in front of his male peers. He openly made fun of the female students (mostly outside of class in the school's courtyard), which he believed demonstrated his masculinity. A soft-spoken girl named Katja, also a 10th grade student, received many of Luis' belittling comments. Katja's friends sadly informed her Luis had created offensive memes of her and had proudly displayed them to others on his phone. All of this occurred less than three weeks after Luis arrived.

Soon thereafter, Dr. Mueller learned about these unfortunate incidents from Katja's friends who knew Katja herself was too shy to report Luis on her own. The principal found out that one of the school's newest young female teachers was also being verbally harassed by Luis. When the teacher reported Luis' inappropriate behaviors to Dr. Mueller, she blamed herself for not having the necessary classroom management skills to resolve this problem on her own. She in fact took it personally that Katja had repeatedly been the victim of Luis' cyberbullying actions.

In mid-March, Renata Mueller received an email message from Katja's parents (the mom is an alumna of the gymnasium), demanding that she expel this "horrible Brazilian guy who is making our daughter anxious and utterly afraid to come to school!! He is a blatant cyberbullying criminal who has no right to be in the same classroom with our Katja!" As she stared at the terse statement on her computer screen, Renata reflected on her long tenure as both a teacher and leader for the school's many stakeholders.

2.2   Questions to Ponder

1.   What actions should Principal Renata Mueller take at this point?
2.   Are there any legal issues she should be considering?
3.   What additional information does Dr. Mueller need before taking any action (E.g., school district's policies regarding bullying/cyberbullying)?
4.   How do you anticipate her actions and/or decisions will impact the persons involved (e.g. Luis, Katja, other students, teachers, social workers, community-at-large, etc.)?

2.3   What Actually Occurred?

Rather than responding to the email message, Dr. Mueller felt it best to call the parents to speak with them directly. Prior to making the call, she decided to see if Katja was actually in class that day. She located her in a music class and invited her to come to the office for a private conversation. Despite her shyness, it didn't take much coaxing by Renata to convince Katja to confide in her. She ultimately gathered the additional evidence (e.g., images from Katja's iPhone) needed to determine what consequences might ultimately be appropriate for Luis. Once Katja had been taken back to class, Principal Mueller called her mother informing her their message had been received, and she was investigating the alleged series of events.

Dr. Mueller next located Luis, and escorted him to her office to discuss the alleged behaviors that had been brought to her attention. Luis was decidedly less brazen as she described the inappropriate cyberbullying actions of which others had accused him. He neither denied the allegations, nor claimed responsibility for the verbally abusive statements. The principal contacted Luis' father while the young man was still in her office, and asked him to come to the school to meet with her and his son. Mr. Lopez appeared surprised when Dr. Mueller reported the allegations that had been made against Luis, and the boy remained quiet and withdrawn throughout the discussion.

Luis received a one-week suspension for his behavior that had clearly, and repeatedly violated the school's Code of Conduct. During Luis' absence, Dr. Mueller received word from her School Resource Officer (SRO) that Katja's father had also contacted him to complain about Luis' despicable behavior. Feeling like they were not making sufficient headway with the principal, the parents came to him demanding he do what he could to have Luis expelled.

He had therefore taken it upon himself to conduct his own investigation, and was surprised to learn that Luis had never acted entirely on his own where the cyberbullying incidents were concerned. In fact, some of the other 10th grade boys had more or less dared him to create the memes of Katja. Luis had seemingly done so to both prove his masculinity, and preserve the nascent friendships he had established.

This new information confused Renata, and, regretting she had not done so earlier, immediately consulted with the school's social worker to determine if he had ever had occasion to meet with Luis. The social worker admitted to having had at least two conversations with Luis, and they had scheduled a third session to be held in a couple of weeks. The boy was apparently dealing his own desperate issues, and felt like he could never live up to his dad's expectations, especially when forced to live outside his native country of Brazil!

The social worker further explained to Renata he felt it would be in Luis' best interest if he were allowed to return to school sooner vs. later at this point. Knowing she could not easily, nor ethically, rescind the suspension, Renata decided to have a private follow-up meeting with Mr. Lopez, and invited the social worker to attend. It was during this conversation the social worker recommended Luis receive therapy for his depression, and the father vehemently disagreed this was necessary.

When Luis returned to school the following week, Katja's parents immediately called Dr. Mueller again insisting he should not be allowed to attend. Fearing their request would not be granted in a timely manner, they transferred their daughter to another secondary school in the region, one that unfortunately would not provide the quality and depth of music instruction Katja had in Renata's building.

Since Luis was himself scheduled to return to Brazil with his father at the end of the year, Dr. Mueller did not take any additional action to have him relocated. She did however submit her full report to the District Office, and requested Luis not be placed in her school should he return to Germany the following year.

And sure enough, HE JUST SHOWED UP UNEXPECTEDLY in late December, right before the Christmas holiday. Renata and the SRO respectfully escorted him out of the building, and explained he was no longer approved to attend this school. A month later, Luis showed up again with his father on the "Open Day" and Renata found it necessary to ask them both to leave. Demonstrating her understanding of the young man's cultural background and educational interests, Dr. Mueller provided written instructions regarding where the district had placed Luis Lopez for his 11th grade classes for the remainder of that school year.

2.4   *Follow-up Questions*

1.   To what extent did Principal Renata Mueller demonstrate (or fail to demonstrate) the selected leadership competencies identified above for PSEL #2 – *Ethics and Professional Norms?*

2.   What might Dr. Mueller have done differently in response to the cyber-bullying activities occurring among her school's students?

3   Where Have You Been?

PSEL – **Standard 2:** Effective educational leaders act ethically and according to professional norms to promote each student's academic success and well-being.

Selected Elements:

2a – Act ethically and professionally in personal conduct, relationships with others, decision-making, stewardship of the school's resources, and all aspects of school leadership.

2b – Act according to and promote the professional norms of integrity, fairness, transparency, trust, collaboration, perseverance, learning, and continuous improvement.

2e – Lead with interpersonal and communication skill, social-emotional insight, and understanding of all students' and staff members' backgrounds and cultures.

2f – Provide moral direction for the school and promote ethical and professional behavior among faculty and staff.

3.1   *The Story*

Upon completing her School Administrator's Certification, Ms. Camille Delgado was appointed to be one of two Vice Principals at a large urban middle school. When her Principal Dr. Quentin Waters was promoted, and moved into the District Office three years later to become the Director of Secondary Curriculum, Ms. Delgado was encouraged to apply for his vacated position. The other Vice Principal, Pamela Cookstone, who had been at the middle school for several years prior to Camille's arrival, also applied for the job. Ms. Delgado was ultimately the candidate appointed to lead the middle school which enrolled 1400 students in grades 6–8, and employed 72 teachers.

As she began her first year as Principal, the District Office placed a new Vice Principal in the middle school to fill Camille's previous position. Dr. Waters contacted Camille privately to give her a bit of background on this person whose name was Benjamin Brooks. Mr. Brooks had been in the district for more than 28 years, and had served as a Vice Principal in two of the district's elementary schools, and in one of its high schools. He had started and nearly finished a doctoral program in Educational Leadership, but had not yet completed his dissertation. Everyone who worked closely with Ben believed he was on a solid career path toward one of the district's many school Principal positions. And then something unforeseen happened.

At some point during his tenure as a high school Vice Principal, Mr. Brooks was implicated in a case of missing inventory, and also suspected of being under the influence of drugs while performing his duties during the work day. He was subsequently placed on administrative leave while a thorough investigation took place. Benjamin Brooks was ultimately cleared of any offences, and there were no records of the allegations placed in his personnel file. Regardless, the District Office thought it prudent to move him to the middle school to start anew with Ms. Delgado.

Therefore, as Ms. Delgado launched into her first year as Principal, she found herself supervising two very different Vice Principals. One, Benjamin Brooks, was new to the school, but had accrued many years as both a teacher and administrator in the district. He was grateful to have a fresh start, and interested to work with someone new. The other, Pamela Cookstone, had been Camille's peer for three years, and was disappointed she herself had not landed the job as Principal. Ms. Cookstone also had a reputation for being a very rigid disciplinarian, and she didn't care one bit for Camille Delgado's more innovative style of transformational leadership. In fact, many of the teachers perceived Pamela actually tried to make things more difficult for Camille as she transitioned to her new role as Principal.

The District Office informed Vice Principal Brooks and Principal Delgado that they would be periodically sending an officer to the school, who was authorized to randomly test Ben for the presence of drugs in his system. Given the nature of the earlier allegations and subsequent investigation involving the Vice Principal, the Superintendent believed this precautionary process was in the best interest of all stakeholders, especially the middle school students with whom Ben would be working on a daily basis.

Things ran very smoothly for the first few months of the year as Mr. Brooks complied with the random drug tests without difficulty, and he always passed them. Ben's good natured personality made him a hit with the middle school students, and he enthusiastically supported Ms. Delgado's innovative ideas. The Vice Principal assisted Camille in numerous ways as she worked to introduce new initiatives to the middle school teachers and professional staff members. Simply stated, the two leaders trusted one another both explicitly and implicitly, and they enjoyed working together as a team. In a variety of ways, Ben Brooks' unconditional support and respect for Principal Delgado mitigated Pamela Cookstone's vitriolic attitudes toward her.

At some point during the second half of the school year, Vice Principal Brooks didn't show up to work for an entire week. There were no apparent reasons for his absence, and he neglected to respond to Ms. Delgado's repeated phone and text messages. When he finally returned to his office, Principal Delgado exclaimed "WHERE HAVE YOU BEEN?! Why didn't you answer my calls? I was worried something terrible had happened to you or a member of your family!" He somberly reported his mother was sick, and he had been called out of town to monitor her care. Camille accepted his explanation, and they finished out their first year without further incidents of this nature.

During their second year together in the middle school, Ms. Delgado learned that Mr. Brooks' son was playing Varsity Basketball, and was also one of the team's star players. As might be expected, Ben requested time off to attend his son's practices and games. Since Ben had accrued considerable vacation/personal time within the school district, these were considered excused absences.

Mr. Brooks' behaviors became more unpredictable during the third year he served as Vice Principal. He continually requested time off to either care for his mother, attend his son's basketball games, or even to work on completing his unfinished dissertation. In a few of these cases, as had occurred during year one, he neglected to inform Camille he would be away for a few days! While he was in school however, Vice Principal Brooks carried out his duties and responsibilities in a respectable manner, and Principal Delgado valued him as her "right hand co-leader."

Regardless, Camille remained totally committed to providing moral direction for the school, and promoting ethical and professional behavior among faculty and staff. She therefore wrote a detailed email message to Benjamin Brooks laying out her expectations moving forward, stating "Unexcused absences will no longer be tolerated. You are dangerously close to having no accrued time left for any type of absence. We must strictly follow the school district's policy from here on out." Benjamin Brooks knew the employment contract inside and out, and acknowledged that Principal Delgado had been perhaps too lenient in her response to his often cavalier use of his personal days. He thanked her for her personal, yet unofficial email message, and promised her things would change. Their third year as a leadership team in the middle school proceeded as Camille hoped it would.

During the summer following this third year, Camille Delgado applied for and obtained another leadership position in the district as a high school Principal. The large high school enrolled 70% students of color, but employed fewer than 5% teaches of color. Her loyalty to and respect for Ben Brooks, who was African American, compelled her to request he be transferred with her to the high school to assume one of its four Vice Principal positions. The District Office approved her request, and they made the move together in August.

It didn't take long for Vice Principal Brooks, who was now called Dr. Brooks, to build rapport with the high school students – they loved him! Having finished his dissertation during the summer, Benjamin Brooks felt rejuvenated and ready to take on a new portfolio of responsibilities, while working alongside Camille Delgado for whom he had sincere admiration and respect. Ben quickly became very popular with many of the high school teachers, who respected him for his vast knowledge and expertise in pedagogical strategies to promote social and emotional learning.

Without warning, Dr. Brooks neglected to show up for work during the first week of February. Without success, Ms. Delgado attempted to get in touch with him to find out where he was.

3.2 *Questions to Ponder*
1. What actions should Principal Camille Delgado take at this point?
2. What ethical considerations come into play in this case?
3. Are there any legal issues she should be considering? (See Chapter 12, Section 2)
4. How do you anticipate her actions and/or decisions will impact the persons involved (e.g. Benjamin, other VPs, students, District Office Administration, etc.)?

3.3 *What Actually Occurred?*
Needless to say, Principal Delgado was quite exasperated with Dr. Brooks' unprofessional disregard for the school district's written policies regarding excused vs. unexcused absences from the workplace. When he returned to work after being gone an entire week, she confronted him directly in his office. Ben sadly informed her his mother had died. Camille offered her sincere condolences, and still reminded him he needed to follow district policy which certainly allowed time away for bereavement.

Shortly thereafter, Benjamin missed work again, for several days in a row. He offered various somewhat weak excuses, and seemed rather distraught a lot of the time. By this point, the teachers and students were all noticing he was gone, and wondered why this was happening so often. Dr. Brooks had used up all of his personal leave days and his vacation time as well. Ms. Delgado contacted the Superintendent to seek advice in this complicated personnel matter. The Superintendent responded with "You requested Ben Brooks be transferred to the high school with you, so you need to figure out how to fix it now!"

Principal Delgado believed she had made a series of progressive disciplinary attempts to provide effective supervision for her vice principal. Realizing these efforts had not been entirely successful, Principal Delgado consulted with the Director of Human Resources, and wasted no further time to schedule a formal meeting with Dr. Brooks together with his union representative. After working with Benjamin for nearly four years, Ms. Delgado finally prepared a formal counseling memo to be placed in his personnel file. Ben's union representative later recommended he should probably be seeking employment elsewhere. This official counseling memo was quite serious and perhaps long overdue, and it was likely the district would be hard pressed to support him in the future.

At the end of that school year Dr. Benjamin Brooks landed an appointment as Principal of a Charter School in the region. He worked in that location for about a year and a half when he contacted Camille Delgado to request she write him a letter of recommendation. He had apparently decided to leave his administrative position and apply for one of the district's teaching vacancies. Ms. Delgado provided a standard reference letter for him highlighting his competencies, and acknowledging his deep institutional memory in the school district. To her knowledge, he was not hired to teach in the district, and she is not sure where (or if) he ultimately found employment in an educational setting.

3.4   *Follow-up Questions*

1.   To what extent did Principal Camille Delgado demonstrate (or fail to demonstrate) the selected leadership competencies identified above for PSEL #2 – *Ethics and Professional Norms?*
2.   What additional strategies might Ms. Delgado have tried to guide (or reprimand) Vice Principal Brooks as he continually missed days of work?

4   We Can't Find the Error

PSEL – **Standard 2:** Effective educational leaders act ethically and according to professional norms to promote each student's academic success and well-being.

Selected Elements:
2a – Act ethically and professionally in personal conduct, relationships with others, decision-making, stewardship of the school's resources, and all aspects of school leadership.

2b – Act according to and promote the professional norms of integrity, fairness, transparency, trust, collaboration, perseverance, learning, and continuous improvement.

2c – Place children at the center of education and accept responsibility for each student's academic success and well-being.

2f – Provide moral direction for the school and promote ethical and professional behavior among faculty and staff.

4.1   The Story

Following fourteen years of service as a teacher in a rural school district where most parents and family members held blue collar jobs, Anneke Quincy decided to complete a graduate program in educational leadership. Ms. Quincy earned her School Administrator's Certification and obtained a position as principal of one of the district's two elementary schools. The school enrolled 365 students in grades K–6, and employed 25 teachers. It was during Ms. Quincy's second year as principal when the events in this story occurred. Since many of the teachers had taught with Anneke in this school, they were still becoming acclimated to her leadership style in this new administrative role.

The school district had also hired Samuel Hayes as the new Business Manager that same year. Mr. Hayes had many years of experience as the Chief Financial Officer of a construction firm, and had also spent three years at the Director of Budget and Finance for an urban school district in another State.

At the time Principal Quincy assumed her position as principal, two persons shared the duties of her Administrative Assistant in the Main Office. Together they managed the principal's schedule, interacted with students and family members, monitored the reports submitted by the Attendance Office, and generally kept track of the building's activities. Several years prior to Ms. Quincy's appointment, her predecessor authorized them to manage the school's fundraising account – a practice Anneke had endorsed, and was continuing to review as she settled into her job as building leader.

The school's Fall Fundraiser was launched in late September each year, and included all grade levels. Teachers distributed order forms and sales instructions to their students. They encouraged them to get out into their neighborhoods, with parents and family members as appropriate for the younger children, and sell a variety of unique wrapping papers to interested customers. The monies accrued through the students' sales were distributed to their grade level teachers later in the semester, and could be used to purchase additional classroom materials. In other words, the profits earned through all sales made by 3rd grade students were allocated to the 3rd grade teachers, and were intended to be spent that same year. The practice was mirrored at all grade levels.

Without forewarning, one of the two part-time Administrative Assistants (Felicity) informed Principal Quincy she was leaving the position, effective immediately. Fortunately, her work partner Lydia was willing to assume the important clerical role on a full-time basis, thus providing continuity for both Ms. Quincy, and the Main Office as a whole.

It was during this transition period that the principal discovered some inconsistencies in the accounting records for the Fall Fundraiser. As just noted, Anneke was still gaining information about how these discretionary funds were being managed, and regularly spent time studying the various spreadsheets that had been created by Felicity and Lydia. She discovered they both had electronic access to the accounting records, and found they also maintained/monitored a large file of paper records. The inconsistencies did not appear to be egregious, but Anneke nonetheless had discovered them. For example: some teachers were allowed to carry fund balances over from one year to the next; teachers generally, but not always, submitted receipts for their classroom purchases; a few deposits showed up in one spreadsheet, but were not included in the final balance on that same document. Most disturbingly, Principal Quincy's calculations indicated a shortage of $2,500 in the general ledger. She wondered where the monies had disappeared to, and felt she had an ethical responsibility to locate the source of the discrepancy.

Since the Fall Fundraiser was already in full swing, and knowing the teachers would soon be receiving their students' order forms with customers' payments, Ms. Quincy wanted to be sure the accounting records were accurate before any new deposits were made, so all grade levels would receive the correct allocation of funds based on the students' hard work. Anneke did not want teachers or their students to be penalized for accounting mistakes for which they were not responsible. She therefore spent the better part of a full work week reviewing several years' worth of bank statements, deposit slips, order forms and receipts.

Feeling somewhat exasperated, Ms. Quincy sat down with her Administrative Assistant to discuss the less than satisfactory results of her intensive review of the fundraising records. She asked Lydia if she, or perhaps Felicity, might be able to provide any additional information about the account's history, to which Lydia responded "I've shared all of the pertinent documents with you, we are not hiding anything." Ultimately, Principal Quincy quietly concluded:

> Since WE CAN'T FIND THE ERROR, I need to schedule a brief meeting with
> Mr. Hayes to seek his advice in this matter. Will you please accompany

me, since you have co-managed this complex fundraising account for quite a few years?

Lydia's immediate and succinct response to the principal's request was "No, I prefer to not be involved in that discussion."

4.2   Questions to Ponder

1. What actions should Principal Anneke Quincy take at this point?
2. Are there any legal issues she should be considering? (See Chapter 12, Section 2)
3. What ethical considerations come into play in this case?
4. How do you anticipate her actions and/or decisions will impact the persons involved (e.g. Lydia, Felicity, students, teachers, family members, herself, etc.)?

4.3   What Actually Occurred?

Given the fact Samuel Hayes was very new to the school district as its Business Officer, Anneke had hoped Lydia would be willing to provide important institutional history regarding the school's Fall Fundraiser activities, and the evolution of the account's management procedures. Regardless, she respected her Administrative Assistant's desire to not be included in what she perceived to be an administrative meeting beyond the purview of her clerical duties in the elementary school's Main Office.

Principal Quincy therefore met with the Business Officer on her own, and described in detail all of her findings regarding the Fall Fundraiser, noting she believed the account was short $2500. Mr. Hayes thanked Anneke for her candor, and for her diligence as she tried to locate the source of the accounting error. He then respectfully asked her if she could think of anyone who may have either taken the money outright, or misappropriated the funds elsewhere. Ms. Quincy had prepared herself for this unpleasant question, and was forthright in her conclusion that

> I can think of no one in our school who would do such a thing. And I trust both Lydia and Felicity always acted responsibly, as they worked collaboratively with my predecessor to ensure each teacher received her/his correct allocation.

Samuel Hayes, by virtue of his experience managing a variety of budgets, surmised the shortfall was unlikely due to one gross mistake. He was not interested in making staff members nervous unnecessarily, since it was also improbable that any one person had been dishonest. The Business Officer explained it was most likely that small portions of the "missing" funds had been mistakenly distributed over a number of years, and it was Anneke's careful scrutiny that uncovered the larger deficit that had accrued. Principal Quincy remained steadfast in her desire to reconcile the $2500 shortfall, insisting she did not want to inform any of the teachers they would be receiving a lesser amount of money for classroom materials than they had anticipated.

The Business Officer offered a partial solution wherein he agreed to allow Ms. Quincy to locate receipts for recent purchases within her building's Main Office, which could then be submitted to him for reimbursement out of the District Office's account for miscellaneous discretionary expenditures. Anneke questioned the integrity of this course of action, and Samuel assured her the practice was compliant with district policy. Principal Quincy and her Administrative Assistant Lydia subsequently found and submitted receipts for minor office improvements totaling $1650. Mr. Hayes authorized the transfer of this amount into Anneke's fundraising account which partially made up the lost monies. Still unable to accept the negative balance, Anneke Quincy decided to quietly cover the $850 difference out of her own pocket. In her mind's ethical/moral compass, this was the only acceptable solution to make the account whole for her teachers and their students.

Throughout the entire unexpected ordeal, Ms. Quincy always believed her colleagues had acted judiciously, and never wanted to raise suspicions about her predecessor's decisions, or the abilities of the school's two administrative assistants. Anneke therefore placed the topic of school-based accounting procedures on the agenda for the Superintendent's next leadership team meeting.

The Superintendent delegated oversight of these accounts to the Business Officer who then worked individually with the school principals to revise, where necessary, the process for managing their future fundraising events. Moving forward, Mr. Hayes' office became the central depository for all schools' accounts, and teachers were held accountable to expend all of their classroom monies in the same year they were earned. Unexpended funds remained in the District Office's aforementioned discretionary account. Building principals were responsible for maintaining their own account records as a check/balance for the DO. Furthermore, all principals were encouraged to hold monthly meetings to examine these records with whomever they identified to be the school's fundraising coordinator (e.g., teacher, counselor, administrative assistant, or even a small committee).

4.4   *Follow-up Questions*

1.   To what extent did Principal Anneke Quincy demonstrate (or fail to demonstrate) the selected leadership competencies identified above for PSEL #2 – *Ethics and Professional Norms?*
2.   If you were Ms. Quincy, would you have felt compelled to contribute your own money to the school's fundraising account? Why or why not?
3.   Do you believe there were other possible solutions for this case?

Note

1   Contributing author: Frederik Ahlgrimm, Ph.D.

Equity and Cultural Responsiveness

1 Your Son Has Great Potential[1]

PSEL – Standard 3: Effective educational leaders strive for equity of educational opportunity and culturally responsive practices to promote each student's academic success and well-being.

Selected Elements:

3a – Ensure that each student is treated fairly, respectfully, and with an understanding of each student's culture and context.

3c – Ensure that each student has equitable access to effective teachers, learning opportunities, academic and social support, and other resources necessary for success.

3d – Develop student policies and address student misconduct in a positive, fair and unbiased manner.

3f – Promote the preparation of students to live productively in and contribute to the diverse cultural contexts of a global society.

1.1   *The Story*

Mrs. Gretchen Hollister is the Founding Principal of a small elementary school located in a large city in Germany. At the time the events of this story occurred, the school had been in existence for three years, enrolled 265 students in grades 1–5, and employed 15 teachers. A plan to include a 6th grade class was in place for the following year. Principal Hollister described the very close-knit, collaborative culture she had fostered in her building since it opened. All members of the instructional staff believed that *all* learning was both social and emotional, and they practiced pedagogical strategies to help young students develop critical skills for success inside and outside of their classrooms.

Gretchen was proud to say the teachers rarely reported classroom management issues – the children who attended this school were well behaved, respectful of one another, and dedicated to their learning.

In the midst of what might be perceived as an idyllic educational environment, Principal Hollister next described an emerging reality wherein an increasing number of refugee students were being placed in her school. A refugee shelter had recently been established near her school building, so it was essential for her to become especially familiar with the school district's nascent policies and procedures for assigning these displaced school-aged children to their appropriate grade levels. One new requirement entailed the establishment of a mixed-age "welcoming class" in many of the district's school buildings where refugee students would be taught German language skills during a portion of the day.

In late September of that year, Barend arrived in her office with his parents. The family had migrated from Syria to Germany in late August and were staying in the refugee shelter. The School District Coordination Center had tested Barend, who was 11 years old, and determined he should be placed in the school's "welcoming class" for children with little German knowledge as described above. And, based on his math proficiency, Barend was to be placed in the 5th grade classroom for the remainder of the school day. This young boy was one of perhaps a dozen other refugee students who Mrs. Hollister welcomed to her school that year.

Within a few weeks of his arrival, Barend's teachers observed his increasingly erratic behaviors, many of which occurred for no apparent reason. He appeared to be very anxious all the time, and had great difficulty concentrating during class sessions. He ran up and down the hallways, and became very agitated whenever anyone came near him during these outbursts. While Barend was not disrespectful to his teachers, nor did he attempt to strike out at them, they reported to Gretchen they were feeling overwhelmed. As noted above, they had not dealt with classroom management issues to any great extent, and were largely unfamiliar with new strategies being tried/used in other locations to foster trauma sensitive school settings.

With a translator, Barend's father attended his son's first teacher conference in October. It was common for both the principal and the teacher to meet with family members, together with their sons or daughters, during these semi-annual conferences. Principal Hollister, being cognizant of the behaviors Barend's teachers had described, happily observed that he was very calm in the presence of his dad. At the conclusion of that conference, after Barend's teachers had reviewed his academic progress with the father, Principal Hollister suggested they have a follow-up meeting to further discuss the child's special needs.

Both of Barend's parents came in to see Mrs. Hollister the following week; again they were accompanied by a translator from the refugee shelter. Sensing Barend's mother was feeling very uncomfortable and out of place in her office, Gretchen decided to move the group to a more comfortable location in the teacher's lounge where they could have coffee during their meeting. As the principal assessed Barend's academic competencies in various subject areas, she stated to the parents on more than one occasion "I know YOUR SON HAS GREAT POTENTIAL!"

However, as Gretchen described Barend's difficulty when it came to controlling his emotional outbursts, the parents became quite defensive. The father shouted vehemently – "What do you all expect? Barend has witnessed gunfire right in our front yard, and he is definitely dealing with a huge number of traumatic memories for a boy his age!" Principal Hollister calmly allowed Barend's dad to express himself, and then respectfully suggested they might want to consider having their son meet with a psychotherapist who could help him address these post-traumatic stress (PTS) symptoms. Upon hearing the suggestion their son potentially needed "psychiatric care," Barend's dad grabbed the mother's wrist and pulled her with him as he angrily left the meeting, and departed from the school building.

1.2   Questions to Ponder

1.   How should Principal Hollister proceed to address Barend's special needs?
2.   Can you identify any ethical considerations she should be taking into account while attempting to resolve this case?
3.   With whom should she consult to take actions regarding Barend's future in her school?
4.   How might her ultimate decisions impact the persons involved (e.g. Barend, classmates, family members, teachers and other staff members, etc.)?

1.3   What Actually Occurred?

Principal Hollister sat in a state of disbelief for several minutes following the unexpected, swift closure to her conversation with Barend's parents. She next made it a top priority to learn more about the family's cultural background, and the context for their distinctive beliefs and traditional practices. Here is one noteworthy fact she discovered: In many Middle Eastern cultures, any reference to "psychotherapeutic practice" was inferred to mean the person in question was to be destined for severe clinical treatment, and possibly declared insane. Apparently, the notion of a middle ground wherein simple "counseling interventions" might be helpful did not exist.

Gretchen discussed her concerns with district-level administrators who directed her to bring Barend's case before the members of the district-wide Special Education Committee (SEC). Together with Barend's teachers, Mrs. Hollister prepared a succinct record of his academic proficiencies, progress with learning German, and an accounting of his recurrent social and emotional flare-ups both inside and outside of the classroom. She was given space on the agenda for the next SEC meeting. The SEC members concluded Barend needed a licensed psychotherapist to provide an official report denoting he needed additional support for his PTS symptoms above and beyond what Mrs. Hollister's school could address on its own. Once that report was submitted, additional staffing could be provided.

With the SEC's assistance, the principal found Dr. Lauren Graham, a psychotherapist who was knowledgeable of the school district's policies and procedures for handling these types of cases. She was also trilingual in German, Arabic and English. Gretchen took the additional time outside of the school day to meet with Dr. Graham to discuss Barend's case with her in detail. Together they crafted a plan of action whereby Principal Hollister could begin to establish a more personal relationship with Barend's family members. Dr. Graham seemed to believe this was necessary before the mother and father would ever trust Gretchen's recommendations, and consent to having their son meet with her on a professional basis.

Over the course of another couple of months, Gretchen Hollister continued to monitor Barend's progress in his various subjects. While his emotional outbursts still occurred more than she and his teachers would have wanted, Barend displayed an increased interest in many more of his class assignments as time passed. Mrs. Hollister also went to the refugee shelter on several occasions to visit with Barend's family members.

As they learned to trust her, Gretchen offered to assist them as they were required to complete a series of official government forms regarding their status to remain in Germany. She also reviewed the requirements for eligibility for being able to find their own flat in the city. In other words, the principal went above and beyond what might normally be expected of her as she endeavored to promote each student's academic success and well-being.

Ultimately, Barend's father agreed to allow Dr. Graham to meet with his son. This was decidedly one of the conditions Principal Hollister had set in place as she agreed to help the family become qualified to move into a flat near the school. Once they eventually moved out of the shelter into their own place, Barend would be allowed to continue his studies the following year as a 6th grade student in her building.

1.4   *Follow-up Questions*

1. To what extent did Principal Gretchen Hollister demonstrate (or fail to demonstrate) the selected leadership competencies identified above for PSEL #3 – *Equity and Cultural Responsiveness?*
2. Describe additional actions Gretchen Hollister might consider to gain the trust and confidence of Barend's parents and family members?

2   I Never Said Any of Those Things

PSEL – **Standard 3:** Effective educational leaders strive for equity of educational opportunity and culturally responsive practices to promote each student's academic success and well-being.

Selected Elements:
3a – Ensure that each student is treated fairly, respectfully, and with an understanding of each student's culture and context.
3d – Develop student policies and address student misconduct in a positive, fair and unbiased manner.
3e – Confront and alter institutional biases of student marginalization, deficit-based schooling, and low expectations associated with race, class, culture and language, gender and sexual orientation, and disability or social status.
3f – Promote the preparation of students to live productively in and contribute to the diverse cultural contexts of a global society.
3g – Act with cultural competence and responsiveness in their interactions, decision making and practice.

2.1   *The Story*
The school where Ms. Shana Barnes has been principal for twelve years is located in a middle class suburban neighborhood. The elementary school enrolls 450 students in grades K–6, and employs 30 teachers. There are three homerooms for each grade level. Throughout her tenure, Ms. Barnes had observed a great deal of stability in the school's student population, meaning most children entered as Kindergarteners and remained through the 6th grade when they moved to one of three middle schools in the district. She had therefore gotten to know the students and their family members quite well over time. Case in point, the three 6th grade boys whose names are identified in the events described in this story had all attended Shana's school since they were in Kindergarten.

It was shortly after lunch, on a Thursday afternoon in early March, when Principal Barnes found herself in a meeting that was interrupted by a call from the nurse's office. The school nurse informed her Tomas Kovac had been delivered to her with a bloody nose. The teaching assistant who brought him in from the playground reported he had been punched in the face by another 6th grade boy, and was then pushed into a snow bank. Ms. Barnes excused herself from the curriculum meeting and went directly to the nurse's office to speak with Tomas.

When she arrived, the nurse was sitting with him, and he was holding an ice bag next to his nose which had not yet stopped bleeding; he was also starting to get a black eye. Shana first acknowledged his injuries, and then asked him how he was feeling. Tomas bravely assured her he was doing fine, and just wanted his nose to stop bleeding. She asked him what happened, and he said "Alex Peterman just came up and punched me and then pushed me into the snow, for no good reason." The principal of course asked him "are you sure you did nothing to provoke Alex?" And he insisted he had been minding his own business waiting for the bell to ring so he could come inside out of the cold weather. Principal Barnes instructed the nurse to stay with him, and asked her to call Tomas' homeroom teacher to have someone bring his personal items to the office so he'd have them when it was time for dismissal. She informed Tomas she'd be back shortly.

As she left the nurse's office, en route to Alex Peterman's classroom, Shana remembered an incident involving the same two boys that had occurred the previous year. While no physical altercations had taken place, Tomas and Alex were seen having a heated argument during the 5th grade lunch period, and one of the boy's lunch trays was subsequently shoved onto the floor. The cafeteria monitor asked the boys to clean up the mess, after which she escorted them to Ms. Barnes' office.

Shana recalled she interviewed Alex first, and he accused Tomas of making a derogatory statement directed at yet another 5th grade boy named Garret Foster. She probed to determine what had been said, and learned Tomas had asked Garret "How do you people breath in the shower if you're not wearing a gas mask?" Garret is Middle Eastern American. Shana called Tomas in to speak with her, and asked him if he had made an insulting remark to anyone during the lunch period. He admitted he had jokingly asked Garret if he needed to wear a gas mask while in the shower. Ms. Barnes reminded Tomas about her expectations that all students be treated fairly, and with a respectful understanding of each person's cultural background. The type of remark Tomas had made would not be tolerated; ethnic slurs were never to be considered a joking matter. Following the district's Code of Conduct, Tomas had received a three-day suspension for making that specific statement the previous year.

With this incident in the back of her mind, Principal Barnes entered Alex Peterman's classroom and requested he be excused from class to meet with her. In her office, the principal asked Alex to tell her about what had happened earlier when the 6th grade classes were outside for their recess period. Alex admitted he had punched Tomas in the face, and then shoved him into a snow bank. He said he knew it was wrong to behave that way, and he apologized for showing his anger. He further stated he had overheard Tomas saying horrible things to Garret Foster, several words he didn't even want to repeat. Ms. Barnes patiently asked him to tell her what he could say – Alex responded – "Tomas said to Garret: *If you don't go back to your own country, I'll beat you to death! President Trump doesn't even want you here, so just leave.*"

Alex went on to say he knew Garret would not stand up for himself, so he felt compelled to defend him against a person he believed to be an inconsiderate bully. He further confided to Ms. Barnes "I know what it's like to be discriminated against since I am from a Jewish family, and we reside in a neighborhood dominated by families who attend Christian churches." The principal acknowledged Alex's candor, and explained there would be consequences for his aggressive actions against another student. The district's Code of Conduct specified an out-of-school suspension for this offense, and she told Alex she'd be calling his parents shortly thereafter.

Alex returned to his classroom, and Shana Barnes proceeded to the nurse's office to have another conversation with Tomas Kovak. When she arrived, Tomas was resting, his nose had stopped bleeding, and the nurse was still sitting with him. The principal questioned him a second time about the allegations Alex had reported, and he vehemently denied having made any insulting remarks to anyone. Reminding Tomas he had previously admitted making anti-Muslim comments, Shana asked him to reconsider his response to her inquiry about the immediate playground incident. More than once he screamed at her "I NEVER SAID ANY OF THOSE THINGS! Garret is just paranoid, and everything he told Alex was a lie."

By that point, it was nearly time for dismissal. Ms. Barnes asked Tomas if he felt well enough, both physically and emotionally, to ride the bus home. He insisted he was fine, and the nurse confirmed he had not displayed any visible signs of discomfort during his stay in her office. The principal instructed her to keep him there until dismissal, at which point he could be released to board his bus to go home.

As she returned to her office, Shana Barnes began to wonder which of the two boys (Alex or Tomas) was telling her the truth. She generally trusted her instincts, and prided herself in her ability to speak with young students in such a way they usually felt comfortable being honest with her. In this instance however, she did not have a definitive answer in her head. She knew she had at least two sets of parents to contact, and when she arrived in the Main Office her administrative assistant informed her about another incident demanding her immediate attention.

2.2   *Questions to Ponder*

1.   What actions should Principal Shana Barnes take immediately? Long term?

2.   What consequences should Alex and Tomas receive?
3.   Are there any legal issues she should be considering? (See Chapter 12, Section 2)
4.   What additional information/data might she obtain prior to taking action?
5.   How might her ultimate decisions impact the persons involved (e.g. Tomas, Alex, Garret, other students, family members, teachers and other staff members, etc.)?

2.3   What Actually Occurred?

Principal Barnes quickly read the note the administrative assistant had handed to her, and learned that one of her school's 5th grade girls had posted several pictures on social media that were quite alarming. The student claimed she had assembled weapons at home, and was planning to end her own life since her family life was horrible. Ms. Barnes immediately contacted the girl's family members to alert them about the information she had received. Together they discussed a series of necessary interventions, and Ms. Barnes continued to monitor that situation for many weeks following. (Note: While this brief vignette is unrelated to the story being analyzed, it illustrates the fact that this principal is being pulled in multiple directions to simultaneously resolve two serious incidents involving her young students.)

Shana's next call was to Tomas Kovak's parents. She informed them their son had been in a fight during the afternoon recess period, and invited them to come in to meet with her the following day. Shana explained the allegations that had been made against Tomas, and the mother and father both agreed to attend the meeting.

The principal then consulted with her team of 6th grade teachers and the school counselor to discuss the consequences for Alex's behavior. She recounted the conversation she had had with Alex, and concluded he should receive a one-day suspension. The teachers disputed her decision, and reminded her the normal consequence for hitting or punching another student was a five-day suspension. Shana thanked them for their insights, and noted Alex's remorse and willingness to stand up for another classmate who had (allegedly) been the brunt of extreme cultural insensitivity. Principal Barnes therefore stood by her decision, contacted Alex's parents to let them know about the playground incident, and informed them he was to be suspended for one day.

That evening, as she reflected on the day's chaotic events, Shana thought about the impending meeting with the Kovak family. Over the years, she noticed a greater number of parents and family members had become less willing to collaboratively support the school district's disciplinary policies and procedures. More often than not, persons were quick to deflect blame away from their sons or daughters concluding the fault lay with the teachers or other classmates. She hoped things might be different when she met with Mr. and Mrs. Kovak the following day.

Principal Barnes welcomed the Kovaks into her office, and asked the administrative assistant to call Tomas to the office to attend the meeting. Before the meeting even started, Mr. Kovak let her know he was furious to hear "Alex Peterman had only received a one-day suspension for beating up on our son for no reason!" [Word travels quickly via social media.] Ms. Barnes adeptly redirected the discussion to the primary purpose of the meeting which was to question Tomas about the remarks he may have made to Garret Foster. To which Mr. Kovak responded,

> We are from Bosnia, so why would Tomas say anything like *go back to your own country?* Tomas never even tried to defend himself against Alex, so why is he the one whose integrity is being questioned?

At this point Tomas' mother urged her husband to calm down so they could all have a civil conversation. When Tomas arrived, he reaffirmed his innocence in all matters regarding any defamatory comments toward Garret.

Ms. Barnes decided to bring the session to a close in this manner. She said to the Kovaks,

> I need your help here. These allegations are very serious and demand further investigation on my part. I suggest you take Tomas home today, and I will work to collect additional data so we can all be confident in the final course of action to be taken.

Having already met with the three 6th grade teachers, Shana Barnes decided it would be prudent to speak directly with all of the 6th grade students (n = 74, minus Alex who was suspended, and Tomas who had gone home for the day with his parents). She delivered the same presentation to all three classes, using the forum to remind them about the school district's policies designed to address student misconduct in a positive, fair and unbiased manner. The principal was very specific when she asked the students to not simply recall the playground incident, but wanted to know if any one of them had actually witnessed/heard Tomas make the racially biased remarks to Garret.

Ms. Barnes set herself up at a small table in the hallway and waited patiently. The first student to come out to see her was a very quiet, painfully shy girl who confirmed she had heard Tomas "say those nasty things to Garret." Shortly thereafter, a boy who was actually close friends with Tomas came out to tell her "I didn't want to get him in trouble, but he did say some mean things to Garret, and it's not the first time I've heard him talk like that." Finally, one more female student appeared in the hall to say she "was embarrassed to hear one of her classmates speaking in that manner about Garret, who is a pretty nice guy." With that evidence in hand, Shana quickly re-visited each class to thank the students for their assistance.

That afternoon, following the district's Code of Conduct, Principal Barnes contacted Mr. Kovak to inform him she had the evidence necessary to issue a five-day suspension for Tomas, along with a Superintendent's hearing which would take place on Wednesday the following week. She explained the home tutoring services to which Tomas was entitled, and the father refused them stating "we can do a better job educating our son. I'm fed up with all of this, and will contact the superintendent myself!"

At the Superintendent's hearing the following week, it was Mrs. Kovak who displayed her anger, and made derogatory comments directed at Shana Barnes. She stated "My son was locked up by himself for two hours in the nurse's office and no one ever checked on him." The principal asked Tomas if he remembered the conversations she had had with him, and he admitted he had never been alone. The hearing officer continued to question Tomas and ultimately gathered enough evidence to conclude the incidents, as reported by Alex and the other students, could have occurred beyond a reasonable doubt.

Tomas was then assigned an additional ten days of out-of-school suspension for his verbally abusive behavior toward one of his 6th grade classmates. Not surprisingly, Tomas almost proudly posted details of his "unwarranted punishment" on social media. Home tutoring services were declined by Tomas' parents, and they agreed to receive/monitor all of his lessons and assignments electronically. Given the extended length of the suspension, the principal worked collaboratively with his teachers and the school counselor to create a detailed re-entry plan for Tomas.

2.4   *Follow-up Questions*

1. To what extent did Principal Shana Barnes demonstrate (or fail to demonstrate) the selected leadership competencies identified above for PSEL #3 – *Equity and Cultural Responsiveness?*

2. What might Shana Barnes have done differently as she sought to find the true story in this incident?

3. Can you identify any ethical considerations she should be taking into account while attempting to resolve this case?

4. What additional steps should Ms. Barnes, and other building leaders in her district, be taking to create a more inclusive learning environment?

3   I Don't Want To – You Can't Make Me

PSEL – **Standard 3:** Effective educational leaders strive for equity of educational opportunity and culturally responsive practices to promote each
student's academic success and well-being.

Selected Elements:
3a – Ensure that each student is treated fairly, respectfully, and with an
understanding of each student's culture and context.
3b – Recognize, respect, and employ each student's strengths, diversity, and
culture as assets for teaching and learning.
3d – Develop student policies and address student misconduct in a positive,
fair and unbiased manner.
3e – Confront and alter institutional biases of student marginalization, deficit-based schooling, and low expectations associated with race, class, culture and language, gender and sexual orientation, and disability or special
status.
3h – Address matters of equity and cultural responsiveness in all aspects of
leadership.

3.1   *The Story*

Mrs. Evelyn Cummings-Getz has been a member of this school district's
leadership team for more than 20 years, and has seen her share of superintendents come and go during her tenure. At the time the incidents in this story
occurred, Evelyn was the principal of a large elementary school located in a
suburban city that borders an extensive agricultural region; she was nearing
the end of her eighth year in this position. The school enrolls 630 students in
grades K–5, and employs one vice principal, and 44 teachers and professional
staff members. The school district's superintendent was newly appointed to
his position in the preceding year, and quickly found himself in the midst of
a petition being circulated by a group called *Families Rallying Against Racist
Actions* (FRARA).[2]

Approximately 17% of the students in Principal Cummings-Getz's school
are persons of color, a percentage slightly below the region's overall population wherein 25% identify as members of a racial minority group. When Miss
Cummings finished her graduate program in the late 1990s, and moved into
the district to assume her first administrative appointment as the middle
school's vice principal, the geographic area was largely agrarian, and nearly

100% Caucasian. The shift in demographics had thus occurred gradually over a couple decades as more families relocated away from the larger urban center nearby.

Over the years, Mrs. Cummings-Getz had worked persistently to establish supportive and trusting relationships with the parents and family members of the students in her building. Evelyn very much enjoyed seeing the children, and their siblings, advance through the elementary grades, and often followed up with them after they moved on to the middle school. She was understandably troubled when she read FRARA's petition, as it highlighted several examples that implied an unmitigated level of distrust in the school district's administration. The authors of the petition listed their expectations, one of which specified the need for the school district to develop, and implement succinct policies and protocols regarding anti-racism. All told, the FRARA group was essentially demanding a zero-tolerance policy on all racist actions, including discrimination, harassment, silencing, bullying, and ostracizing.

Although Principal Cummings-Getz had established good rapport with a majority of her students' families, she had occasionally dealt with disgruntled family members who believed her to be discriminatory against their children. Evelyn reflected on one such case involving Mitchell Weigelt that had gone on for months, and she wondered if it would ever be resolved.

Chandra Weigelt is the single mother of five children, one of whom was distressingly lost to a drowning accident at the age of three. Her two daughters previously attended Evelyn's school, and are now in college and high school. Mitchell, one of her two sons, is presently in 5th grade, and her youngest will begin Kindergarten next year. For the past two years, Mitchell has had an IEP that details his social and emotional learning goals.

Prior to that in the earlier grades, Mitchell's teachers rarely reported him as displaying any difficult behaviors in their classrooms, or elsewhere in the school building. Mrs. Cummings-Getz met with the school psychologist on several occasions, to discuss the changes she and others had observed in Mitchell's temperament starting near the end of 3rd grade, which was at the time he lost his brother. The young boy was no longer content to engage in classroom activities. He instead began wandering the halls aimlessly, used offensive language, and displayed outbursts for no apparent reason. One of Mitchell's favorite responses to the principal, when she spoke with him about the school's Code of Conduct, was something like "I don't' have to! I DON'T WANT TO! YOU CAN'T MAKE ME!"

It was also around this time that Chandra Weigelt decided it was necessary to move her family out of the school district, and closer to the nearby metropolitan center. Since the children's grandmother also had a home in the district, Mitchell and his high school-aged sister lived with her during the week in order to remain in their same schools. For this reason, and since Chandra no longer had a phone, when Principal Cummings-Getz needed to contact a family member regarding Mitchell's unacceptable behaviors, she often spoke with his grandmother. And these conversations had become more frequent this year.

Tom Gervais, Mitchell's 5th grade teacher, found it increasingly difficult to manage the boy's repeated tantrums during classroom exercises. Specifically, and shortly before the Thanksgiving holiday, Mr. Gervais witnessed Mitchell and another boy punching one another in the hallway as they returned from their physical education class. Both boys were sent to Mrs. Cummings-Getz's office. Mitchell's grandmother was contacted and she came in to meet with the principal; the school psychologist was also present during this meeting.

When Evelyn described the incident to the grandmother, she became quite defensive, insisting her boy was being targeted. Mitchell claimed the other boy had made fun of him during gym class, and had told him he "should move back to live with his mom, so he could go to school in the city with all the other black kids." Hearing this, the grandmother made the following statement to Principal Cummings-Getz:

> You have no idea what it's like for us in school! I know how the teachers treat people like us. I still have a scar on my forehead where a teacher hit me years ago, for absolutely no good reason. And, it appears things are no different today, so you can be damn well sure I will tell my grandson to fight back and defend himself!

The principal listened to Mitchell's grandmother's story respectfully, for several minutes, before explaining the district's Code of Conduct, and the consequences for students who get involved in physical fights in school, or anywhere on the school's property.

Unfortunately, Mrs. Cummings-Getz, still unable to get in touch with Chandra Weigelt, found herself in another very similar meeting with Mitchell's grandmother less than two weeks later. Again, the grandparent fully defended her grandson, and accused Evelyn of showing favoritism toward the "other" students.

Principal Cummings-Getz showed compassion as she patiently described all of the options Mitchell's teachers had provided, in order to help him manage his own proclivities for overt emotional outbursts during class. She concluded by suggesting, "Perhaps your daughter might want to consider another educational setting for Mitchell, if you both believe we are not providing an inclusive, engaging, and safe school environment for him here." To this Mitchell's grandmother responded, "Well! You obviously don't want him here!" and ultimately called Evelyn a *racist white princess*, as she stomped out of the office.

3.2   Questions to Ponder

1. How should Evelyn Cummings-Getz proceed to address this escalating situation?
2. Can you identify any ethical considerations she should be taking into account while attempting to resolve this case?
3. With whom should she consult to make decisions regarding Mitchell's future in her school?
4. How might her actions impact the persons featured in this story (e.g. Mitchell, Chandra Weigelt, Mitchell's siblings, grandmother, other students, teachers and other staff members, etc.)?

3.3   What Actually Occurred?

With the winter holidays approaching, Principal Cummings-Getz decided to schedule a meeting with the district's Assistant Superintendent, Special Education Director, School Psychologist, Tom Gervais, and several other teachers who had worked closely with Mitchell. Feeling quite disheartened that the young boy's family seemed unwilling to support the school's efforts to keep him, and others safe, Evelyn envisioned an outcome where a new behavior intervention plan would be developed to augment Mitchell Weigelt's existing IEP. The principal expected to have this new plan in place when the students were back in session in early January. She was optimistic this expanded group could collaboratively devise strategies that would make the most of Mitchell's strengths, and cultural heritage as assets for his learning.

Coincidentally, two days before this meeting was set to occur, Chandra Weigelt showed up in the school's Main Office requesting to speak with Mrs. Cummings-Getz. Mitchell's grandmother had informed Chandra about the several discussions she had had with the principal about her son's behavior issues, and this prompted mom to take time off from work to visit the school in person. Upon entering the principal's office, Chandra was excited to report that she had spent her last paycheck to purchase a new mobile phone!! From there, the conversation moved on to address Mitchell's social and emotional well-being, both in school and at home. While Ms. Weigelt reiterated her own mother's sentiments about telling all of her children to "defend themselves at all costs," she also expressed a firm desire to support the principal's actions on Mitchell's behalf.

By the end of this unplanned, and somewhat lengthy meeting, Principal Cummings-Getz felt gratified knowing Mitchell's mother would not be undermining the school's efforts to assist her son when he displayed anxiety or other disruptive behaviors. Evelyn informed Chandra about her ideas regarding a new behavior intervention plan for Mitchell, and suggested ways she, and Mitchell's grandmother, might provide incentives at home to reinforce the teachers' activities.

The aforementioned leadership/instructional team successfully created a new plan for Mitchell that included restorative practices, and strategies to promote self-regulation, resiliency, and positive behavior. Principal Cummings-Getz proactively submitted a proposal to the Superintendent requesting funding to support ongoing and targeted professional development for teachers and staff members – topics she proposed should be covered in these sessions included: implicit bias, cultural competence & responsiveness, institutional racism, and restorative practices.

Mitchell Weigelt returned to school in January, and his teacher Tom Gervais noted he seemed calmer, and perhaps more focused on the classroom activities than previously. Principal Cummings-Getz made it a point to visit Mitchell several times throughout the week, and perceived she had started to make some headway in gaining his trust and respect.

At some point in late March, Mrs. Cummings-Getz learned from the school psychologist that Mitchell's grandmother had been hospitalized after suffering a stroke. Further consultation revealed Mitchell's biological father had begun a serious court battle for custody, claiming Chandra Weigelt to be an unfit mother, and a drug addict who had no rights to his kids. In her heart, Evelyn wanted to believe young Mitchell was ready to move on to middle school, and had a promising educational career ahead of him. In her mind, she sadly knew her school's many interventions could only go so far to guide Mitchell's future path, and his case was quite far from being resolved at this point.

3.4   *Follow-up Questions*

1.   To what extent did Principal Evelyn Cumming-Getz demonstrate (or fail to demonstrate) the selected leadership competencies identified above for PSEL #3 – *Equity and Cultural Responsiveness?*
2.   How might Evelyn Cummings-Getz have handled Mitchell Weigelt's case differently to ensure his well-being in her school?
3.   On the positive side, what did Evelyn do that worked well in this case, so she might rely on these practices in future situations?

4   My Wedding Plans

PSEL – Standard 3: Effective educational leaders strive for equity of educational opportunity and culturally responsive practices to promote each student's academic success and well-being.

Selected Elements:
3a – Ensure that each student is treated fairly, respectfully, and with an understanding of each student's culture and context.
3c – Ensure that each student has equitable access to effective teachers, learning opportunities, academic and social support, and other resources necessary for success.
3d – Develop student policies and address student misconduct in a positive, fair and unbiased manner.
3e – Confront and alter institutional biases of student marginalization, deficit-based schooling, and low expectations associated with race, class, culture and language, gender and sexual orientation, and disability or social status.
3h – Address matters of equity and cultural responsiveness in all aspects of leadership.

4.1   *The Story*
Ms. Venera Jorgensen is the Founding Principal of a new elementary school located in a suburban residential neighborhood. At the time these incidents occurred, she had been principal for two years, following 20 years of service as principal in another elementary school in the same district.

Venera essentially had the unenviable task of closing one school, and then immediately opened the new one. The district's Board of Education approved a recommendation wherein all employees interested in moving to the new school, were required to submit updated applications to be considered for appointments there. Therefore, many veteran teachers were displaced during this transition. Subsequently, Principal Jorgensen's school enrolls 670 students in grades K–5, and employs 102 staff members, 45 of whom are certified classroom teachers.

Principal Jorgensen prides herself in making connections with the parents and family members of the students who attend her school. Venera makes it a point to come out of her office to greet moms and dads in the school's Main Office, whenever they happen to be in the building to drop off or pick up their students. Nevertheless, over the course of her long career in school administration, there had always been a handful or so of family members who, for one reason or another, she had difficulty satisfying.

In early May on a Saturday afternoon, Ms. Jorgensen received a call from her superintendent alerting her that he had received a call from a distressed parent – one of the few who Venera placed in this category of persons who were hard to please. The parent of a 4th grade girl had called him to report, in her words, "yet another incident where her daughter had been bullied." Earlier that day, the School Board Chairperson had called the superintendent to report that she had also received an angry call from the same parent. The superintendent had no additional details to share, and subsequently let the principal know Mrs. Martinez would likely be in to see her the following Monday morning.

Leah Martinez is the single mother of Valerie, Marcus and Andrew. Valerie is currently in the 4th grade, and her two brothers are both in high school. The Martinez family had relocated to this school district when Valerie was in the middle of 2nd grade, at about the time the children's father abandoned them.

From the beginning, it was apparent to Principal Jorgensen that Mrs. Martinez was going to be the classic, overly protective "helicopter mom." Throughout Valerie's two years as a student in her building, Mrs. Martinez made it a point to make her displeasures known about all sorts of things, including, to name a few: your physical education classes are quite dangerous; the lunch selections are not appealing; Valerie's 3rd grade teacher is too bossy; there is not enough supervision on the school's playground; many of the girls in her class are bullies, and my daughter is afraid to use the girl's bathroom for fear of being ridiculed; and the homework assignments are too hard.

Ms. Jorgensen had therefore had many meetings with Leah Martinez prior to this most recent incident. Allegedly, what she was about to learn, Valerie's hair had been pulled as she walked down the hallway with a 5th grade boy named Kyle, who was African American. Valerie informed her mother that Kyle's sister had violently pulled her hair for no good reason, and it was not the first time she had done this. Venera was suitably prepared for Mrs. Martinez's visit on Monday morning, but she did not expect her to arrive accompanied by a member of the local police force.

On Saturday, when the superintendent re-directed her to Ms. Jorgensen, Leah apparently decided to call the police, and accused the principal of not protecting her daughter from the African American girls who constantly ganged up on her. When they arrived, Principal Jorgensen escorted the police officer and Mrs. Martinez into her office. She listened intently as Leah further charged her as being way too deferential to the minority population in the district, stating "you favor this little in-group of black girls, and you treat them better than any of the other students in the school!" The police officer observed the discussion for perhaps fifteen minutes, and determined he no longer needed to be present. As he departed, the officer acknowledged Ms. Jorgensen's capable leadership, and informed Leah Martinez she would be directed back to the school if she called the Police Department again to report routine disciplinary incidents like this one.

The officer's casual reprimand left Mrs. Martinez feeling more infuriated. Finding herself alone with Venera, she shared additional news about her daughter Valerie. Over the weekend, while searching through Valerie's knapsack, she discovered a very elaborate chart, drawn with colored crayons, and it was labeled "MY WEDDING PLANS." Here is a loose replica of what Leah briskly shoved in the principal's face:

My Wedding Plans

My Promises to Kyle	Activities at the Wedding
I agree to be married.	Dress Code ~ Fancy
I will party and drink.	Spin the Battle Bottle
I will have sex.	Dancing
I will treat him nice.	Caryoky Karaoke
I will make his lunch.	Truth or Dare

As Venera Jorgensen stared at the drawing, Leah Martinez screamed at her "What are you going to do about this? Someone else put whatever this is in Valerie's knapsack. My daughter would never write these things, and she certainly isn't interested in being with anyone named Kyle!" Principal Jorgensen knew Valerie's handwriting, and also recalled several incidents where the young girl had been dishonest with her. Additionally, the principal suspected Valerie actually wanted to hang out with the small group of African American girls, and she herself had instigated arguments with them so they would pay attention to her.

4.2   Questions to Ponder

1. How do you think Principal Venera Jorgensen should respond to Mrs. Martinez?
2. Can you identify any ethical considerations she should be taking into account while attempting to resolve this case?

3.   What additional information/data might she obtain prior to taking any action?

4.   How might her ultimate decisions impact the persons involved (e.g. Valerie, Leah Martinez, Kyle, other students, family members, teachers, etc.)?

4.3   *What Actually Occurred?*

Principal Jorgensen endured Mrs. Martinez's criticisms for several more minutes. Venera then stood up and seated herself closer to Leah, thus indicating her own desire to be heard. Before asking her administrative assistant to call the 4th grade classroom teacher, and have Valerie come to the office, the principal asked Mrs. Martinez a few questions.

She asked her to describe the hair pulling incident Valerie had complained about, and inquired as to when it was supposed to have occurred. She probed a bit about how much Leah's daughter had discussed the idea of having a boyfriend at her young age. Venera asked Leah what Valerie had said to her when she discovered the wedding plans. And finally, without ever suggesting Valerie had lied to her in the past, the principal asked the mother if she had ever noticed situations when her daughter had perhaps exaggerated stories to bend the truth a bit.

In each instance, Mrs. Martinez fervently defended her daughter. Leah informed the principal that Valerie's hair had been pulled by that boy Kyle's sister last week on Thursday, but Valerie had not told her about it until Friday morning when it was time for her to leave for school. To the second question, she responded "all girls at this age dream about having a boyfriend, but my Valerie is not interested in being with a black kid." Third, Valerie denied making the wedding plans, and insisted one of the other girls in her class must have made it, and then stuck it in her knapsack. Leah awkwardly admitted her daughter occasionally told some tall tales, but insisted she was telling the truth about all of the issues currently on the table.

When Valerie came into the principal's office, she didn't look surprised to see her mother sitting in the room with Ms. Jorgensen. She did however seem to blush a bit when she saw the chart that detailed the wedding plans sitting on the table. Venera invited Valerie to sit with them, and explained the main purpose of the meeting was to hear the truth about what had happened to her while walking in the hallway last week. Valerie repeated her same story, stating Kyle's sister had yanked on her hair for no good reason. The principal asked her if she and Kyle were hanging out together, to which she responded "no way!" At this point, Ms. Jorgensen decided to re-direct the discussion to the drawing, but noted she would later review the videotape captured by the cameras in the hallway to determine the appropriate course of action regarding Valerie's allegations against one of her classmates.

Venera pointed to the wedding plans, and asked Valerie if she had made the drawing, to which she replied "No!" The principal recognized the girl's handwriting, and asked her again if she was telling the truth. Valerie then said "the girls made me do it, and they told me what I was supposed to write in the chart." Ms. Jorgensen calmly asked her "to which girls are you referring, and why do you think they made you draw this chart?" Mrs. Martinez remained silent throughout this portion of the conversation.

Ultimately, Valerie admitted she enjoyed being around the small group of African American girls in her class, since they were cool, and she wanted them to like her. One of them was Kyle's younger sister Brianna, who told Valerie she could be Kyle's girlfriend. Brianna had shown her how to fix her hair, and described the kinds of clothes Kyle would like to see her wear. Venera thanked her for being honest, and asked her if she understood the meaning behind the things she had written in the chart. Leah Martinez spoke up then, stating she would discuss these personal things with her daughter in private.

Later that day, Principal Jorgensen reviewed the building's videotape to determine what had actually occurred in the hallway the previous week. She saw Valerie walking closely next to Kyle, and noted they were not holding hands or otherwise displaying affections toward one another. Brianna entered the picture briefly as she passed by the two of them, smiled at Valerie, and sweetly touched her hair – seemingly indicating she liked the way it looked.

Ms. Jorgensen followed up with Mrs. Martinez to let her know her daughter had not been bullied as alleged. Surprisingly, Leah did not contest the report, and actually thanked Venera for showing compassion toward Valerie. She also apologized for accusing the principal of marginalizing the majority group of students in the school.

Principal Jorgensen made it a point to visit Valerie's classroom several times during the few weeks remaining in the month of May. Venera observed her participate in a variety of classroom activities, and listened to the responses she gave when prompted to do so. In some ways, the principal found it painful to watch Valerie trying to "be liked by" or "fit in with" Brianna's group of girls, both during class and in the cafeteria.

When Ms. Jorgensen discussed Valerie's learning habits with her 4th grade teacher, they both determined she might be better served in a 5th grade classroom with a more structured environment. The master schedule was still being created, and the principal made a mental note about Valerie's ultimate placement for the following school year – if at all possible, the young girl would be assigned to a male 5th grade teacher who routinely practiced "mindfulness" in his classroom. Brianna's small group would be dispersed so not all were in the same 5th grade classroom, and Brianna herself would not be placed in the same class with Valerie Martinez.

4.4 *Follow-up Questions*

1. To what extent did Principal Venera Jorgensen demonstrate (or fail to demonstrate) the selected leadership competencies identified above for PSEL #3 – *Equity and Cultural Responsiveness?*
2. Do you agree with Venera Jorgensen's plans regarding Valerie Martinez's future classroom placement? Explain the reasoning behind your response.

Notes

1 Contributing author: Frederik Ahlgrimm, Ph.D.
2 FRARA is also a pseudonym.

Curriculum, Instruction and Assessment

1   I Never Thought I Was Cheating

PSEL – **Standard 4:** Effective educational leaders develop and support intellectually rigorous and coherent systems of curriculum, instruction and assessment to promote each student's academic success and well-being.

Selected Elements:
4b – Align and focus systems of curriculum, instruction, and assessment within and across grade levels to promote student academic success, love of learning, the identities and habits of learners, and healthy sense of self.
4d – Ensure instructional practice that is intellectually challenging, authentic to student experiences, recognizes student strengths, and is differentiated and personalized.
4e – Promote the effective use of technology in the service of teaching and learning.
4f – Employ valid assessments that are consistent with knowledge of child learning and development and technical standards of measurement.
4g – Use assessment data appropriately and within technical limitations to monitor student progress and improve instruction.

1.1   *The Story*
Mr. Stuart Gomez is one of three full-time Vice Principals at a high school, located in a suburban district, which enrolls 1300 students in grades 10–12, and employs 80 teachers. Mr. Gomez is in his fourth year in the district; he spent three years at the district's middle school before moving to the high school to assume the role of 12th grade Vice Principal. In addition to his administrative certifications, Stuart holds permanent certification in English for grades 7–12.

All teachers in this high school are expected to align their lessons to both the national content standards for their disciplines and the associated college/ career readiness anchor standards. Special education certified teachers regularly co-teach with their content certified colleagues in inclusive classrooms. The school district has continuously provided differentiated professional development for teachers and professional staff members within vertical

© KONINKLIJKE BRILL NV, LEIDEN, 2020 | DOI: 10.1163/9789004436862_005

and cross-disciplinary learning communities (PLCs), and has maintained an impressive high school graduation rate (90+%) for many years.

Approximately two weeks prior to the first quarter marking period, the high school's executive principal asked Vice Principal Gomez to investigate a report she had received from two of the school's tenth grade teachers – Justine, certified in ELA, and Michael, dually certified in Special Education and Literacy Education. Even though Mr. Gomez had been hired and assigned to work primarily with 12th grade students, the principal chose him to handle this specific case since he had been a highly effective secondary English teacher for many years in a nearby school district.

Justine and Michael were both tenured, and highly respected by their colleagues. Michael was an active member of the building's Parent Teacher Association, and Justine was the lead instructional facilitator for the vertical PLC that had been established for ELA and Social Studies teachers. While neither of them claimed to be "tech-savvy," as a team they had demonstrated an operative use of technology within their pedagogical strategies. When 9th grade students met with school counselors to plan their 10th grade schedules, many requested to be placed in Justine and Michael's co-taught ELA classes. Word had gotten out these teachers provided students with a variety of intellectually challenging assignments that required collaborative discussions and authentic writing exercises.

Mr. Gomez was initially perplexed when he read the report submitted by Justine and Michael. He therefore went to their classroom to hear their story first-hand. Justine described the key assessment to him – students worked in teams to review three historical documents, and were then required to compare/contrast the authors' descriptions of "freedom" in each publication. Michael noted that "peer editing" strategies had recently been introduced to the class, and students were becoming acclimated to this collaborative writing process. Both teachers highlighted two college and career readiness anchor standards for writing (grades 6–12) which guided their design of this assessment: *Develop and strengthen writing as needed by planning, revising, editing, rewriting, or trying a new approach. Use technology, including the Internet, to produce and publish writing and to interact and collaborate with others.* Each student was required to submit her/his own completed essay into a shared Google drive.

Two students, Sasha and Roberto, were identified in the report. Sasha and Roberto had been assigned to work as partners in this sophomore ELA class; both were above average students who had been nominated for the National Honor Society. Roberto was on the JV soccer team, and also tutored elementary school students in reading several days a week after school. Sasha was vice president of the sophomore class, a member of the chorus, and volunteered her time at the community's senior center. It goes without saying both students were engaged in their own learning, and had numerous commitments outside of class.

As instructed, both students had submitted their completed papers electronically into the designated shared Google drive. When Justine opened Sasha's document, she quickly reviewed the edit history and discovered that Roberto had been the last person to enter copy into the essay, and the time stamp read 10:41 PM the night before the assignment was due. She then reviewed Roberto's essay to see that he had uploaded his own essay at 1:20 PM during his study hall on the afternoon before it was due. Despite the fact the content of each essay was unique and well written overall, Justine believed the evidence proved Sasha had submitted work that was not entirely her own and should earn a zero for the assignment. She was firm in her stance that Sasha's actions violated the school's Code of Conduct, and her co-teacher Michael backed her up.

After meeting with the teachers, Vice Principal Gomez next called Roberto into his office, informed him that he had been implicated in a case involving plagiarism, and asked to hear his side of the story. Roberto acknowledged he and his partner Sasha had peer edited each other's papers several times during the course of completing this assignment. He noted the teachers expected them to work together to help each other understand and examine different points of view. Mr. Gomez asked Roberto directly "Did you complete and submit Sasha's paper for her?" Roberto responded by sharing a screen shot of a Facetime conversation he had had with Sasha the night before the paper was due – the time stamp read 9:52 PM. He explained Sasha was working late at the senior center and had asked him to help her put the finishing touches on her paper. Roberto stated "She dictated the copy she wanted me to include, and I just typed it for her. We accomplished this together via Facetime, and I uploaded her document into the Google drive just before 11:00 PM."

Shortly thereafter, Sasha was called into the vice principal's office, and Mr. Gomez let her know she had been accused of plagiarism by her ELA teacher. He respectfully asked to hear her side of the incident, and she easily corroborated Roberto's story. Mr. Gomez asked Sasha specifically "Is ALL of the written material in the essay your own? Why was it necessary for Roberto to submit the work for you?" Without hesitation, Sasha responded emphatically

> Of course it's my own work – we are *expected* to work together in this class! And, I knew I might not get home from the senior center before

11:00 PM, so I asked Roberto to upload the document for me. Our teachers require us to get our work submitted before that time, or it is marked as late and we lose points!!

1.2   *Questions to Ponder*

1. What actions should Vice Principal Gomez take at this point?
2. What consequences should Sasha and Roberto receive?
3. Can you identify any ethical considerations he should be taking into account while attempting to resolve this case? (See Chapter 12, Section 1)
4. How will his decisions impact the persons potentially involved (e.g. students, ELA teacher, Special Education teacher, parents, other teachers in the PLC)?

1.3   *What Actually Occurred?*

Vice Principal Gomez expected the two veteran teachers were likely to hold the line and insist that Sasha receive a zero for the "plagiarized" paper she submitted as her own. Having not had any previous experience with Roberto and Sasha, Stuart Gomez was not entirely certain he could trust their honesty. He nevertheless felt torn between standing behind the decisions rendered by Justine and Michael, and digging deeper into the actions the students had reportedly taken to complete the ELA writing assignment as instructed.

His first step was to contact Sasha's parents to inform them about the teachers' report regarding her writing assignment, and invited them to come in for a meeting with him and their daughter at their earliest convenience. They agreed to come in the next day after school. Stuart contacted Justine and Michael and asked them to be present at the meeting as well.

During the meeting Stuart asked the teachers to share their reasons for concluding Sasha had plagiarized her paper. Sasha was then allowed to respond to their accusations. She explained her understanding that peer editing was an essential component of learning new writing styles in 10th grade. She added that many of her classmates simply exchanged laptops during class to edit each other's drafts without logging into the shared Google drive. Justine did not deny knowing this occurred, but seemed a bit surprised when this information was shared with the group. Sasha concluded by saying

> I didn't try to hide anything. I just ran out of time to finish my essay before I had to go to volunteer at the senior center. I texted Roberto and asked him to Facetime with me after his soccer game. He agreed and

then logged into his own account to help me make the final edits and additions to my paper. If I had wanted to be devious, I would have given him my password so he could just log in as me... **I NEVER THOUGHT I WAS CHEATING!**

Sasha's parents, who are both active PTA members, defended her actions intently. They were adamant about her not receiving a zero on the assignment stating it could jeopardize her admission into the National Honor Society as a sophomore. They admitted their own ignorance regarding the guidelines or protocol for peer editing in Sasha's ELA class. Vice Principal Gomez thanked all for attending the meeting – the parents left stating they'd take this to the superintendent if Sasha received a failing grade for the assignment. Justine and Michael departed feeling less than celebratory since they realized there might be some ambiguity in their peer editing instructions.

Mr. Gomez met again with the two teachers the next day to inquire about the rubric/protocol they had established for the peer editing component of their writing assignments. He reassured them he would uphold their ultimate decision, knowing they all wanted to best support the students and help them not make similar mistakes in the future. They admitted this was a new approach for them, and it was still a "work in progress." They also realized Sasha and Roberto had most likely not behaved inappropriately or unethically. Justine agreed to allow Sasha to re-write her essay without a late penalty. She and Michael worked with their PLC colleagues to create a more prescriptive rubric for peer editing. All 10th grade students received detailed instructions about the new rubric at the start of the second quarter marking period.

The vice principal met individually with Sasha and Roberto to counsel each about making good choices. His cogent advice to Sasha was "Don't make yourself vulnerable to this type of accusation in the future – manage your time well and be mindful of how others will interpret your actions."

1.4   *Follow-up Questions*

1. To what extent did Vice Principal Stuart Gomez demonstrate (or fail to demonstrate) the selected leadership competencies identified above for PSEL #4 – *Curriculum, Instruction and Assessment?*
2. What might you have done differently to resolve Sasha and Roberto's case if you were Stuart Gomez?
3. What professional development is needed for teachers to effectively integrate instructional technology in their curriculum and pedagogy?

2   Silent Night

PSEL – **Standard 4:** Effective educational leaders develop and support intellectually rigorous and coherent systems of curriculum, instruction and assessment to promote each student's academic success and well-being.

Selected Elements:
4a – Implement coherent systems of curriculum, instruction, and assessment that promote the mission, vision, and core values of the school, embody high expectations for student learning, align with academic standards, and are culturally relevant.
4b – Align and focus systems of curriculum, instruction, and assessment within and across grade levels to promote student academic success, love of learning, the identities and habits of learners, and healthy sense of self.
4c – Promote instructional practice that is consistent with knowledge of child learning and development, effective pedagogy, and the needs of each student.
4d – Ensure instructional practice that is intellectually challenging, authentic to student experiences, recognizes student strengths, and is differentiated and personalized.
4g – Use assessment data appropriately and within technical limitations to monitor student progress and improve instruction.

2.1   *The Story*
Ms. Hannah Garcia is Principal of a suburban middle school, and has one Assistant Principal reporting to her. This school enrolls 500 students in grades 5–8, and employs 50 teachers. At the time the incidents in this story occurred, Ms. Garcia had been the building's leader for nine years. The school district's mission and vision highlight its focus on the arts across the curriculum at all grade levels. Each year, community members look forward to attending contemporary musical performances at both the high school and the middle school.

Hannah Garcia earned her permanent teaching certification in PK–12 Art Education. She prided herself in making time in her schedule to join the students and the music teachers as they practiced and rehearsed singing many of the songs featured in the shows. One of her favorite events of the school year is the Opening Night Performance of popular musicals like *Grease* and *Annie*.

In addition to the annual theatrical production which typically takes place in March, the middle school students also perform orchestral and choral ensembles in December and May. These events are very well attended by parents, families and community members.

Fraternal twins Bridget and Brian Emory were in 7th grade. Brian played clarinet in the middle school band, and Bridget was optimistic she would land a singing role in *The Little Mermaid*, which had been selected for that year's musical production. The students' parents were actively engaged in many of the school's initiatives, and Mr. Emory had been elected to be Vice Chair of the Middle School Parent Teacher Organization (PTO).

The Emory family moved into the district when the children were entering the 6th grade, and Principal Garcia had found several opportunities to meet the parents, especially since the father had immediately become an active PTO participant. On the other hand, she had only gotten to know Bridget and Brian marginally over the course of their first year in her school. Both students excelled academically, and each had seemingly made friends easily.

On the morning two days after the Middle School's "Holiday Concert" Ms. Garcia received an urgent call from the Superintendent's Office. The principal was asked to come to the District Office immediately for a discussion of certain songs her students had performed at the recent concert. When she arrived for the meeting, the Superintendent recounted the heated discussion she had had with Mr. Emory the previous afternoon.

Unbeknownst to Ms. Garcia, the Emory family members were very public about their atheism, and emphatically denied the existence of a superior or higher power. The Superintendent noted:

> Mr. Emory came storming into the office yesterday to let me know he was outraged that his son had been forced to play SILENT NIGHT during the concert! His words to me were pretty graphic, many of which I will not repeat. He vehemently complained his family's rights had been violated, and our insistence on calling the performance a *holiday* concert was complete hogwash!

Brian's father further accused the school district of failing to honor his children's First Amendment rights (e.g., *Establishment Clause ~ Congress shall make no law respecting an establishment of religion*). The Superintendent eventually asked Principal Garcia if she had reviewed the list of songs the Band and Choral Directors had selected to perform, and Hannah responded affirmatively. While she did not specifically defend the Music Department's decision to play *Silent Night*, Ms. Garcia inquired as to whether Mr. Emory had also complained about the band's performance of *Harambee: A Song for Kwanzaa*. This inquiry prompted the two leaders to engage in further discussion about various elements found in the State's learning standards for Music, and the Arts in general.

Most importantly at this juncture, the Superintendent informed Principal Garcia that Mr. Emory had left his meeting with her feeling satisfied his perspectives had been heard, and she informed him the district would strictly review its policies regarding students playing, singing or performing music with religious themes. Mr. Emory vowed to bring the issue before the PTO, and also insisted on removing his son Brian from the band. He did however allow his daughter Bridget to remain actively engaged in the middle school's choral group. As Hannah drove back to her office, she reflected on this somewhat disturbing conversation, knowing it was imperative to meet very soon with the members of her Music Department, all of whom taught both in her building and in the high school.

2.2   *Questions to Ponder*

1. How should Principal Garcia structure the agenda for her formal meeting with the music teachers, Band and Choral Directors?
2. What additional information should she acquire prior to scheduling this meeting?
3. Are there any legal issues she should be considering?
4. How will her decisions impact the persons potentially involved (e.g. Brian & Bridget Emory, other middle school students, members of the school's Music Department, other teachers, family and community members)?

2.3   *What Actually Occurred?*

Having served as a school building administrator for nearly ten years, Hannah Garcia had earned much respect among her colleagues. She had also been elected to hold an officer's position in her State's professional association for educational leaders. In carrying out the duties of that role, Ms. Garcia had garnered a statewide reputation for improving student achievement, and for supporting the autonomy of teachers in the design/delivery of their standards-driven curricula.

Principal Garcia met with her Assistant Principal to bring him up to speed on the situation that had developed. They spent time reviewing the Arts Learning Standards and the specific elements included in the anchor standards for Music curricula in grades 5–8. Both of them knew the district did not have a policy in place that explicitly banned music with religious themes at school-sponsored events, and members of the community had heretofore been more or less silent on the matter.

As they reviewed the standards together, two phrases stood out as being salient in this matter: *Students should be able to identify: (1) The musical qualities that give persuasive music its effect on the perspectives and beliefs of the listener; and (2) The ways in which music is used to inform or change the beliefs, values, or behaviors of an individual or society.*

During her time as President of the school leaders' professional organization, Ms. Garcia had learned about a few districts across the State, and in neighboring States, where School Board members had campaigned for a more secular playlist for their school's holiday concerts. A number of these districts had subsequently banned many of the historically popular Christmas Carols she herself had grown up singing. She wondered if this was the prudent direction for her own district at this point in time when public schools are becoming more sensitive to the religious, political and social beliefs students bring to the classroom. Just the same, in her mind the diverse nature of the playlist her own teachers had developed for this year's holiday concert distinctly emphasized the school's neutrality toward religion.

Ms. Garcia respected her teachers' decisions implicitly, and had therefore established a very collaborative culture in her middle school building over the years. It was essential to ensure the teachers in her Music Department had an opportunity to explain the logic and reasoning behind their curricular decisions, and resultant musical selections for both the school's band and choral group. The principal sent a personal note to each of three Music teachers and the Band and Choral Directors inviting them to meet with her during their common planning period at the end of that week. Her note included the agenda for the meeting which allowed time for all persons to discuss strategies they were using to prepare students to contribute to the diverse cultural contexts of their society. The resultant meeting also provided time for the group to collegially discuss the school's past, present and future musical selections and productions.

As promised, Mr. Emory brought his issues before the members of the PTO, and they ultimately received time on the agenda to make a formal presentation to the School Board. Even though not all PTO members were as vocal about or invested in the topic as their Vice Chair, they showed up in force to support him during the February Board Meeting.

Following this meeting, the Superintendent asked Principal Garcia to work collaboratively with the high school principal to come up with a draft curricular proposal that would both celebrate the district's focus on the arts across the curriculum, and simultaneously respect the School Board's newly formed views regarding the students' future artistic displays, theatrical productions, and musical performances. Principal Garcia and her high school counterpart structured a series of monthly meetings with all faculty members who taught art, design, theater and music for the remainder of the year. They submitted their proposal to the Superintendent in June which largely retained the curriculum, instructional strategies and assessments that had been in place since the new Arts Learning Standards had been adopted.

One notable change however was reflected in the Music Department's decision to change the name of the December performances at the high school and middle school to "The Winter Celebration Concert." Bridget Emory continued to participate in the choral group as an 8th grade student the following year, and her brother re-joined the band. Their father was most pleased with the Choral Director's playlist which included twelve songs, a few of which were: *Ode to Joy*, *Chinese Dance from the Nutcracker*, *Frosty the Snowman*, and *Ukrainian Bell Carol*.

While the school district did not officially adopt a policy banning musical selections with a religious theme, the Music Department has deemed it wise to be culturally aware when determining musical selections, while still focusing on challenging and interesting musical pieces.

2.4   *Follow-up Questions*

1. To what extent did Principal Hannah Garcia demonstrate (or fail to demonstrate) the selected leadership competencies identified above for PSEL #4 – *Curriculum, Instruction and Assessment?*
2. What more could Hannah Garcia have done to respond to the complaints brought forward by Mr. Emory?
3. What conversations might Ms. Garcia have with other building leaders to ensure a consistent district-wide approach to this issue in the future?

3   How Did They Override the System?

PSEL – **Standard 4:** Effective educational leaders develop and support intellectually rigorous and coherent systems of curriculum, instruction and assessment to promote each student's academic success and well-being.

Selected Elements:

4c – Promote instructional practice that is consistent with knowledge of child learning and development, effective pedagogy, and the needs of each student.

4d – Ensure instructional practice that is intellectually challenging, authentic to student experiences, recognizes student strengths, and is differentiated and personalized.

4e – Promote the effective use of technology in the service of teaching and learning.

4f – Employ valid assessments that are consistent with knowledge of child learning and development and technical standards of measurement.

4g – Use assessment data appropriately and within technical limitations to monitor student progress and improve instruction.

3.1 The Story

Mr. William Roberts was recently hired as the Principal at a rural middle school which enrolls approximately 500 students in grades 5–8, and employs 36 teachers. Immediately prior to this appointment Mr. Roberts had been an Assistant Principal in a neighboring school district for two years. Since he had worked as both a second grade teacher, and then an instructional coach in the current district for many years, William was delighted when the superintendent called to inform him about the opening in the middle school. He holds permanent teaching certifications in elementary education and literacy education.

Along with many others across the nation, Mr. Roberts' school district adopted an online data reporting and analysis system called *ManGO/360*.[1] Beginning with the 2007–08 school year, this diagnostic assessment tool enabled teachers in grades K–8 to monitor their students' growth in literacy and numeracy. William Roberts first received training to use *ManGO/360* with his elementary school colleagues when he was a second grade teacher. At three times during the year, all teachers at that time were expected to administer both the Literacy and Math assessments to their own students. These assessments changed each year, and teachers gave them to their students face-to-face, in a one-on-one format within the regular classroom during the times set aside for testing.

Over the next few years, by virtue of having its elementary and middle school teachers using *ManGO/360*, the school district's administrative team learned that a large percentage of K–8 students were identified as being at high risk of falling behind in both Math and ELA. This data subsequently drove the district's development of a very robust K–8 Response to Intervention (RtI) plan, and also led to targeted professional development programs for the entire educational staff.

Five years after teachers began using *ManGO/360*, Mr. Roberts interviewed for and received one of his elementary school's three positions as an instructional coach. It was around that same time the State approved new components within the annual professional performance reviews for teachers. Moving forward, school districts were expected to measure student growth, and use it as one of several indicators of a teacher's effectiveness. As a result of this regulatory change, teachers were no longer permitted to administer the *ManGO/360* benchmark assessments to their own students. As a newly appointed instructional coach for ELA, William Roberts worked with the other two coaches to devise a cooperative way for teachers to administer the assessments in an equitable and efficient manner.

The first scheduling configuration set aside one full day for teachers to complete the testing. Each grade level had four classrooms of 20 students, and four equal time blocks were arranged for teams of teachers to move from one room to the next and test each other's students one-on-one. For example, here is how the 2nd grade team worked together:

Time block & Grade 2 classroom for *ManGO/360*	Grade 2 teachers administering *ManGO/360*	Grade 2 teacher in planning period	Grade 2 students with substitute teacher
1. Class A	B, C, D	A	B, C, D
2. Class B	A, C, D	B	A, C, D
3. Class C	A, B, D	C	A, B, D
4. Class D	A, B, C	D	A, B, C

With this configuration, teachers soon began to complain to the administration about how their own colleagues were administering the assessments to their students. They even began to blame one another if their own students didn't earn high scores, stating things like:

> I know my own students well, and know when to turn pages more slowly, and know not to mark a kid wrong for having a speech impediment. It's not fair to be dinged for someone else's fallacies!

Mr. Roberts and the other instructional coaches went back to square one, and devised an alternate plan for the elementary school's teachers to complete the *ManGO/360* assessments.

A second plan allowed grade level teachers to simply switch with their neighbor colleagues (i.e., A and B worked together, and C and D worked together). Critical information regarding students' special learning needs could be shared ahead of time, so teachers knew what testing strategies were necessary to enable kids to do their best and be successful. This plan also had its naysayers, since teachers complained about being out of their own class-rooms for an extended period of time.

The third plan William Roberts helped create unexpectedly coincided with a statewide change in the teacher evaluation system – student growth would now be measured independent of teacher effectiveness. Mr. Roberts, together with the other ELA coach, math coach, school psychologist and three reading teachers formed a *ManGO/360* team, and they administered all of the assessments to the K–4 students from that point on. On average, it took the team about two weeks to test all students individually. It was during this school year when Mr. Roberts completed his educational administration certification, and took an assistant principal position in another school district, one that had also adopted *ManGO/360*.

By the time William Roberts returned to his current district to assume the middle school principal position, Philip Das had been hired as Director for Curriculum, Instruction and Assessment (DCIA). The district had also purchased services from a countywide data coordinator, whose findings revealed a strong correlation between scores the students received on *ManGO/360* exercises and the State assessments for grades three through eight. The district had therefore modified its RtI plan, and the new DCIA spent a good portion of his time learning about *ManGO/360*. In so doing, he earnestly reviewed student growth indicators, as reported within that data analysis tool.

Mr. Das, having completed his graduate education and prior administrative experience in another part of the country, was not immediately familiar with *ManGO/360*. He often relied on persons like Principal Roberts to provide a historical perspective regarding its use by teachers and the administration. One such instance is essentially at the heart of this story.

Rather than use the *ManGO/360* data primarily to identify the special learning needs of individual students, Philip Das had discerned it was also possible to look at specific teacher's student growth rates to determine which kids were actually getting the best instruction. Teachers had gotten wise about this new administrator's interest in making connections between their students' growth scores, and their own teaching competencies. As a result, several had become overly anxious about how well their kids performed on the *ManGO/360* assessments.

One afternoon, just before the district's weekly leadership team meeting, the DCIA shared some disquieting *ManGO/360* reports with Principal Roberts. Mr. Das discovered data that revealed a huge discrepancy between the early literacy scores one cohort of 1st grade students received, and the scores received by the same cohort when they started 2nd grade. Philip asked William directly,

You were both a teacher and an instructional coach in that building, so **HOW DID THEY MANAGE TO OVERRIDE THE SYSTEM**? Is it possible to manipulate scores when administering these assessments?

3.2   *Questions to Ponder*

1.   How should Principal Roberts respond to the Director of Curriculum, Instruction & Assessment's request for information in this case?
2.   What investigatory actions should William take in order to obtain additional evidence prior to having a follow-up meeting with Philip?
3.   Can you identify any ethical considerations he should be taking into account while attempting to resolve this case?
4.   How will his decisions impact the persons potentially involved (e.g. students, teachers, instructional coaches, himself, DCIA, etc.)?

3.3   *What Actually Occurred?*

Principal Roberts found himself in a quandary, as he stared at the *ManGO/360* data charts Philip Das had placed on his desk. For this cohort in first grade, only 5% of students were in tier one for early literacy in the fall; remarkably, by the time the spring assessments were given, 92% of them were in tier one. Conversely, when the same cohort entered second grade, only 12% of the students were in tier one; and, when they completed the spring assessments that year, only 25% had moved up to tier one.

While the data seemed to suggest something was strangely awry, William had absolutely no reason to suspect his former elementary school colleagues would have knowingly misreported the results of the assessments for this specific cohort of students. Furthermore, the *ManGO/360* team was still in place, which removed the 1st and 2nd grade teachers from the entire process of administering the assessments, and uploading the students' scores. Being new to his leadership position in this district however placed Mr. Roberts in an unenviable position. As a building administrator, he was expected to do whatever was necessary to ensure all teachers and professional staff members were promoting every student's academic success and well-being. Ethically, on the other hand, he knew the *ManGO/360* system had not been scientifically designed to monitor or measure teacher effectiveness.

As William Roberts reflected on the DCIA's questions regarding this data, he decided to seek advice from his own professional mentor who had just retired from a superintendency in an urban district located several hundred miles away. Her name was Sarah McKenzie, and William trusted she could provide insightful guidance, especially in this matter. As it turns out, she had been a member of the State Education Department's Technology Assessment

Committee who had initially examined the practicality and unique features of *ManGO/360*.

William's resultant conversation with Sarah proved incredibly constructive. One of the first things she suggested he might consider is the extent to which Mr. Das' request for historical information was actually somewhat rhetorical. Sarah inferred the following possibility – "Since Philip himself was new to the district, perhaps he was simply testing the waters to determine how to best work with William who was the newest member of the district's leadership team." With Ms. McKenzie's assistance, here are some of the notes Principal Roberts made for himself as he prepared for his next meeting with Director Das:

- The DCIA's focus on the student growth data charts should not be ignored, but celebrated. When used properly *ManGO/360* provides valid, comprehensive assessments that are consistent with knowledge of child learning and development, and reliable/technical standards of measurement.
- The data William was asked to examine was more than three years old, so perhaps we can be better served by focusing on long-range trends in the results as opposed to single snapshots.
- Many of the same elementary teachers are still there, and the members of the *ManGO/360* team are largely the same as when the abnormal results were reported. Since then, the growth rates for that cohort of students, who are now in middle school, have normalized. Maybe it was just a fluke in the data analysis, and we should not spend any more time pondering those erroneous charts.
- *ManGO/360* has been shown to be a valid predictor of student performance on the statewide assessments. For this reason, some teachers have altered their instructional strategies to prepare kids for the *ManGO/360* exercises. Is this teaching to the test? And, should we expect, or even prepare, all teachers to follow this strategy?
- We should be mindful about the external variables that could be significantly impacting the students' scores on the *ManGO/360* assessments (e.g., location of the testing, time of day the tests are given, students' familiarity with the person(s) administering the assessments, etc.).
- Since *ManGO/360* has not been proven to be a valid predictor of teacher effectiveness in the classroom, ethically we should not be using it for this purpose.

3.4   *Follow-up Questions*

1. To what extent did Principal William Roberts demonstrate (or fail to demonstrate) the selected leadership competencies identified above for PSEL #4 – *Curriculum, Instruction and Assessment?*

2. Are there additional items you might place on the list of topics William Roberts plans to discuss with Phillip Das?
3. What forward-thinking conversations should occur between staff members and the administration regarding the use of data, and teacher accountability for that data?

Note

1 *ManGO/360* is also a pseudonym.

Community of Care and Support for Students

1   Not Mine, Smoking Stinks!

PSEL – Standard 5: Effective educational leaders cultivate an inclusive, caring, and supportive school community that promotes the academic success and well-being of each student.

Selected Elements:
5a – Build and maintain a safe, caring, and healthy school environment that meets the academic, social, emotional, and physical needs of each student.
5b – Create and sustain a school environment in which each student is known, accepted and valued, trusted and respected, cared for, and encouraged to be an active and responsible member of the school community.
5c – Provide coherent systems of academic and social supports, services, extracurricular activities, and accommodations to meet the range of learning needs of each student.
5d – Promote adult-student, student-peer, and school-community relationships that value and support academic learning and positive social and emotional development.
5e – Cultivate and reinforce student engagement in school and positive student conduct.

1.1   *The Story*

It was early during the first year of her appointment as principal of a small city elementary school that Ms. Shelia McIntyre learned about the role *law guardians* played in her building. State Statute defines law guardian as an attorney admitted to the practice of law in this State, regularly employed by the Office of the Public Defender or appointed by the court, and designated under this act to represent minors in alleged cases of child abuse or neglect and in termination of parental rights proceedings. Principal McIntyre's K–6 school enrolls approximately 370 students and employs 39 teachers, 74% of whom have been teaching there for more than three years.

On the morning when the following incident occurred, the law guardian for Dennis (3rd grade student) arrived unannounced to meet with him. This being a common monthly practice, the attorney was given space in the vicinity of

© KONINKLIJKE BRILL NV, LEIDEN, 2020 | DOI: 10.1163/9789004436862_006

the Main Office to have her private meeting with Dennis (i.e., no other school building leaders or professional staff members were present during this session which lasted approximately a half hour). Unlike representatives from other community agencies (e.g., Child Protective Services, Social Workers), law guardians do not typically spend time meeting with school building leaders to discuss the academic performance or the learning needs of the students for whom they are providing care/representation.

Simultaneously, one of the building's 5th grade teachers came to Ms. McIntyre's Office to inform her she had found a cigarette butt on the floor in front of Cheryl's (5th grade student) locker. The principal thanked the teacher for her report, and prepared to begin her investigation which would begin with bringing the student in to question her about this incident. Shelia knew Cheryl's father had recently been incarcerated, and her parents were now divorced. At this time however, the mother had been granted full legal/physical custody of her daughter and, to the best of Shelia's knowledge, Cheryl's home life was safe and secure.

Before Principal McIntyre was able to leave her office to go find Cheryl in her classroom, her administrative assistant called to inform her Cheryl's mother was on the phone to speak with her, and her tone was fairly volatile. Shelia, feeling somewhat perplexed, accepted the call and lightheartedly greeted Cheryl's mother with "good morning Mrs. Phillips – are you psychic? I was actually just on my way to Cheryl's classroom!" Mrs. Phillips was fuming mad and did not find this greeting at all cordial. She screamed at the principal demanding to know why her daughter was being accused of bringing a cigarette to school, further stating she didn't even have any tobacco products in her home. When Ms. McIntyre asked her how she had received this information, she responded "I just received a text message from my daughter's *former* law guardian!"

1.2   *Questions to Ponder*

1.   What action(s) should Principal McIntyre take at this time?
2.   Are there any legal issues she should be considering? (See Chapter 12, Section 2)
3.   How will her decisions impact the persons involved (e.g. Cheryl, other students, parent, law guardian, teachers, herself, etc.)?
4.   Can you identify any ethical considerations she should be taking into account while attempting to resolve this case?

1.3   *What Actually Occurred?*

Principal McIntyre quickly surmised the law guardian in her building had overheard the brief conversation she had had with her 5th grade teacher, not more than 15 minutes prior. She took a look out her office door and noted the attorney was still meeting with Dennis, but had apparently neglected to close the door to the room to which she had been assigned. Clearly, this was a direct breach of confidentiality on the part of the law guardian who had pre-maturely managed to cause a parent considerable stress and anxiety. Before Shelia went to get Cheryl from her classroom, she made a call to the Assistant Superintendent for Student Services (ASSS) and described the events that had transpired thus far that morning. This district level administrator assured Shelia she would immediately contact the law office where this person was employed to submit a formal report about the attorney's unprofessional behavior. The ASSS also requested Shelia call the mother back to determine the exact content of the text message she had received.

Principal McIntyre next called Mrs. Phillips to let her know she was beginning her investigation of the "cigarette butt" incident, and asked her to share the text of the message she had received on her phone from the law guardian. Mrs. Phillips sounded a bit calmer by then and readily shared the message with Shelia – "Cheryl is in trouble for bringing tobacco – cigarette butt – to school and she could get suspended!" The principal promptly relayed this information to the ASSS, and then proceeded to visit Cheryl's 5th grade classroom.

Ms. McIntyre brought Cheryl to her office and showed her the cigarette butt her teacher had found on the floor in front of her locker. When the principal asked her if it belonged to her, Cheryl immediately stated "that's NOT MINE, SMOKING STINKS! My mom doesn't smoke and never allows anyone else to smoke in our house." Thanking Cheryl for her honesty, the principal proceeded to interview other 5th graders who had lockers near Cheryl. It didn't take her long to identify the owner of the cigarette who gleefully admitted it was his, also bragging he planned to share it with his kid brother on the way home that afternoon. Per the district's Code of Conduct, this student's parent was contacted, and he received a one-day suspension for bringing a tobacco product into the building. Shelia also contacted Cheryl's mother once more to apologize to her for the unfounded allegation that had been made about her daughter.

The ASSS later informed Principal McIntyre the law guardian had no legal right to discuss students' cases while in the building to meet with other students to whom she had been assigned. This attorney was presumably reprimanded by her law firm; she is however still acting as a law guardian for students in Ms. McIntyre's building.

Shelia McIntyre dutifully recognized the need to establish a more formalized and rigorous process to handle future school visits by her students' law guardians. Knowing it was her responsibility to maintain a safe, caring and healthy educational environment for all students, Shelia could no longer allow attorneys to casually come and go as they pleased. She set in place a protocol whereby: (1) the law guardian arrives, is asked to provide ID and sign in; (2) a member of her leadership team is sent to bring the student to the office; (3) the law guardian and student are then escorted to a secure room, and the door is closed for the duration of their meeting; (4) the principal or designee remains in the vicinity of the room until the law guardian completes her/his session with the appointed student; and (5) the student is allowed to return to her/his classroom and the law guardian is escorted back to the main office where s/he signs out and leaves the building.

An important lesson Ms. McIntyre learned early in her tenure as a building leader is this – just because a professional with a respected title enters your building, there is no guarantee s/he will behave in an ethical manner – it is not enough to monitor your own ethical behaviors, you must be mindful of all who are assigned to work with or on behalf of your students.

1.4   *Follow-up Questions*

1.   To what extent did Principal Shelia McIntyre demonstrate (or fail to demonstrate) the selected leadership competencies identified above for PSEL #5 – *Community of Care and Support for Students?*

2.   What other actions should Shelia McIntyre have taken in response to the unethical behavior demonstrated by Dennis' law guardian?

2   This Girl Hit My Daughter

PSEL – **Standard 5:** Effective educational leaders cultivate an inclusive, caring, and supportive school community that promotes the academic success and well-being of each student.

Selected Elements:
5a – Build and maintain a safe, caring, and healthy school environment that meets the academic, social, emotional, and physical needs of each student.
5b – Create and sustain a school environment in which each student is known, accepted and valued, trusted and respected, cared for, and encouraged to be an active and responsible member of the school community.
5c – Provide coherent systems of academic and social supports, services, extracurricular activities, and accommodations to meet the range of learning needs of each student.
5d – Promote adult-student, student-peer, and school-community relationships that value and support academic learning and positive social and emotional development.

5e – Cultivate and reinforce student engagement in school and positive student conduct.

5f – Infuse the school's learning environment with the cultures and languages of the school's community.

2.1   The Story

Following more than two decades of school building leadership experience, Ms. Helena Williams accepted the principal's position at a medium-sized urban school that specialized in project based learning and exploration activities at all grade levels. It was during her first year the following incident occurred. Principal Williams' PK–8 school enrolls approximately 360 students and employs 29 teachers; there are 19 homerooms in the building.

Given the diverse nature of her previous administrative appointments, Helena Williams had extensive experience dealing with incidents involving bullying. Over the years she had learned that most persons lacked a clear understanding of what actions or behaviors constituted bullying. In essence, the terms bullying and harassment were often thought to be synonymous. Therefore, in the schools where she had been principal or vice principal, teachers and professional staff members regularly received training sessions so they'd be better prepared to both identify and address bullying issues in their classrooms.

Parents and family members, who had not generally received such training, were often quick to claim their son or daughter had been bullied, the only evidence being that said child had reported the altercation to them. Principal Williams often thought about ways she might better assist parents and family members to understand both the causes and consequences of bullying and cyberbullying in the lives of their young students. She constantly reflected on how critical it was for parents and guardians to provide their children with coping strategies to best deal with potentially confrontational situations, and treat others with respect.

During the first few weeks of the school year Ms. Williams learned that two first grade girls, Maya and Alyssa, were not getting along well at all. According to their classroom teacher Renee Stanton, who was also in her first year at this school, both girls seemed to be highly emotional and often unable to control their own actions. Alyssa was high spirited and seemed to know how to push the right buttons, saying hurtful things to upset her classmate. Maya, who had a history of being a bit rough as a Kindergarten student, did not seem to know how to express herself in words to defend herself against Alyssa's insulting comments. Maya therefore resorted to more physical reactions (e.g., hair grabbing, slapping, hitting), causing Alyssa to report her to Mrs. Stanton.

Principal Williams knew it was essential to have all individuals on the same page this early in the school year. After meeting individually with each girl to hear their stories, she next asked both sets of parents to come in for a meeting with her to discuss the various arguments that had already occurred between Maya and Alyssa. Both of Alyssa's parents showed up, but only Maya's father was able to attend the meeting. While all persons were respectful toward one another during this discussion, there was a distinct level of tension in the room. Alyssa's mom and dad accused Maya of being a bully and treating their daughter badly for no apparent reason. Maya's dad calmly suggested that it was Alyssa who had actually been the verbal aggressor toward his daughter in each incident thus far. He described some of the insulting comments Maya had reported to him multiple times.

Helena allowed each person to have his/her say and she listened intently, taking notes as each one spoke. Both families were insistent their daughters be allowed to remain in Renee Stanton's 1st grade classroom. There was one other first-grade homeroom in the school where Maurice Gauldet had been the primary teacher for more than ten years. As she brought the meeting to an end, Principal Williams provided the girls' parents with a variety of resources they could use to help their young daughters to effectively avoid future confrontations with one another. Driving home that evening, Helena wondered to herself if she had truly resolved the problem, and questioned the extent to which the Maya's and Alyssa's parents would truly help their daughters better manage their anger towards one another.

By the end of that same week, Alyssa's mother posted a comment to the school's blog stating "THIS GIRL (MAYA) HIT MY DAUGHTER! She is most definitely a bully who deserves to be strictly reprimanded for hurting others."

2.2   Questions to Ponder

1.   How should Helena Williams handle the situation at this point?
2.   Can you identify any ethical considerations she should be taking into account while attempting to resolve this case?
3.   How will her decisions impact the persons involved (e.g. Maya, Alyssa, other 1st grade students, family members, Mrs. Stanton, Mr. Gauldet, etc.)?

2.3   What Actually Occurred?

Principal Williams reflected on the meeting she had had with the girls' family members, and studied the policy her school had developed to address these types of incidents when they occurred among the students who attended her school. In the State where her school was located, each School Board was required to approve a Code of Conduct and policy to identify incidents of bullying, adopt a written policy prohibiting intimidation and bullying of any students, and adhere to a process whereby parents and guardians would be notified when their children were involved in such incidents.

Ms. Williams contacted the president of her school's Parent Teacher Organization (PTO) and reassured her that she was both aware of the incidents involving Maya and Alyssa, and was preparing to meet immediately with the family members for the second time in less than two weeks. During that conversation, the PTO president noted it was probably time to re-visit the school's policies and procedures regarding how persons were able to post statements to its blog site.

Helena met with both first grade teachers (Mrs. Stanton and Mr. Gauldet) to gather additional data regarding the behaviors and dispositions they had observed while working with all students in their respective classrooms, especially those exhibited by Alyssa and Maya. Among other things, she learned Mr. Delgado had established a "safe space" in his classroom where he allowed students to be privately reflective in times of stress or anxiety. The principal informed the teachers she planned to have another meeting with the girls' parents and invited them to attend.

During the subsequent meeting with all four parents, Mrs. Stanton was able to describe her first-hand accounting of several of the arguments she had witnessed between the girls. Renee had overheard a few of Alyssa's derogatory comments toward Maya, each time reminding her such language would not be tolerated in her classroom. She also noted that, in more than one instance, it seemed to her that Maya actually wanted to sit close to Alyssa during many of the class activities – to which Alyssa's mother said "why would she do that if she is really afraid of her? Maya is definitely the aggressor here, and we think she should be transferred to another classroom." Maya's parents of course defended her stating

> Why would she lie about the things your daughter has said to her multiple times? Alyssa continually upsets Maya calling her fat and ugly, and makes offensive remarks about her hair. Our daughter deserves to stay in the classroom to which she was assigned at the start of this school year!

As Principal Williams listened to these non-productive statements, she felt bad for both children since it seemed they were not getting proper guidance at home with regard to how to appropriately and respectfully use their words vs. how to not use their hands aggressively toward others. As this heated meeting came to a close, she assured both sets of parents that she would work collaboratively with her teachers and professional staff members to resolve the issues they each were raising.

Ultimately, Helena felt it was in the best interest of both Maya and Alyssa, and for the other young 1st graders in Mrs. Stanton's classroom, that one of them be moved to Mr. Gauldet's homeroom. She consulted with the school psychologist in an effort to gather additional information, and determine which of the two girls might be more successful in each of the two learning environments. Given Maya's history of slightly disruptive behaviors in Kindergarten, the principal decided to move her to Maurice's room, and determined Alyssa would remain with Renee.

Maya's parents were initially very upset with this decision and made their opinions known to Principal Williams. Interestingly though, since Mrs. Stanton had apparently taken Maya to calm down in Mr. Gauldet's "safe space" on a couple of occasions, she actually felt comfortable in the new classroom. Her parents subsequently acquiesced to the principal's decision, the bullying incidents subsided, and Maya became significantly more engaged in her exploratory learning exercises.

2.4   Follow-up Questions

1.   To what extent did Principal Helena Williams demonstrate (or fail to demonstrate) the selected leadership competencies identified above for PSEL #5 – *Community of Care and Support for Students?*

2.   Do you agree with the decision Helena Williams made to move Maya to another 1st grade classroom? Please give one or two reasons for your response.

3   Please Don't Kick Him out of School

PSEL – **Standard 5:** Effective educational leaders cultivate an inclusive, caring, and supportive school community that promotes the academic success and well-being of each student.

Selected Elements:

5a – Build and maintain a safe, caring, and healthy school environment that meets the academic, social, emotional, and physical needs of each student.

5b – Create and sustain a school environment in which each student is known, accepted and valued, trusted and respected, cared for, and encouraged to be an active and responsible member of the school community.

5c – Provide coherent systems of academic and social supports, services, extracurricular activities, and accommodations to meet the range of learning needs of each student.

5d – Promote adult-student, student-peer, and school-community relationships that value and support academic learning and positive social and emotional development.

5e – Cultivate and reinforce student engagement in school and positive student conduct.

3.1   *The Story*

Ms. Brenda Thompson was one of three Vice Principals at an alternative secondary school in a large metropolitan center at the time the events of this story occurred. Her school had been established several years prior to her arrival to provide educational opportunities for students who had fallen behind in traditional junior high/high school settings. Her school enrolled approximately 1350 students in grades 7–12, and employed 52 teachers. The school also housed an adult education program for individuals with special needs (up to age 22). Before assuming this leadership position, Ms. Thompson had been an Assistant Principal for four years at a large urban high school located in the same county. She was therefore quite familiar with the process whereby students, who were struggling academically, could be transferred to the alternative school center to receive more specialized assistance in a non-traditional environment.

Brenda knew too well students could fall behind in their secondary school classes for any number of reasons. In many cases, students who had always earned high grades, and demonstrated proficiency in all courses, suddenly lost interest in their education as they got closer to finishing high school. Benjamin Northfield (called Butch by his family and friends) more or less fit this profile. He was in 10th grade at Vice Principal Thompson's alternative school when she first came to know him. Through his completion of the 9th grade, Benjamin had earned mostly "A" and "B+" grades, and also played for his school's junior varsity baseball team. He had three older siblings who had graduated from the same high school. During the first half of his 10th grade year, Benjamin seemingly lost interest in his classes, and was failing nearly all of them by the end of the first quarter. In December, he was given the choice to transfer to the alternative high school to recover some of the ground he had lost, and he eagerly jumped at the chance to make the move.

Ms. Thompson reviewed Benjamin's transcripts and knew he was a talented and bright young man. Once he was settled into his classes, she made an effort to get to know him, a practice she followed with all new students at varying points throughout the year. Brenda enjoyed her conversations with Butch, noting he always dressed nicely and treated her with respect. By the end of the year, Benjamin had gotten himself partially back on track, but had not fully recovered the typical number of credits for a student entering 11th grade. The vice principal consulted with one of the school's counselors to plan an accelerated course of study for Benjamin to pursue when he returned in the fall.

Brenda Thompson also scheduled a meeting with Benjamin's father, together with Benjamin, to discuss the 11th grade class schedule planned for him. She further suggested some educational activities they could pursue together during the summer months. In her mind, their discussion went well, and she believed Butch would return to school in late August ready to work hard. During the couple of conversations she'd had with Mr. Northfield, Brenda learned he was a single dad whose two oldest sons were successful university graduates, and his only daughter was a sophomore in college.

Vice Principal Thompson made it a point to check in with Benjamin within the first few days of classes in the fall. As always, he was upbeat, very polite, and seemed prepared to delve into his course assignments and class activities. Near the end of October however, as Ms. Thompson reviewed the teachers' attendance records, she noticed he had started to miss school repeatedly. Oddly enough though, Butch began showing up during the lunch period to hang out with his classmates. The cafeteria monitors reported this to the main office, also noting the young man appeared to have a lot of cash on him. At least one of these school employees surmised Butch might be trying to sell drugs to his friends.

The vice principal contacted Mr. Northfield to speak with him about his son's attendance, and informed him that Benjamin had been absent for several days, but had sporadically showed up at lunch to chat with his friends. The father expressed he was not aware Butch had not been attending school, but told Brenda that he had been spending a lot of time at his girlfriend's home in a nearby neighborhood. Ms. Thompson pressed on to let Mr. Northfield know his son had been seen flashing around a lot of cash during his recent lunchtime visits. She further reminded him about the school's attendance policy, to which Mr. Northfield pleaded

> PLEASE DON'T KICK HIM OUT OF SCHOOL! Ever since he started dating this new girl, I've been worried Butch might be involved with something bad. I just haven't been able to figure out what he is up to. He's my youngest kid and I want him to graduate from high school. This is probably his last chance to do so.

The vice principal reassured Mr. Northfield she would do what she could to encourage Benjamin to be an active and responsible member of the school community. Mr. Northfield promised he'd get on Benjamin's case, and persuade him to stop skipping school.

The very next day, Brenda began to position herself in the cafeteria in anticipation she'd "see" Butch in action during one of his drop-in lunchtime visits. Shortly thereafter, the young man showed up in nice clothes and proceeded to join some of his friends at their lunch table. Ms. Thompson approached Benjamin and invited him to her office for a friendly conversation. She asked him to explain why he had not been attending school in recent weeks. In a respectful, still somewhat cavalier fashion, Butch told her he had gotten a job working for his girlfriend's father, which made it difficult to get to school on time. When she asked him if he was in any kind of trouble or engaged in anything illegal, Benjamin promised her things were fine and he'd get things in order so he could start attending his classes again. He said emphatically "my dad worries too much, and he is way too strict, so it's easier for me to just stay at my girlfriends' place." Ms. Thompson let him know this plan was not acceptable, nor did it meet the school's attendance policy. She warned him that he would be at risk of expulsion if this behavior continued.

A few of Benjamin's teachers confirmed his renewed attendance over the next few days, but also observed he seemed to be distracted during their classes and, was never fully engaged in the group discussions. Brenda continued to monitor his sporadic lunchroom activities and eventually witnessed him remove hundreds of dollars of cash in front of his friends. She immediately contacted the School Resource Officer (SRO) to accompany her as she brought Benjamin to her office. Given the pattern of suspicious behavior, the SRO searched Benjamin and found no drugs or any other contraband on his person. She did discover he had $1500 in cash in his coat pocket, and Butch explained he had just gotten paid. Ms. Thompson inquired about the nature of his employment, and he stated "I'm just doing a bunch of odd jobs for my girlfriend's dad." The vice principal again reminded him that she had kept him enrolled despite his lack of attendance, but she could not continue to do this indefinitely. Butch politely responded "Please don't worry about me Ms. T, I'll be just fine! You already have my cell phone number, so you can check on me whenever you want."

3.2   *Questions to Ponder*

1.   How should Vice Principal Brenda Thompson handle the situation at this point?

2. Are there any legal issues she should be considering?
3. What additional information should she be seeking before taking action in this case?
4. Can you identify any ethical considerations she should be taking into account while attempting to resolve this case?
5. How will her decisions impact the persons involved (e.g. Benjamin, Mr. Northfield, Butch's friends, teachers, SRO, etc.)?

3.3   *What Actually Occurred?*

After Benjamin left her office to return to one of his classes, Brenda sat and talked with the SRO for a while, using her as a sounding board as she considered her next moves. In her heart, she suspected the 17-year old might be caught up in something illegal. She also felt empathy for Butch's father, and knew he desperately needed her help to get the boy back in school full time. The vice principal had already bent the rules for Butch by keeping him enrolled in the alternative school, and she didn't feel she had enough evidence to summon law enforcement to investigate at this point. Brenda seriously wanted to believe Benjamin was telling her the truth.

The vice principal consulted with each of Benjamin's teachers. They all said the same thing to her – "He's a very smart kid. We are both sorry and frustrated he is not more motivated to complete the class assignments, or even show up for class on a regular basis." Ms. Thompson also spoke with the school psychologist to determine if he had further insights regarding Benjamin's social interactions and/or emotional state-of-mind. Neither of these avenues provided Brenda any additional peace of mind. She therefore started to send reminder text messages to Butch every morning encouraging him to get to school on time.

This went on for a few weeks, and Benjamin attended all of his classes at least some of the time, but his attendance was never 100%. Late one afternoon, the SRO came into Ms. Thompson's office requesting a *confidential* conversation. Through her contacts at the Department of Juvenile Justice, the SRO had learned Benjamin was apparently caught up in a burglary ring that was allegedly being led by his girlfriend's father. Following multiple break-ins where home residents were held at gunpoint, the local police had begun monitoring the situation, but had not yet caught any of the offenders in action.

Knowing she could not breach confidentiality, Brenda still felt compelled to become more assertive, and thus began calling Benjamin to insist he "get his butt into school immediately." She called Mr. Northfield and urged him to do the same thing. Perhaps in defiance to both of them, Butch then ceased coming to school at all.

One month later, Butch, along with two other boys in the burglary ring, were instructed to head out to a neighborhood location to purchase firearms. They arrived at the identified rendezvous site at the appointed time. As they went to make the exchange of cash for the weapons, they realized the sellers were undercover agents. One of the boys reached for one of the handguns, and this resulted in all three being shot and killed by the officers. Benjamin was the only one of the three who was a high school student.

Brenda Thompson continually asks herself if she could have done anything differently. Why did Butch start showing up to hang out in the cafeteria? Was he trying to recruit others to join the ring, or was he merely bragging about the money he was making? None of the students he spoke with ever came forward to inform her about the content of these conversations. Perhaps she should have brought them in to talk with her directly? Ms. Thompson stayed in contact with Mr. Northfield for a few months. He was of course devastated by the death of his son, and still never blamed her, or held her responsible for what had happened to Butch. Brenda Thompson decided to leave the alternative school, and landed a new leadership position at a traditional high school the following year.

3.4 *Follow-up Questions*

1. To what extent did Vice Principal Brenda Thompson demonstrate (or fail to demonstrate) the selected leadership competencies identified above for PSEL #5 – *Community of Care and Support for Students?*
2. What additional strategies might Brenda Thompson have used to provide social and emotional support for Butch Northfield?
3. Which stakeholder groups should this school district's top administrators consult with to better prepare themselves to prevent future tragic events of this nature?

4 You Must Show Me That Tape

PSEL – **Standard 5:** Effective educational leaders cultivate an inclusive, caring, and supportive school community that promotes the academic success and well-being of each student.

Selected Elements:

5a – Build and maintain a safe, caring, and healthy school environment that meets the academic, social, emotional, and physical needs of each student.

5b – Create and sustain a school environment in which each student is known, accepted and valued, trusted and respected, cared for, and encouraged to be an active and responsible member of the school community.

5d – Promote adult-student, student-peer, and school-community relationships that value and support academic learning and positive social and emotional development.

5e – Cultivate and reinforce student engagement in school and positive student conduct.

5f – Infuse the school's learning environment with the cultures and languages of the school's community.

4.1   *The Story*

Prior to being appointed as principal of this rural elementary school, Dr. Gregory Buchanan had served for six years as principal of the other elementary school in the same district. He had also been a teacher in his current school for ten years before he completed his administrative certifications. Dr. Buchanan's K–6 school enrolls 466 students, and employs 31 teachers, 20% of whom were hired by him. Principal Buchanan was in his sixth year as principal when the incidents in this story unfolded.

In the preceding school year, it was sometime during February when Principal Buchanan received word Tommy Porten, then a 4th grade student, had been misbehaving on the school bus. While Tommy lived most of the time with his mother, older sister, and half-brother, he was occasionally picked up from school by his father who had remarried, and moved out of the district to a neighboring village. When the driver asked the students who were riding his bus to provide their home addresses on an information card, Tommy, for whatever reason, refused to complete the card stating he had more than one address.

The District Office had apparently received complaints from family members whose children had been dropped off at the wrong addresses, so had instructed all bus drivers to update their records to ensure these mistakes would not occur moving forward. When Tommy defiantly returned his blank address card to the driver, he was written up for disrespectful behavior, and issued a warning. Principal Buchanan made it a point to have an informal conversation with Tommy Porten during which he explained the reason behind the bus driver's request for the home address information. Tommy completed the card for Dr. Buchanan, who gave it to the driver, and there were no additional disciplinary issues on the bus for the remainder of that year.

Also during the 4th grade, Tommy Porten was diagnosed as having Attention Deficit Hyperactivity Disorder (ADHD), and had been prescribed medication by his pediatrician. The school psychologist and Tommy's teachers subsequently created a 504 Plan for him. Dr. Buchanan and the school psychologist reviewed the resultant plan with his mother, and explained to her the accommodations outlined were to be modified if necessary, and continued into the following grade year.

Approximately ten weeks into the following school year, Ms. Porten called Principal Buchanan to report that her son had been sexually harassed by a 1st grade female student, and the incident had occurred on the school bus. This was *not* the first time Gregory Buchanan had spoken with Ms. Porten. In fact, for most of the time her son had been enrolled in the school, she had made it a point to call the office every couple weeks to make excuses for Tommy. For example, she either explained or reported: why his assignments were not completed; he forgot to take his medication; other children distracted him during class; the teacher failed to follow the 504 Plan as expected; he didn't want to play outside if it was too cold, and so forth.

Therefore, Dr. Buchanan patiently asked Tommy's mom to explain what she believed happened on the bus. Ms. Porten informed the principal a first grade student by the name of Sally Bowman had "grabbed Tommy's butt" as he passed by her seat on the bus. She further stated this young girl had repeatedly demonstrated flirtatious behaviors toward other boys besides her son. Gregory politely ended the call and promised her he would investigate the allegation right away. Since the end of the day was approaching, Principal Buchanan decided to postpone his interview with the students, and made it a point to take a ride on Tommy's bus route that afternoon. This was a practice he had employed for many years, as it allowed him to be visible to students and their families, and to other professional staff members in the district. Gregory also felt it cultivated positive student conduct both inside and outside of the school's walls.

Dr. Buchanan contacted the district's School Resource Officer (SRO) the following morning, and requested that she join him to watch the bus videos. Together they reviewed several days of video records taken during Tommy Porten's bus routes. In no instance did they see any contact between Sally Bowman and Tommy, nor between the little girl and anyone else for that matter. They did however observe Tommy having an argument with the bus monitor as he refused to sit in the seat to which he was assigned.

The principal next interviewed Tommy Porten who insisted Sally had grabbed him as he walked past her on the bus. He stated "Sally is always telling boys she is in love with them. I think she is a pervert since she is always trying to hug me, so I just push her away when she does that stuff!" When Dr. Buchanan told the young 5th grade boy he had seen no evidence of this when he reviewed the videos taken on the bus, Tommy screamed back "why don't you believe me?!?" Gregory continued the conversation in an effort to calm the boy down, and tried to get him to understand Sally's behaviors from a wider perspective of acceptance and respect.

Later in the day, most likely after receiving an emotional text message from her son, Ms. Porten showed up in the office demanding to see Dr. Buchanan. Gregory escorted the mother into his office at which point she shouted "How dare you accuse my son of being a liar!? He is so upset right now, that he can't even stand being in this school building another minute. YOU MUST SHOW ME THAT TAPE immediately!"

4.2   Questions to Ponder

1. What action(s) should Dr. Buchanan take at this time?
2. Can you identify any ethical considerations he should be taking into account while attempting to resolve this case?
3. How will his decisions impact the persons involved (e.g. Tommy, Sally, other students, Ms. Porten, family members, teachers, bus driver, etc.)?

4.3   What Actually Occurred?

Principal Buchanan allowed Ms. Porten to speak her piece for as long as she needed. As she went on with her accusatory outburst for several more minutes, Tommy's mother further informed Gregory that she had already taken it upon herself to report Sally Bowman's parents to Child Protective Services (CPS), "since no 1st grade girl would be demonstrating those deviant behaviors unless she herself were being sexually abused!"

While this new information caught him slightly off guard, Dr. Buchanan steadily explained the school district's policy regarding bus videos to Ms. Porten. He informed her these recordings were never shared with anyone other than the SRO and members of the school district's administrative team. Gregory also reiterated he had seen no evidence of aberrant misconduct on the part of Sally or any of the other students who rode Tommy's bus with him. Ms. Porten responded to this news by pulling Tommy out of school for the remainder of the year during which time he was home-schooled (Note: his older sister and younger half-brother were not removed from school). Dr. Buchanan directly contacted the District Office, and filed all of the necessary documents that would allow this to happen.

Soon thereafter, the principal received a call from the Village Police Department as they followed up on a report that had been filed by CPS regarding the Bowmans. Dr. Buchanan agreed to meet with them, and asked the school psychologist to be present during the discussion that focused on Sally Bowman's behavior in school. The principal and psychologist concurred that

Sally was perhaps a bit unusual in her overly demonstrative actions – she likes to hug other kids, boys and girls alike. Her teachers continued to remind Sally to be respectful of other students who had "personal space" into which she should not intrude. Academically, Sally was advanced for her 1st grade level, so her teachers always sought ways for her to take on more challenging tasks alongside her classmates. The police officer departed feeling satisfied with the meeting, and no further actions were taken against the Bowman family.

Several months later, as the school year was drawing to a close, Tommy Porten's mom called Principal Buchanan to ask a favor. The 5th grade class was planning an all-day field trip to a large amusement park, and Ms. Porten wanted her son to be able to attend with his former classmates. Since Tommy had not been suspended, and his mom had the right to request he be home-schooled, Dr. Buchanan approved her request, and Tommy was allowed to participate in the field trip activities.

Interestingly though, many of the teachers in the building were displeased with Gregory's decision stating it was setting an untenable precedent. Even still, the decision had the beneficial effect of promoting a positive, and ultimately more collaborative relationship between the school and Ms. Porten. As Tommy's 5th grade year as a home-schooled student ended, Ms. Porten informed Principal Buchanan that her son would be returning to attend 6th grade as an in-school student the following year. While she remained very defensive of Tommy, Ms. Porten also acknowledged he was not perfect. She admitted to Gregory that her son, like all young adolescents, could find lots of ways to exaggerate the truth, and blow simple things out of proportion.

4.4   Follow-up Questions

1.   To what extent did Principal Gregory Buchanan demonstrate (or fail to demonstrate) the selected leadership competencies identified above for PSEL #5 – Community of Care and Support for Students?

2.   What might Dr. Buchanan have done differently to both investigate and resolve the incident alleged to have occurred on Tommy and Sally's bus ride?

Professional Capacity of School Personnel

1 But I'm a Good Teacher

PSEL – Standard 6: Effective educational leaders develop the professional capacity and practice of school personnel to promote each student's academic success and well-being.

Selected Elements:
6b – Plan for and manage staff turnover and succession, providing opportunities for effective induction and mentoring of new personnel.
6e – Deliver actionable feedback about instruction and other professional practice, through valid, research-anchored systems of supervision and evaluation to support the development of teachers' and staff members' knowledge, skills and practice.
6f – Empower and motivate teachers and staff to the highest levels of professional practice and to continuous learning and improvement.
6h – Promote the personal and professional health, well-being, and work-life balance of faculty and staff members.

1.1 *The Story*

Mr. Aaron Robischon is one of two full-time Vice Principals at a PK–8 school, located in a large urban district, which enrolls 900 students and employs 80 teachers and professional staff members. The school year during which this story occurred marked his fifth year in this leadership position, and he had reported to four different executive principals during that time frame. At this point however, the principal with whom he was working had been in the building for three years, and she had established a very cohesive leadership team with her two vice principals, school psychologist and school counselors. Aaron therefore participated fully in the teacher recruitment, selection and retention process throughout the year. He also led the 7th grade professional learning community (PLC) for mathematics.

On average, due to expected retirements and staff attrition for various other reasons, this school typically hired five to eight new teachers each year. Mr. Robischon recalled the difficulty they had hiring a well-qualified math teacher that year. Working with a very small applicant pool in June, the

© KONINKLIJKE BRILL NV, LEIDEN, 2020 | DOI: 10.1163/9789004436862_007

team interviewed six candidates; not one was stellar, nor did any one of them seem to fit the vision/culture of this very diverse PK–8 school. The administrative team worked throughout the summer and ultimately interviewed one more candidate who had just completed his initial certification in secondary mathematics. With time running out, the team agreed this candidate possessed the knowledge, skills, and dispositions to be successful in their school. Two weeks before the start of the academic year, Roy Atkinson was hired into a tenure track teaching position and assigned to teach 7th grade mathematics.

More than a decade ago, the school district had set in place a well-researched process whereby all new teachers were assigned to work with a PAR mentor (Peer Assistance and Review) for a period of one year. The program's development and implementation evolved over several years (1999–2005); the entire process was fraught with a variety of challenges that required collaborative efforts and compromises on the parts of the district-level administration, principals' union, and teachers' association. The primary function of the PAR mentor is to assist new teachers in the district in developing and improving skills required to be a proficient educator, and to be an effective participating member of departmental teams, and school building committees. Vice Principal Robischon, having previously taught in this school district, was a member of the first cohort of new teachers who had been assigned PAR mentors, and knew firsthand how beneficial their assistance can be.

Roy Atkinson was introduced to his PAR mentor – Shana Harris – immediately after he was hired and the school year began. Shana quickly established guidelines for Roy, and she articulated her expectations regarding submission of lesson plans, curriculum standards, analysis of assessment data and classroom management. She also discussed the rubric the district had adopted for the annual professional and performance review of its teachers, and let Roy know when he would be meeting with her on a weekly basis. Ms. Harris explained to Roy that she was expected to submit regular reports regarding his teaching effectiveness and overall performance to the district's PAR Panel which met in December, March and May. The PAR Panel is co-chaired by a Deputy Superintendent and the President of the Teachers' Association, and its membership consists of four additional teachers and three administrators.

Vice Principal Robischon worked collaboratively with the PAR mentors in the building, and kept the building principal apprised of any issues or concerns that might come up as new teachers became acclimated to their new roles and responsibilities. Mr. Atkinson was expected to attend and contribute to the 7th grade PLC that Aaron Robischon convened on a daily (40 minutes) basis. Since the vice principal was meeting with Roy every day, he was able to let the PAR mentor know how to best assist him unpack the math modules, create re-teaching plans, and analyze interim assessment data for his students.

Robyn Harris noted the first signs things were not going well when Roy neglected to submit his lesson plans to her on time beginning in October. Aaron Robischon also noted Roy was either not showing up for the PLC meetings at all, or showed up late and generally unprepared to make meaningful contributions to the discussions. More than once Mr. Atkinson stated "BUT I'M A GOOD TEACHER, and some of your expectations are unreasonable given the number of students I am assigned to teach." Both Robischon and Harris explained that these activities were essential components of his professional obligations as a teacher in the building, and they were non-negotiable aspects of his signed contract.

Ms. Harris delivered her report regarding Roy Atkinson to the PAR Panel in December. Shortly thereafter, Mr. Atkinson was required to meet with the building principal, vice principal and PAR mentor and was informed he was being officially placed on a teacher improvement plan (TIP). His bitter reaction to this news resembled his previous behaviors, and he again exclaimed "but I am a good teacher – and don't see a need for a TIP!" Regardless, Vice Principal Robischon spent 90 minutes per day with him after school for nearly a week, and fully documented all of his efforts to help Roy re-structure his room, re-design his lesson plans, and study in depth the upcoming math modules. In other words, the vice principal devoted individualized attention to Mr. Atkinson ensuring he understood the gravity of his situation and was fully aware of the need to hit the "re-set" button driving his teaching performance.

Despite these interventions, Mr. Atkinson's 7th grade students were a full module behind in mathematics by early February, parents had begun calling the principal to complain about Roy's lack of teaching effectiveness, and students reported they were not learning math during his class. The PAR mentor informed Vice Principal Robischon she had to prepare her next report for the March meeting of the PAR Panel, and requested his guidance regarding Roy Atkinson.

1.2   *Questions to Ponder*

1.   What recommendation(s) regarding Roy Atkinson should Vice Principal Robischon make to the PAR mentor?
2.   Can you identify any ethical considerations he should be taking into account while attempting to resolve this case?

3.   How will his decisions impact the persons involved (e.g. Roy, other teachers, PLC, PAR mentor, students, himself)?

1.3   *What Actually Occurred?*

Vice Principal Robischon believed he had dedicated considerable time supporting and re-directing Roy Atkinson as a new teacher. Still, he wondered if he had actually done everything he could to help him be successful. As he recounted Mr. Atkinson's somewhat cavalier reactions to both himself and Ms. Harris as they tried to mentor him, he knew he had to make a recommendation that was in the best interest of the students in his building. Based primarily on the teacher's ineffectiveness and his unwillingness to follow several of the building's policies and procedures, the vice principal recommended Roy Atkinson be terminated immediately. Robyn delivered this report to the PAR Panel and it was unanimously accepted. The teachers' contract in this district permits first-year teachers to be terminated at any time during the year. Roy was instructed to travel to the district office to receive this news from the PAR Panel co-chairs. He was given the opportunity to resign, and did so without dispute.

When he returned to the school building however, he expressly bad-mouthed the vice principal and PAR mentor claiming they had done nothing to assist him, and he didn't deserve to be fired, all the while avowing "I am a good teacher!" Mr. Robischon quietly escorted Roy to his classroom so he could pack up his personal belongings and return his keys to the building.

With this unpleasant task behind them, the administration faced the reality they had no qualified math teacher for the 7th grade students who would be expected to take the State assessment for mathematics in less than two months. They were able to hire a long-term substitute who was not adverse to teaching math, but was also not certified to do so. Since Vice Principal Robischon was certified in secondary mathematics, and had himself been an instructional coach for math before earning his administrative certification, the principal approved a plan whereby he co-created lesson plans with the substitute teacher and taught the first period class each day. This plan held together for about six weeks, and the substitute teacher was able to replicate Aaron's teaching strategies with considerable fidelity. A new well-qualified math teacher was hired to replace Roy Atkinson near the end of April. The building was essentially down one full-time administrator for part of the day during that time, but the principal fully supported everyone's efforts to ensure the students were receiving thorough math instruction.

At some point in early April, Mr. Robischon received an email request from Roy Atkinson for a letter of recommendation. He respectfully declined to submit a letter into the online application system, but later received a telephone request for a recommendation from a superintendent in another district who was considering hiring Roy as a middle school teacher. The vice principal responded honestly stating "I really don't feel comfortable providing a recommendation for this candidate, and wish you success filling this position."

1.4 *Follow-up Questions*

1. To what extent did Vice Principal Aaron Robischon demonstrate (or fail to demonstrate) the selected leadership competencies identified above for PSEL #6 – *Professional Capacity of School Personnel?*
2. What additional instructional supports (if any) do you believe Aaron Robischon could have provided to help Roy Atkinson improve his overall performance in the classroom?

2   Measure Twice, Cut Once

PSEL – **Standard 6:** Effective educational leaders develop the professional capacity and practice of school personnel to promote each student's academic success and well-being.

Selected Elements:
6a – Recruit, hire, support, develop, and retain effective and caring teachers and other professional staff and form them into an educationally effective faculty.
6c – Develop teachers' and staff members' professional knowledge, skills, and practice through differentiated opportunities for learning and growth, guided by understanding of professional and adult learning and development.
6e – Deliver actionable feedback about instruction and other professional practice, through valid, research-anchored systems of supervision and evaluation to support the development of teachers' and staff members' knowledge, skills and practice.
6f – Empower and motivate teachers and staff to the highest levels of professional practice and to continuous learning and improvement.
6 g – Develop the capacity, opportunities, and support for teacher leadership and leadership from other members of the school community.
6i – Tend to their own learning and effectiveness through reflection, study, and improvement, maintaining a healthy work-life balance.

2.1   *The Story*

Dr. Rita Fiorini is in her eighth year as the principal of a large high school located in an expansive urban school district. The school now enrolls 2000 students in grades 9–12, and employs over 100 teachers and professional staff members. Dr. Fiorini's school had experienced significant growth in recent years. This growth in enrollment, coupled with expected retirements, increased the need for more teachers. More than 70% of the teachers at this school had therefore been hired since Dr. Fiorini was appointed as Principal.

Rita values collaborative decision-making, and is fully committed to developing the leadership capacity of the four full-time vice principals who report to her. And, while she provides oversight for the hiring of all new staff members, the vice principals have been given both the responsibility and autonomy to recruit, select, and recommend the appointments of the teachers for their assigned subject areas and/or grade levels.

Being a "leader of leaders" is an admirable quality, and one that Dr. Fiorini aspires to maintain, and continually improve within herself. One piece of advice she routinely provides to her Vice Principals, specifically when they discuss hiring priorities, is this – always remember to MEASURE TWICE, CUT ONCE! This familiar adage has its roots in carpentry and fine furniture making, where the unintended consequences of cutting too soon might result in the total loss of expensive materials. In the educational profession however, the consequential measurements and cuts are not taken of wood or metal. They are made every time a new teacher or professional staff member is selected, and appointed to provide academic and social supports, services, and extracurricular activities to meet the wide range of learning needs of each student.

Rita reminds the vice principals they are expected to make informed personnel decisions based on a thorough review of prospective employees' credentials and qualifications. Everyone must live with the recommendations and subsequent decisions made by her leadership team, especially the adolescents and young adults in their school, with whom these new teachers and professional staff members will be working for many years to come.

Despite these efforts, Dr. Fiorini's vice principals occasionally made ill-advised decisions when it came to hiring, or recommending the hiring of new employees. In one such case, a vice principal, who had been on the team for four years, hired a behavioral specialist to work with 9th and 10th grade students. On paper, this person was highly qualified, but had not yet accrued much experience. What Dr. Fiorini did not know, was that this new employee was also a close personal friend of the vice principal. Subsequently, whenever the behavioral specialist's performance occasionally fell short of Rita's expectations, the Vice Principal took his failures personally, and felt compelled to defend him during their leadership team meetings.

In a second very different case, Principal Fiorini authorized another, newly hired vice principal to consult with the high school's head custodian as they set about hiring a custodian to work during the night shift. The vice principal was also assigned to supervise the Head Custodian, who in turn oversaw the work of the entire custodial staff. The person selected by the vice principal to be the new night custodian was not Dr. Fiorini's first choice, but she allowed the VP's recommendation to move forward. Eight months later, it had become apparent this new hire was not working out – he was showing up late, not completing tasks, and was reportedly seen in the parking lot on his phone, and smoking cigarettes during his shift. The head custodian reluctantly went around the vice principal to inform Dr. Fiorini about this unfortunate situation. When Rita later met with the vice principal, she realized this new leader was terrified of having a difficult supervisory conversation with the head custodian.

A third case involved yet another vice principal, Angus Hill, who had previously been Rita Fiorini's peer at an elementary school earlier in her career. Being somewhat familiar with Mr. Hill's leadership abilities, Dr. Fiorini hired him three years after she became this high school's principal. Vice Principal Hill was given responsibility for the Math and Science Departments for all grade levels, and was empowered to oversee the hiring process for the teachers in these disciplines.

Maggie Scott was one of the new teachers Mr. Hill had hired to teach Chemistry, and once again this person would not have been Dr. Fiorini's choice for this assignment. During the screening process the team learned that Maggie had initially thought she'd go to medical school, but then changed her mind. Team members observed she had a somewhat strident personality during the interview which required her to deliver a sample lesson to students. Nevertheless, Ms. Scott became Vice Principal Hill's top choice for the Chemistry position, and Dr. Fiorini endorsed his recommendation.

Over the course of the first year of Maggie Scott's employment in the Science Department, Vice Principal Hill observed her teaching on several occasions, but did not report any concerns to Dr. Fiorini during their weekly leadership team meetings. On the other hand, at some point near the end of the school year's third quarter, two other science teachers and at least a dozen students alerted Principal Fiorini about some of Maggie's unconventional instructional practices. Maggie's department colleagues remarked that she seemed to have no clue about how to manage a classroom, let alone a chemistry lab.

The students cited examples of Ms. Scott's lack of judgement, and complained about her boring lectures. They also reported her continual use of derogatory comments and foul language during class. The incident that tipped the scale for Dr. Fiorini was this – one of the students confessed to forgetting to bring his lab notes to class, and said "Ms. Scott reacted in a crazy manner," and further stated, "She grabbed a cupful of flour, called me a lazy moron, chased me out into the hallway, and threw the flour in my face!"

2.2   *Questions to Ponder*

1.   What actions should Dr. Fiorini take at this point?
2.   Can you identify any ethical considerations she should be taking into account while attempting to resolve this case?
3.   How do you see the "Measure Twice, Cut Once" maxim playing out in this case?
4.   How will her actions (both short- and long-term) impact the individuals involved (e.g. Angus Hill, Maggie Scott, other Vice Principals, teachers, students, etc.)?

2.3   *What Actually Occurred?*

As Rita Fiorini looked back on her eight years of leading this high school, she brought to mind all of the times she had empowered the Vice Principals to lead critical initiatives, and make pivotal decisions. She inherently trusted her leadership team members to think things through, and make the best decisions for all stakeholders. In most of those instances, she was truly proud of and satisfied with their actions, and the students largely benefitted in numerous ways. Conversely, there were those few times when she wished she had intervened earlier to prevent misguided decisions from occurring in the first place.

With this in mind, and having listened to the disturbing complaints about Maggie Scott, Dr. Fiorini quickly summoned Vice Principal Hill for a meeting, and requested he be prepared to discuss his teacher evaluation reports with her. As they reviewed the notes taken during his observations of Maggie Smith, Rita noted Angus had given her scores that were in the "Effective" and "Developing" range on the district's teaching performance rubric. When she pressed him to see if he had noticed her apparent lack of classroom management skills, he responded with "she's still young and inexperienced, and I've asked one of the other science teachers to mentor her." And, when she informed him about the allegations the students had made about her lack of professionalism, Angus said in Maggie's defense "She's an intelligent scientist, so she probably just intimidates them."

Following this session, Dr. Fiorini made it a point to visit Maggie Scott's classroom herself, and, after three observations, surmised it was in the best interest of the students, and the entire Science Department to not renew Maggie Scott's teaching contract. To maintain continuity within the procedures she had established with her leadership team, she instructed Vice Principal Hill to "let Maggie Scott go." This course of action did not occur. Angus Hill was seemingly afraid to fire this new teacher he had hired, and didn't know how to express this to Dr. Fiorini. Maggie Scott's contract was renewed, and Angus Hill was simultaneously transferred to another school in the district. While the two incidents were unrelated, Principal Fiorini, along with her staff and students, was forced to live with Vice Principal Hill's decision.

In the State where this school is located, it is extremely difficult to terminate a teacher once he/she has been retained after the first year. Maggie Scott's pedagogical skills have not improved, despite the fact she has received extensive mentoring and professional development. Rita Fiorini knows the students are the ones who are losing out, but remains optimistic the tides will eventually turn in a positive direction.

Upon serious and lengthy reflection, Dr. Fiorini determined she needed to modify her own leadership style in ways that might truly enhance the professional capacity of school personnel. As a "leader of leaders" she most importantly wanted to continuously strengthen the skills of her school's leadership team. In a few of her "measure twice, cut once" notes to herself, Rita Fiorini:

- Accepted the fact that she, and all school stakeholders, would need to live, and be comfortable with the decisions made by others – everyone would be required to collaboratively support newly hired school employees;
- Recognized the importance of knowing where persons are on their own leadership trajectories, meaning some new administrators would need more guidance than others (e.g., as seen in the three examples in this story);
- Identified and provided differentiated professional development opportunities for the vice principals to learn and grow within their unique leadership roles;
- Practiced, practiced, practiced giving timely and actionable feedback to the members of her leadership team;
- Monitored and revised the ways she coached and mentored vice principals, professional staff members, and teacher leaders; and (perhaps most importantly)
- Reminded herself on a daily basis to confront issues head-on right away, and to have those difficult conversations with staff members, even when doing so might threaten the positive relationships she had worked so hard to establish.

2.4 *Follow-up Questions*

1. To what extent did Principal Rita Fiorini demonstrate (or fail to demonstrate) the selected leadership competencies identified above for PSEL #6 – *Professional Capacity of School Personnel?*
2. Why do you think Vice Principal Angus Hill was: (a) Unwilling to terminate Maggie Scott's teaching contract? And (b) Unable to inform Dr. Fiorini about his decision to go against her instructions?
3. What additional steps might Rita have taken to help her vice principals learn to have the difficult personnel conversations that are essential for retaining the highest quality teachers for their students?

3 She's So Disorganized

PSEL – **Standard 6:** Effective educational leaders develop the professional capacity and practice of school personnel to promote each student's academic success and well-being.

Selected Elements:
6a – Recruit, hire, support, develop, and retain effective and caring teachers and other professional staff and form them into an educationally effective faculty.
6d – Foster continuous improvement of individual and collective instructional capacity to achieve outcomes envisioned for each student.
6e – Deliver actionable feedback about instruction and other professional practice, through valid, research-anchored systems of supervision and evaluation to support the development of teachers' and staff members' knowledge, skills and practice.
6f – Empower and motivate teachers and staff to the highest levels of professional practice and to continuous learning and improvement.
6 g – Develop the capacity, opportunities, and support for teacher leadership and leadership from other members of the school community.

3.1 *The Story*

Mr. Charles Douglass is the principal of a large TK–5 school, located in a sprawling suburban district, which enrolls 715 students and employs 30 teachers and professional staff members. This elementary school includes a TK grade level (Transitional Kindergarten) which allows a small number of children, who are not five years old on the September 1st cut-off date to attend classes in an age- and developmentally-appropriate classroom. In most years, there are 24 children in TK, and they move on to Kindergarten the following year. One vice principal reports to the principal, and she was appointed one year after Charles Douglass arrived to lead the school. Nearly 85% of all teachers and staff members are tenured, and were hired prior to Mr. Douglass' initial appointment four years ago.

A Master Scheduling Committee, consisting of the school counselors, vice principal, two representatives from the school's parent organization, and a teacher from each grade level, assists the principal who finalizes the new class schedule each year. A great deal of pre-planning goes into creating the schedule in order to best utilize the collective instructional capacity of the entire staff to achieve optimal learning outcomes envisioned for each and every student. The size of the school requires four or five sections per grade level, and Mr. Douglass has instilled his vision to create heterogeneous groups of students in all classrooms. Family members generally receive notification of their children's classroom and teacher assignments in mid-to-late July.

Principal Douglass spends a good percentage of his time each day making personal visits to the teachers' classrooms, and uses a simple "walk-through form" to provide formative feedback to each staff member several times a year. Over his four years as the school's principal, Charles has worked diligently to establish trust and rapport with the teachers, many of whom, as previously noted, have been with the school for more than 20 years. Claire Sheldon is a member of the school's 5th grade teacher team, and she had just completed her 25th year of service at the time the following incident occurred.

When Jacob Foster's parents received notification their son had been assigned to Mrs. Sheldon's classroom, they immediately sought a meeting with Principal Douglass. At the start of every meeting he had with family members, Mr. Douglass always posited the same two questions following their brief exchange of greetings: First, what specific concerns do you bring to the table today? And second, what outcomes do you expect at which time we conclude our meeting? Charles found this consistent approach useful to keep his meetings on point, and ensure all members present had a common understanding of where the conversation should be focused.

The Fosters had one outcome in mind when they were seated in Principal Douglass' office on a warm August afternoon. They wanted their son Jacob to be transferred out of Claire Sheldon's 5th grade classroom, and they didn't specify which alternate teacher they preferred. When the principal asked them to explain their reasoning behind this request, Jacob's mom replied

> Our son needs a teacher who will provide individualized instruction regarding homework assignments, and also needs structured routines

each day during class. We've heard a number of stories about Mrs. Sheldon's classroom, and know SHE'S SO DISORGANIZED! Jacob will surely struggle amidst the chaos Claire seems to thrive in, and we don't believe she will understand our son's learning style.

Charles Douglass listened to the Fosters as they made their case, and then politely explained the school's collective 5th grade educational environment, and the team's expectations for these older students to gradually take on more responsibility for their learning. He described a variety of strategies all of the 5th grade teachers used to foster greater independence among their students as they prepared to "graduate" and move on to the middle school. To this explanation Mr. Foster responded

> We don't need to hear your educational jargon! If we don't leave your office knowing Jacob will be moved OUT of Claire Sheldon's classroom, our next stop will be in the superintendent's office across town.

3.2   Questions to Ponder

1. How should Principal Charles Douglass respond to Jacob Foster's parents' request?
2. Can you identify any ethical considerations he should be taking into account while attempting to resolve this case?
3. With whom should he consult prior to taking any actions regarding Jacob's placement?
4. How might his ultimate decisions impact the persons involved (e.g. Jacob, Claire, other 5th grade teachers, staff members, family members, Charles himself, etc.)?

3.3   What Actually Occurred?

Charles Douglass stood by his window and watched the Fosters, who were still quite animated, walk out to their car and depart from the parking lot. He made a quick call to the superintendent's office to alert the staff about the possibility of the Fosters' unscheduled visit. The principal spoke with the superintendent's administrative assistant and provided a quick summary of the meeting he had just concluded with Jacob Foster's parents.

While Charles knew it was unlikely the Foster's son, their only child, would be transferred to another 5th grade classroom, he took a few moments to search through the informal notes he had taken during his drop-in visits to Claire Sheldon's classroom. Early in his tenure as principal, he himself had described Claire's room as disorderly, and a bit out of control. Even still, the students all seemed to be happily engaged in one form of learning activity or another, so Principal Foster continually tried his best to provide Claire with actionable feedback regarding ways she might modify her classroom management procedures. A handful of other family members had expressed their concerns about Claire's unconventional pedagogical tactics, but this was the first time in his tenure that parents had been so confrontational demanding their child be moved out of her classroom.

Interestingly, a couple of the 4th grade teachers reported how much they enjoyed visiting Mrs. Sheldon's classroom, and loved seeing how she worked so energetically with their former students to give each one her undivided attention as often as possible. As Charles reviewed his more recent classroom notes for Claire Sheldon, he came across this statement he had written:

It is rare to find Claire standing in front of the classroom delivering a one-way lecture. She is always in motion moving around the room from one cluster of students to another encouraging them to pose questions, offer solutions, take risks, and think creatively about the topic at hand. The kids are responsive, on task, and adaptive to this teacher's instructional environment – it is one of organized chaos.

As expected, the superintendent contacted Charles Douglass the following morning to recap the brief meeting she had had with the Fosters. She further assured him that she would support whatever decision he believed was in the best interest of the student, and had offered that same statement to Jacob's parents. Principal Douglass reviewed Jacob's academic records including classroom grades and statewide assessment scores, along with attendance reports, and the school counselor's notes regarding the child's career aspirations. Jacob rarely missed school, had scored above the 75th percentile on the 3rd and 4th grade State assessments, generally performed slightly above average in his classroom assignments, and wanted to become a large animal veterinarian. He did however see this notation written by his 3rd grade teacher – "Jacob often has difficulty understanding the homework instructions. He requires additional written guidelines to ensure punctual completion of the take-home assignments."

Mr. Douglass waited until the end of the week to contact the Fosters. He spoke with Jacob's mom to let her know the child's classroom assignment would remain intact. The principal further explained the actions he intended to pursue with Mrs. Sheldon regarding their son's learning needs. Specifically, Jacob would be provided with a daily homework log; each Monday afternoon, Claire would send a weekly email message to Jacob and his parents listing all of the homework assignments for the following days; and the parents would be given access to the classroom's web portal allowing them to review the classroom activities, and interact with Mrs. Sheldon as necessary.

Even still, the Fosters were highly displeased with the Principal Douglass' decision which they viewed as thoughtless and autocratic. To their credit just the same, Jacob was not informed about any of their interactions with his school's principal, and he spent the remaining weeks of summer playing on his little league baseball team, and innocently enjoying all the other activities associated with being a ten-year old boy. He showed up to Claire Sheldon's 5th grade classroom unbiased, and ready to start his final year at the elementary school he had attended since Kindergarten.

Charles Douglass had a fruitful meeting with Claire and the other members of the 5th grade team during their professional development sessions in late August. He reviewed with them the special needs of all students entering their 5th grade classrooms, and reminded each of his plans to continue his drop-in visits throughout the year. Each teacher was given an opportunity to describe any new instructional strategies or classroom management procedures planned for the upcoming year. Claire shared some new knowledge she had gained through attending a district-funded summer research conference on the topic of *Authentic Integrated Learning*, and described a few new projects she intended to incorporate into the curriculum.

Several weeks into the fall term, and prior to the first parent/teacher conferences, Mr. Douglass contacted Jacob Foster's parents to determine the extent to which their negative attitude toward their son's 5th grade teacher had begun to wane, if at all. Charles was pleasantly surprised to hear Mrs. Foster report that her son was "really enjoying Mrs. Sheldon's teaching style, and all the ways she helped him make connections between their classroom activities, and what was actually happening in his everyday life at home."

Serendipitously, Jacob Foster's placement in Claire Sheldon's classroom proved favorable. The Fosters made a point to come into the office toward the end of the year to express their gratitude to Principal Douglass for allowing Jacob to stay put, despite their requests that he be transferred. They admitted Mrs. Sheldon truly guided Jacob to become more self-confident and independent as the year progressed. The principal asked them if he could share these sentiments with the teacher, and they readily agreed he should do so. As Charles watched the two parents leave the building and walk to their car that afternoon, he couldn't help feeling elated by the unexpected positive consequences that resulted by virtue of holding his ground with them back in August.

3.4   *Follow-up Questions*

1. To what extent did Principal Charles Douglass demonstrate (or fail to demonstrate) the selected leadership competencies identified above for PSEL #6 – *Professional Capacity of School Personnel?*

2. Describe a few more strategies Charles Douglass might have used to either respond to Jacob Foster's parents' demands, or provide support for veteran teacher Claire Sheldon.

4   Do Summative Reviews Ever Make a Difference?

PSEL – **Standard 6:** Effective educational leaders develop the professional capacity and practice of school personnel to promote each student's academic success and well-being.

Selected Elements:
6b – Plan for and manage staff turnover and succession, providing opportunities for effective induction and mentoring of new personnel.
6c – Develop teachers' and staff members' professional knowledge, skills, and practice through differentiated opportunities for learning and growth, guided by understanding of professional and adult learning and development.
6d – Foster continuous improvement of individual and collective instructional capacity to achieve outcomes envisioned for each student.
6e – Deliver actionable feedback about instruction and other professional practice, through valid, research-anchored systems of supervision and evaluation to support the development of teachers' and staff members' knowledge, skills and practice.
6f – Empower and motivate teachers and staff to the highest levels of professional practice and to continuous learning and improvement.

4.1   *The Story*

Nearly all school building leaders spend a considerable portion of their time compiling written evaluations of teachers and professional staff members. In most instances, employee contracts dictate both the nature and quantity of the reviews administrators are required to complete on an annual basis. Ms. Kim Lenkiewicz was nearing the end of her eleventh year as an academic assistant principal (AAP) in a rural high school when she recounted the events in this story. She, along with another assistant principal, and two deans report to the executive principal. The school employs 103 teachers (40% of whom are probationary), and enrolls approximately 1500 students in grades 9–12. During her tenure in this administrative role, Kim had reported to three different executive principals, the newest of whom had been recently appointed near the end of the previous year.

A little over a decade ago, the State enacted legislation that allowed school districts to apply to participate in a program wherein funds would be allocated to support school improvement within collectively bargained plans. Two among the list of initiatives eligible for funding were teacher evaluation, and performance pay. Ms. Lenkiewicz's school district became one of several dozen selected to receive funds through this program, and many of its teachers therefore had been receiving discretionary salary awards (also called bonus pay) for a good number of years.

Contractually, administrators are required to prepare summative evaluations of teachers, thereby making them eligible to receive these awards. In AAP Lenkiewicz's district, summative reviews were completed once a year for tenured teachers, and three times a year for probationary teachers. AAP Kim Lenkiewicz and Executive Principal (EP) Timon Davis were the only two high school administrators authorized to complete these reviews, and compile the online summative reports. The contract specified that all classroom visitations used to gather evidence for the reports had to be announced ahead of time.

The evaluation framework adopted by this district used the following scale to "score" various criteria pertinent to teacher effectiveness, especially with reference to student achievement: (1) Developing, (2) Proficient, (3) Accomplished, and (4) Distinguished. Both administrators had received training, and were subsequently knowledgeable users of the standards-based McREL[1] evaluation tool adopted by the district. Oddly enough though, Ms. Lenkiewicz had surmised over the years that her summative reviews generally seemed more rigorous than those completed by Mr. Davis, and by the previous two EPS as well. Even still, all teachers who received at least a "2 – Proficient" on most indicators, were automatically awarded bonus pay.

One such teacher was Candace Turner, who was hired to teach Math at about the time Ms. Lenkiewicz had been AAP for five years. And, since Kim was responsible for evaluating those educators who taught Mathematics, Science, Foreign Language, Music, Technology, and Business, Candace was assigned to her. EP Timon Davis reviewed teachers of Social Studies, English, Special Education, Physical Education, and Family & Consumer Science. The two administrators often consulted with one another if they had concerns about the effectiveness of any one teacher, regardless of academic discipline.

As per the union contract, a summative review was completed for Ms. Turner by the AAP three times annually. Each clinical observation cycle was announced, and scheduled in advance – one in October, one in February, and one in May. Ms. Lenkiewicz was generally satisfied with Candace's pedagogical strategies, and observed her doing a variety of creative project-focused math exercises with her students each time she visited her classroom. During her first two and a half years in this position, Candace also seemed to work well with her Math department colleagues, and regularly took advantage of the assistance afforded by the high school's instructional coaches. Ms. Lenkiewicz's summative reviews of Ms. Turner's teaching effectiveness therefore reflected scores of 2 (proficient), 3 (accomplished), and even occasionally 4 (distinguished) on the rubric.

It was shortly after the October review in Ms. Turner's third year that one of the instructional coaches informed Kim about several concerns he had regarding Candace's teaching abilities. He had noticed Candace seemed somewhat bored while working with her students, and she had begun to give the kids work sheets to complete while she sat at her desk for major portions of the class reviewing various Internet sites. The AAP was somewhat surprised to learn about this since she had only seen Candace deliver well-constructed, innovative lessons. Furthermore, Ms. Lenkiewicz was essentially planning to recommend this math teacher be tenured on schedule at the end of her third year. Kim thanked the instructional coach for bringing his concerns to her attention, and she made it a priority to make some unannounced visits to Ms. Turner's classroom.

Although these walk-through visits could not be used for the official summative reviews, they gave the AAP a different view of a teacher who heretofore had not been on her radar. Ms. Lenkiewicz knew it was important to visit non-tenured teachers often, but frequent drop-in sessions were also time consuming. Kim checked in with EP Davis to see if he had received any less than satisfactory comments regarding this teacher. Interestingly, Mr. Davis echoed the concerns expressed by the instructional coach, and recalled hearing from a few teachers that Candace was underperforming.

As the time for the mid-year classroom observation arrived, Kim couldn't help but wonder to herself if the MANDATORY SUMMATIVE REVIEWS EVER MADE A DIFFERENCE. Shortly after this scheduled visitation, Ms. Lenkiewicz completed her February summative report for Candace Turner, and there were considerably more scores of 1 (developing) than she had previously recorded.

During the post-observation conference with Candace, the AAP shared her feedback, and, among other things, described her pedagogical strategies as being significantly less engaging than earlier. Candace immediately became defensive saying

> all these years you've given me glowing reviews, I've been given discretionary salary awards, and now you're telling me you see a problem with my teaching! What a joke this whole evaluation process has become.

Ms. Lenkiewicz listened to the young teacher who was clearly distraught, and encouraged Candace to spend some time reflecting on the actionable feedback she had provided. As she walked back to her office, and knowing it was always a challenge to find qualified math teachers, Kim thought about the imminent tenure decision looming on the horizon for Ms. Turner.

4.2 *Questions to Ponder*

1. If you were Academic Assistant Principal Lenkiewicz, what recommendations would you make regarding tenure for Candace Turner?
2. Can you identify any ethical considerations she should be taking into account while attempting to resolve this case? (See Chapter 12, Section 1)
3. How can summative performance reviews be used effectively to make a difference for all teachers (both tenured and non-tenured)?
4. How will Kim's actions (both short- and long-term) impact the individuals involved (e.g. Candace Turner, students, math department colleagues, other teachers, instructional coaches, etc.)?

4.3 *What Actually Occurred?*

Candace Turner immediately went to meet with Executive Principal Timon Davis to complain about the AAP's unfounded and unfair critique of her teaching performance. Mr. Davis supported Ms. Lenkiewicz's actions, and advised Candace to seek additional guidance from her math colleagues, and the instructional coaches assigned to work with her department. The disgruntled teacher then took her grievance to her union representative which culminated in a series of meetings with AAP Lenkiewicz, EP Davis, and the district's Assistant Superintendent for Human Resources & Professional Development (ASHR&PD).

Two months later, when it came time for Ms. Lenkiewicz to complete her third summative review of Ms. Turner in May, various aspects of the case had been reviewed multiple times, and Kim had made more than a dozen walk-through visits to Candace's classroom. Also during that span of time, a number of the students enrolled in her Statistics course had come forward to alert the AAP that Ms. Turner had "pretty much stopped teaching, and our class has become an extra study hall."

In June, Ms. Turner received the official letter from the District Office which informed her she had been given a fourth probationary year, during which a teacher improvement plan (TIP) would be established for her. Feeling demoralized, Candace sought counsel from the Math Department Chair, who strongly suggested "she get on board, and follow the TIP if she wanted to remain employed in this school district." There were ten teachers in the math department including Ms. Turner, and all but her were tenured. The department chair and four others were somewhat disappointed in the administration's decision to extend Candace's probationary appointment, and believed she should have been given a positive recommendation for tenure at the end of year three. Conversely, the other four math teachers felt strongly that Ms. Turner's appointment should have been terminated, perhaps even prior to year three.

When Candace Turner began her fourth year that fall, Ms. Lenkiewicz was informed by the ASHR&PD that she would no longer be responsible for completing summative reviews for this math teacher. At the behest of the union, that duty had been transferred to Mr. Davis to ensure Ms. Turner would receive a non-biased review of her teaching skills. At the end of this school year, Candace was awarded tenure. Amidst a small group of department colleagues who were undoubtedly unhappy with this decision, Ms. Turner taught in the high school for four more years, and then agreed to take on a new assignment as an instructional coach for mathematics in the middle school.

Candace Turner was returned to Ms. Lenkiewicz's supervisory roster for the duration of her time in the high school's math department. To the best of her ability, within the time she had available for completing a large number of summative reviews, Kim continued to provide what she believed was timely/relevant feedback to all teachers assigned to her. Regardless, she never stopped questioning herself about the extent to which these somewhat perfunctory reports really made a difference for teachers over the long term of their professional careers.

4.4   *Follow-up Questions*

1. To what extent did Academic Assistant Principal Kim Lenkiewicz demonstrate (or fail to demonstrate) the selected leadership competencies identified above for PSEL #6 – *Professional Capacity of School Personnel?*

2. As either a future or practicing school building leader, what additional supports (beyond those provided by Kim Lenkiewicz) will you (or do you) provide to teachers in an effort to help them continually improve their instructional practices?

3. In a similar vein, at what point will you (or do you) commit to making the hard decision to not recommend tenure, and enact the process in place to remove a teacher in the best interest of all students' education?

Note

1 McRel International offers a comprehensive personnel review system that uses sound research on educator effectiveness to evaluate teachers, principals, and superintendents on what matters most to student achievement and help them reach their full professional potential. See: https://www.mcrel.org/personnel-evaluation/

CHAPTER 8

Professional Community for Teachers and Staff

1 Just Joking Around

PSEL – Standard 7: Effective educational leaders foster a professional community of teachers and other professional staff to promote each student's academic success and well-being.

Selected Elements:
7c – Establish and sustain a professional culture of engagement and commitment to shared vision, goals, and objectives pertaining to the whole child; high expectations for professional work; ethical and equitable practice; trust and open communications; collaboration, collective efficacy, and continuous individual and organizational learning and improvement.
7d – Promote mutual accountability among teachers and other professional staff for student's success and the effectiveness of the school as a whole.
7e – Develop and support open, productive, caring and trusting working relationships among leaders, faculty and staff to promote professional capacity and the improvement of practice.
7f – Design and implement job-embedded and other opportunities for professional learning collaboratively with faculty and staff.

1.1 *The Story*

Dr. Carole DuBois had been the principal of a suburban elementary school for more than five years when the following events unfolded. This K–6 school enrolls approximately 470 students and employs 35 teachers, many of whom preceded Principal DuBois' appointment. Sometime during the month of October, having already met with her school's union representative, a tenured teacher/media specialist named Danielle informed Carole that she was feeling very uncomfortable working with the teacher assistant (TA) responsible for providing technology support in the building. On several occasions the TA named Kevin had made her feel embarrassed and unpleasant through his use of profanity in the presence of young students, and by making off-color remarks to her personally. By way of example, when Danielle asked for his assistance with her desktop computer in the library, Kevin remarked "Your computer would never have crashed if you hadn't been spending so much time viewing pornographic websites!"

Additionally, when Danielle recounted the interaction she had with the building's union representative several weeks prior, Carole learned that he had dismissed the incident stating

> Relax already! Kevin was **JUST JOKING AROUND!** If you report him to the principal, she will be required to make a report to Human Resources (HR), which will result in him being reprimanded. We don't want that since he recently returned from sick leave having had a heart attack earlier this year. Get some tough skin and just ignore it!

Recognizing the TA's behavior as a form of verbal workplace sexual harassment, Principal DuBois informed the teacher she would make a report to HR, and did so immediately. While waiting to hear back from the HR Assistant Superintendent (HRAS), Carole made an informal visit to Kevin's office to let him know she had been made aware of his foul language in front of the kids, and basically told him she did not want ANY employees to use profanity in her building. The TA dutifully accepted this directive from the building leader.

After several days had passed without word, Dr. DuBois made another attempt to contact the HRAS and left an urgent message with his Administrative Assistant. She followed up a few days letter with email correspondence addressed to both her immediate supervisor (Executive Director for Elementary Education – EDEE) and the HRAS stating she had a serious personnel issue for which she needs guidance. This quickly prompted a telephone response from her supervisor asking her to describe the issue – upon hearing the teacher's allegations regarding the TA's behavior, the EDEE informed Carole he agreed with her assessment stating

> This is most certainly a case that requires HR action, and I will handle it from here. You can consider yourself done with this case, except please inform Danielle she will likely be hearing from the HRAS in the near future, and asked to share the details of her experience for the record.

Principal DuBois relayed this message to the teacher feeling confident she had both respected the administrative chain of command, and followed district protocol for such personnel matters.

More than two weeks went by, and Danielle came into the office to inform Dr. DuBois that she had not yet been contacted by HR, and reported Kevin was still making his disgusting comments to her. Carole maintained her composure without showing frustration, and promised her teacher that she would follow-up again with the HR Office. She called right away to express her surprise that no action on her case had yet been taken – and the Administrative Assistant responded with exasperation "I can't get him to call anyone back!" This motivated Principal DuBois to make a trip to the HR Office to speak with the HRAS directly in an effort to advocate for the teacher with whom she had established a trusting relationship. While in his office, the Superintendent happened to stop by unexpectedly – the three of them had a quick conversation about the matter and the HRAS was directed to handle the case promptly.

Principal DuBois waited patiently for another week and then called her immediate supervisor to press for his assistance stating "This situation in my building needs to be rectified. The TA's unacceptable behavior has gone on far too long!" The EDEE, who was still untenured in his position, more or less told her he had already done all he could stating "The HRAS is really swamped right now, and I don't feel comfortable going over his head to the Superintendent. Perhaps you can handle this issue yourself?"

1.2 *Questions to Ponder*

1. What action(s) should Dr. DuBois take at this time?
2. Can you identify any ethical considerations she should be taking into account while attempting to resolve this case?
3. How will her decisions impact the persons involved (e.g. Danielle, Kevin, EDEE, HRAS, students, other teachers, herself)?

1.3 *What Actually Occurred?*

Principal DuBois pondered her options for a time after having the less than satisfactory conversation with her direct supervisor. Her moral compass compelled her to act in the best interest of the teacher who was being harassed by another tenured employee in her building. At the same time, Carole was well informed about the need to ensure the TA was treated fairly and received due process in the face of the allegations being made about his behavior. She reflected on all that had transpired since the teacher first came to her with the complaint more than two months prior, and ultimately decided to call the TA in to her office for a formal meeting which was scheduled for Monday of the following week.

When Kevin showed up in Dr. DuBois' office, his attitude was a bit cavalier as he stated "What did I do wrong this time boss?!" Carole maintained a serious and professional tone as she asked him to take a seat. She proceeded to have a stern conversation with him letting him know staff members had voiced complaints about his off-color remarks, and gave him specific examples of statements he had been accused of making. Her specific directive to him was "This behavior is egregious and totally unacceptable – it will NEVER happen again in this building." Kevin did not deny the allegation and somberly responded quite simply "You have my word on this."

Carole then went to see Danielle and told her the issue had been resolved. She further explained the HR Office apparently did not need to meet with her, but never revealed the fact that they had not documented these incidents in the TA's personnel file.

The EDEE expressed his satisfaction with her actions, and commended her for her professional resolution of the case.

Within her purview of supervision at the building level, Dr. DuBois provided time for Kevin to attend a professional seminar on the topic of harassment of workplace personnel. She also included the following specific verbiage in the TA's Annual Professional Performance Review summary: "Sarcastic and often crude jokes are sometimes reported by staff members. This type of language is not permitted at any time during your work responsibilities in this building." Kevin acknowledged his receipt of her review with his signature. To date his distasteful behaviors have not recurred.

1.4   *Follow-up Questions*

1.   To what extent did Principal Carole DuBois demonstrate (or fail to demonstrate) the selected leadership competencies identified above for PSEL #7 – *Professional Community for Teachers and Staff?*

2.   Describe several ways Carole DuBois demonstrated ethical leadership, while also respecting the formal chain of leadership authority in her school district.

3.   What documentation should Principal DuBois have kept on file for this particular teaching assistant (Kevin)?

2   My Course Requirements Apply to Everyone[1]

PSEL – **Standard 7:** Effective educational leaders foster a professional community of teachers and other professional staff to promote each student's academic success and well-being.

Selected Elements:
7b – Empower and entrust teachers and staff with collective responsibility for meeting the academic, social, emotional, and physical needs of each student, pursuant to the mission, vision, and core values of the school.

7c – Establish and sustain a professional culture of engagement and commitment to shared vision, goals, and objectives pertaining to the whole child; high expectations for professional work; ethical and equitable practice; trust and open communications; collaboration, collective efficacy, and continuous individual and organizational learning and improvement.
7d – Promote mutual accountability among teachers and other professional staff for student's success and the effectiveness of the school as a whole.
7h – Encourage faculty-initiated improvement of programs and practices.

2.1   The Story

Alexander Krüger is one of two vice principals at a secondary school located in a suburb of a large metropolitan center in Germany. In this leadership role, he also acts as the lead curriculum coordinator in the building, and is therefore responsible for overseeing the master scheduling process. The school enrolls approximately 860 students in grades 5–13 and employs 78 teachers. According to Mr. Krüger, the school's management principles celebrate the inclusion and exchange of all employees' ideas. "Each staff member is expected to set annual goals that are reviewed periodically with the building principal. We believe the principle of delegation increases responsibility, and promotes the innovative development and overall improvement of our school."

Vice Principal Krüger had been in his position for a little more than three years when he found himself involved in a series of conversations that focused on the required curricular assignments within the physical education (PE) courses being offered to students in the upper secondary grades. He became very familiar with one teacher in particular, Franz Chalmers, who taught swimming to all students, and volleyball to the male students. He prided himself in holding all students to very high athletic standards, which created some difficulty, and in many cases a fair amount of anxiety, for those young men and women who did not perform well in these specific sports.

It was not uncommon for students to say they didn't want to swim, and they provided all kinds of reasons for not wanting to do so. Regardless, Mr. Chalmers rigorously insisted they get into the water to complete the required exercises unless they had a written doctor's note. Many more of the females than males routinely brought in their written excuses to avoid having to don their swimming suits, and get into the pool for their PE class during the school day.

As curriculum coordinator, Mr. Krüger found himself fielding calls and email messages from the students' parents who asked him to revise course schedules to give their sons and daughters an approved physical education option other than swimming. On one hand, he found himself wanting to support the teachers who had been empowered to meet the academic and physical needs of all students pursuant to the core mission of the school: *Performance serves the self-discovery, self-realization and general well-being of the individual. Teachers, pupils and parents are equally obliged to contribute to the success of the school.* On the other hand, he empathized with students who, in the case of physical education requirements, did not possess natural athletic abilities. He continually asked himself, "How can I best assist our teachers to become more compassionate, and perhaps willing to provide various levels of options for students with different competencies to earn their PE points for graduation?"

Megan and Bridget Moore were siblings who were one year apart, and both had coincidentally been assigned to Mr. Chalmers' swimming course. The two girls were very different, and it was Mr. Krüger's perception that many teachers didn't seem to know they were sisters. Megan, grade 13, was tall, slender and fairly athletic. She was a popular girl who had many friends, and had been elected to be one of the head girls of her school. Bridget, grade 12, more or less tried to avoid living in her sister's imposing shadow. She was slightly overweight for her medium height, very timid, and did not make friends easily. Bridget also struggled academically, while her older sister had always earned high grades in nearly all of her courses. While Megan actually enjoyed the swimming classes, Bridget would sooner miss an entire day of school than go anywhere near the school's swimming facility.

At some point after the school's December break for the holiday season, two of Bridget's teachers scheduled a meeting with Alexander Krüger to discuss their concerns about her lack of progress in their courses, along with her total lack of interest in attending/participating in many class activities. The vice principal knew Bridget had been having attendance issues with Franz Chalmers' swimming class, but he had not realized her performance was faltering in her core academic courses as well. He therefore asked Bridget to come in to speak with him. During this session she admitted things were not going well, but begged him to not let her parents know she was nearly failing three of her 12th grade courses. She promised him she could improve, and further implored that she be allowed to transfer out of Mr. Chalmers' repulsive swimming course.

Mr. Krüger decided to have another conversation with Franz Chalmers in an attempt to salvage Bridget Moore's current class schedule. He knew there would be repercussions if he transferred Bridget to another PE class when so many other students were equally discouraged by Mr. Chalmers' swimming course requirements. Vice Principal Krüger was optimistic Franz might consider giving students other options to learn about swimming vs. expecting everyone to demonstrate exceptional aquatic competencies in the water. This was not the case. Mr. Chalmers stated emphatically

> MY COURSE REQUIREMENTS APPLY TO EVERYONE! I've been one of this school's lead PE teachers for sixteen years, and I am not going to start making exceptions for students who are just too lazy to get into the pool.

The vice principal returned to his office and reviewed Bridget Moore's 12th grade class schedule for what seemed like the tenth time.

2.2 *Questions to Ponder*

1. How should Vice Principal Krüger respond to Bridget's requests?
2. Can you identify any ethical considerations he should be taking into account while attempting to resolve this case?
3. What additional information does he need in order to take the best course of action?
4. How will his decisions impact the individuals involved (e.g. Bridget, other students, Mr. Chalmers, other teachers, family members, himself, etc.)?

2.3 *What Actually Occurred?*

Vice Principal Krüger pondered his options for a time after having the less than satisfactory conversation with Franz Chalmers. He ultimately determined it was in the best interest of all concerned that he not revise Bridget Moore's class schedule at this mid-point of the school year. While Franz Chalmers was pleased with the vice principal's implied support of his autonomy and high standards, his decision was not well received by Bridget. Her overall attendance subsequently decreased considerably, to the point where her ability to successfully complete the 12th grade was threatened.

It was early April when Mr. Krüger contacted Bridget's mother requesting that she come in for a conference with himself and Bridget's academic advisor. Mrs. Moore agreed to meet right away, and informed the vice principal she was in the midst of divorce proceedings so Mr. Moore would not be attending the session with her. During his discussion with Mrs. Moore, Alexander also learned Bridget had been receiving mental health counseling for her anxiety and depression. Mrs. Moore confirmed that Bridget felt severely threatened by her older sister Megan's popularity, and the impending divorce was causing her additional worries. Her counseling sessions had commenced back in November. She noted her older daughter had been accepted to participate in an internship program in Viet Nam the following year, further concluding Bridget's performance would likely improve once Megan had graduated.

Alexander carefully reviewed Bridget's course grades with Mrs. Moore, and the academic advisor additionally explained she was likely going to be required to repeat some of her 12th grade courses due to her poor performance and lack of attendance. At that point, Mrs. Moore suggested they schedule a follow-up meeting allowing both Bridget's father and Bridget to be present as future plans were formulated. The subsequent meeting took place the following week, during which Bridget resigned herself to repeating the 12th grade.

However, in order for her to even be eligible to receive a new schedule for her second attempt at her 12th grade courses, she needed to earn at least one point per course in the current year (the range of points students earned for each course at the upper secondary level was 15–0; 0 points meaning "fail," 5 "pass" and 15 "outstanding").

All of her teachers except for Mr. Chalmers agreed Bridget had completed a sufficient amount of work to earn the points necessary to repeat, but not pass, their courses. Mr. Krüger knew an ideal solution for Bridget to earn at least one point in her swimming class might be to arrange a private lesson wherein she could perform at least one activity in the water without being embarrassed in front of other students. Mr. Chalmers wanted nothing to do with this option, insisting he could not justify giving Bridget Moore even one point for his *swimming* course when she refused to enter the water during his class.

With some additional persuasion, Alexander finally convinced Franz Chalmers to supervise Bridget in a different discipline instead. Mr. Chalmers agreed to watch her run a lap on the school's track to demonstrate her physical fitness, and ultimately gave her the one point she needed for "physical education," but *not* "swimming."

Vice Principal Krüger and Bridget's academic advisor created a new 12th grade schedule for her to complete the following year that did not include swimming. She was placed in the girls' volleyball course, and she was assigned to new teachers for each of the other 12th grade core courses she had failed previously. Bridget excelled in all of these courses the second time through, and proceeded to move through her 13th grade selections with renewed commitment.

2.4   *Follow-up Questions*

1. To what extent did Vice Principal Alexander Krüger demonstrate (or fail to demonstrate) the selected leadership competencies identified above for PSEL #7 – *Professional Community for Teachers and Staff*?
2. What additional supports might Alexander Krüger have provided for Bridget? For Mr. Chalmers?

3   I Can Show You My Uber Receipts

PSEL – Standard 7: Effective educational leaders foster a professional community of teachers and other professional staff to promote each student's academic success and well-being.

Selected Elements:
7a – Develop workplace conditions for teachers and other professional staff that promote effective professional development, practice, and student learning.
7b – Empower and entrust teachers and staff with collective responsibility for meeting the academic, social, emotional, and physical needs of each student, pursuant to the mission, vision, and core values of the school.
7d – Promote mutual accountability among teachers and other professional staff for student success, and the effectiveness of the school as a whole.
7e – Develop and support open, productive, caring and trusting working relationships among leaders, faculty and staff to promote professional capacity and the improvement of practice.
7g – Provide opportunities for collaborative examination of practice, collegial feedback, and collective learning.

3.1   *The Story*
Dr. Monica Kline was in her sixth year as principal when Derek Lamont was assigned to work in this urban elementary school. Principal Kline's PK–5 school enrolls approximately 470 students and employs 30 teachers. Dr. Kline had hired about one third of these teachers since the date of her appointment, as well as the one vice principal in the building. This school was among several in the district where teachers were contractually required to sign a separate document each year, affirming their agreement to an extended work day for which they would receive an additional stipend. The principal also signed the form known as the *Extended Day Teaching Contract* (EDTC).[2]

At the start of the school year, Dr. Kline submitted a request to the District Office for additional assistance managing student discipline in her building. Monica had worked diligently over the years to foster a variety of school-wide responsive practices, and all teachers and professional staff members had been trained to use them. Even still, several had mentioned to her that it would be helpful to occasionally have an additional pair of hands in their classrooms, and in the cafeteria. Dr. Kline was proud of the professional culture of engagement and commitment to shared vision they had collectively established during her tenure, and was extremely appreciative when the district responded affirmatively to her request.

In October, Derek Lamont was assigned to her building as a teaching assistant (TA) on a part-time basis equating to five hours per day. Since Principal Kline did not officially have a line allocated for this position, she was grateful to welcome Mr. Lamont to her team. Within a few short weeks, it became apparent Derek was working very hard, and often stayed way beyond the twenty-five hours for which he was being paid each week. The students and teachers alike seemed to love being around him. He skillfully facilitated restorative circles, and good-naturedly used his disc jockey skills during a few after school co-curricular enrichment activities. Mr. Lamont easily commanded respect from the students, and this was most apparent during their lunch breaks in the school cafeteria, where monitors reported fewer and fewer disruptions in their established routines whenever Derek was in the room!

Late one evening in March of that year, Dr. Kline received text messages from two of her veteran teachers. The first note came from fourth grade teacher Alan Raycroft who stated: "Monica, this is just a heads-up – Natalie, the student teacher I had last fall, appears to be in some sort of predicament, and it seems she is afraid to tell you about it." Before the principal could respond to Alan, she received a second message from special education teacher Sue Walsh that sounded quite urgent, and it read: "Hey Monica, I looked around for you in the building all day! Where the heck were you? I have something important to discuss, and it involves not only me, but also my student teacher Natalie!!" Knowing from many previous interactions that Ms. Walsh was often overly dramatic, Dr. Kline calmly responded to her saying "Of course you can come in to meet with me first thing tomorrow morning, and, if it is appropriate, please bring Natalie with you." The principal also responded to Mr. Raycroft noting "Thank you for being in touch Alan! Please be sure to let Natalie know she can always come to speak to me privately about any aspect of her student teaching assignment in our building."

Early the next morning, Ms. Walsh and Natalie Valenti arrived in the Main Office to speak with Principal Kline. Sue spoke first and got right to the point when she informed Dr. Kline that Derek Lamont had been harassing her for the past few weeks. By way of example, she described Derek as a stalker who tried to grab her by the arm when she dropped her students off in the Music Room; he later showed up in her classroom, closed the door, and demanded to have a conversation with her. Natalie confirmed these instances, and further noted that Mr. Lamont had been calling her on the phone asking "why have you been avoiding me?" Both concluded they felt uncomfortable and somewhat unsafe in the TA's presence.

As Dr. Kline listened intently and attempted to more fully understand the context for these two instructors' allegations. She ultimately learned that Natalie had established a casual friendship with Mr. Lamont, and admitted to having had a couple cocktails with him back in November. She insisted nothing more serious had developed between them, and she had more or less decided to focus all of her attention on finishing her student teaching requirements. Natalie didn't have time for any outside activities, and was in fact breaking up with her boyfriend.

Principal Kline brought the meeting to a close by judiciously explaining the school district's policy and procedure for staff members to follow when they felt it necessary to file a complaint against another employee. The official process required the complainant to write his/her report, and upload it into the district's personnel database for confidential review by an administrator in the Human Resources Office. Ms. Walsh immediately agreed to do this since she was apparently "afraid to walk through the hallways alone whenever Mr. Lamont was in the building!" Natalie on the other hand insisted she had nothing more to say. She was quite emotional when she left Dr. Kline's office noting that she had made her report, and didn't want to jeopardize her future employment in the district after she completed her teacher certification program in about six more weeks.

Monica Kline thought long and hard about the conversation she'd had with the two female teachers (one Caucasian, one Hispanic) who had each made serious allegations against a TA (African American), who in her eyes had been an exemplary employee. Dr. Kline recalled some of the rumors that had been spread about Sue Walsh having an extra-marital affair with the previous vice principal in the building. She also reminded herself about the only time a grievance had been filed against her – it had occurred two years earlier, and had been brought forward by Sue Walsh. Unsurprisingly, Ms. Walsh could not submit the required evidence to support the grievance against Dr. Kline, and it had been dismissed.

Later that day the HR Office received the online report written by Ms. Walsh, and immediately called Monica Kline to make sure she was aware of the allegations. The first thing the HR Director asked her was "Is Sue Walsh having a relationship with this TA Mr. Lamont?" Dr. Kline responded "No, of course not!" The principal was instructed to bring Derek Lamont in to her office to inform him that an investigation would be taking place, and he would be placed on paid leave for its duration.

Monica went to find Derek Lamont in his office located in the school's Behavior Intervention Center, and escorted him back to her office. She informed him that two individuals had accused him of inappropriate, verbally abusive actions, and HR would be conducting an investigation. Derek responded in an animated, but still respectful manner saying:

> Dr. Kline, you know I love working here, and I am pretty certain who is making me out to be the bad guy. I have spent time with both of these ladies, and have never done anything improper. I had a couple drinks with that student teacher Natalie right before Thanksgiving last year, and I enjoyed talking with her. But things got a lot more serious with Sue – we went out a few times right after I started this job, and we discovered a mutual attraction shortly thereafter. She introduced me to her kids, and I started spending the night at her place on a regular basis, always at her invitation. Our intimate relationship has been going on since late last October. **I CAN SHOW YOU MY UBER RECEIPTS** to prove it!

3.2   *Questions to Ponder*
1.   What action(s) should Dr. Monica Kline take at this time?
2.   Are there any legal issues she should be considering?
3.   How will her decisions impact the persons involved (e.g. Derek, Sue, Natalie, teachers, students, other school employees)?

3.3   *What Actually Occurred?*
Principal Kline remained calm as she continued her conversation with Derek Lamont, despite having just received this surprisingly unexpected news from him. Within a few minutes she learned that Sue Walsh had recently informed him she "needed to take a break from their overnight get-togethers" and had not given him any clear reasons for wanting to do so. Dr. Kline gently reminded him of the need for professional discretion as an employee in the school district, and questioned him as to why he was continuing to call both women. She then learned he had been regularly relying on Ms. Walsh for transportation stating he couldn't afford to take Uber all the time. The principal ended this conversation urging him to stop calling, or otherwise attempting to contact both Ms. Walsh and Ms. Valenti. She further told him she believed he had great potential as a TA, provided him with a bus pass, and escorted him out of her building – reminding him he would be contacted by someone from the HR Office.

When the HR administrator arrived, Monica informed her about the news she had just received from Mr. Lamont. Ms. Walsh was called into the office and questioned about the allegations she had summarized in her formal report, and asked to explain why she suddenly felt unsafe in Mr. Lamont's presence. Sue Walsh mentioned nothing about inviting Derek Lamont to her home, or allowing him to spend time with her children. When Natalie Valenti was interviewed by HR, she admitted to having a couple of casual cocktails with Derek in the fall, but had told him she'd prefer to not meet up again; until just recently, it had been months since she'd heard anything from him outside of school. Alan Raycroft was not interviewed.

That afternoon, Derek Lamont was contacted and invited to meet with the HR administrator in her District Office location. Dr. Kline later received word from HR that Mr. Lamont "was a great guy, very well-spoken and forthright, and had agreed to have no further contact with Ms. Walsh or Ms. Valenti outside of school hours." They determined the case to be closed, and approved Mr. Lamont to return to work for his normal hours the next day.

Meanwhile, Sue Walsh spent time in her building more or less bad-mouthing Derek Lamont. She repeatedly stated "I'm totally afraid of this guy, and hope he is either fired or removed from our building." When Mr. Lamont subsequently reported to work the next day, Ms. Walsh exploded with anger, and interrupted one of Dr. Kline's meetings demanding to know "why this person was ever allowed to return to our school!?" Being a personnel matter, Dr. Kline only noted that HR had found no evidence to support her allegations.

Serendipitously for Derek Lamont, the HR Office contacted Dr. Kline the next day to let her know they had found a full-time position with benefits for him in another school. Monica met with Derek, informed him about the opportunity, and encouraged him to pursue it even though she knew he would be sorely missed in her building. Derek interviewed successfully for the new position in a K–8 building, and was transferred there in less than a week. Principal Kline's leadership colleagues in that school reported they were thrilled to have him.

Sue Walsh continued her ranting and raving about being mistreated and unsupported by the administration. She made a series of accusatory posts directed at the principal on social media, and significantly impacted the building's climate and culture in a negative way on multiple fronts.

As Dr. Kline reflected on Ms. Walsh's most recent unprofessional behaviors, she couldn't help but remember the circumstances under which she was first hired during what would have been her second year as principal in the building. Given the guidelines of the EDTC, Ms. Walsh was a tenured teacher who had requested a transfer to her building, and came highly recommended by the previous vice principal, with whom she was later suspected of having an extramarital affair. During the subsequent four years, when Ms. Walsh had been assigned as the 2nd grade level's special education teacher, four different 2nd grade teachers had themselves requested to be transferred to another building.

Needless to say, this one teacher's presence was negatively impacting many other staff members' opportunities for collaborative examination of practice, collegial feedback, and collective learning on a daily basis. Dr. Kline pondered the clause regarding "mutual consent" in the EDTC, and thought deeply about her administrative options in this difficult personnel case, which had blown out of proportion in a few short days. It had become clear in her mind (and heart) Ms. Walsh was not able to work collegially with others to support the mission, vision and core values of her school. Monica's moral compass therefore guided her to contact HR, and submit her formal request to have Sue Walsh involuntarily transferred out of her building at the end of the school year.

3.4   *Follow-up Questions*

1.   To what extent did Principal Monica Kline demonstrate (or fail to demonstrate) the selected leadership competencies identified above for PSEL #7 – *Professional Community for Teachers and Staff?*
2.   What things did Monica Kline do well as she interacted with the teaching assistant Derek Lamont? What might she have done differently, and why?

4   All Boys Talk That Way

PSEL – **Standard 7:** Effective educational leaders foster a professional community of teachers and other professional staff to promote each student's academic success and well-being.

Selected Elements:
7a – Develop workplace conditions for teachers and other professional staff that promote effective professional development, practice, and student learning.
7b – Establish and sustain a professional culture of engagement and commitment to shared vision, goals, and objectives pertaining to the education of the whole child; high expectations for professional work; ethical and equitable practice; trust and open communication; collaboration, collective efficacy, and continuous individual and organizational learning and improvement.
7d – Promote mutual accountability among teachers and other professional staff for student success, and the effectiveness of the school as a whole.

7e – Develop and support open, productive, caring and trusting working relationships among leaders, faculty and staff to promote professional capacity and the improvement of practice.

7g – Provide opportunities for collaborative examination of practice, collegial feedback, and collective learning.

4.1   The Story

Ms. Judith Oliver is a veteran administrator in this suburban elementary school. Having served as its principal for fourteen years, Judith has hired nearly 50% of the 49 teachers employed in this K–5 school, where 615 students are enrolled. One academic dean reports to the principal; he ensures teachers, staff members and students are fully informed about the district's Codes of Conduct, and also assists the principal to foster school-wide responsive practices within the building's student management system. For the most part, the Dean of Students handles disciplinary incidents involving the younger students in grades K–2, and Principal Oliver responds to those events where students in the higher grades have found themselves in some type of trouble.

During her tenure as principal, Ms. Oliver has worked very intentionally to help new teachers feel welcome in the school. Mentors are assigned to work with newly hired staff members on the basis of subject matter expertise, classroom management strategies, and expressed willingness to go the extra mile for the "newbies." At the start of each new school year, Principal Oliver routinely visits all teachers' classrooms several times within the first few weeks, making sure they have the necessary resources to continuously improve their instructional practices. The building's master schedule is structured to provide time for vertical, cross-disciplinary learning teams to collaborate both during the school day, and after school on Thursdays every other week.

In reference to professional development for the staff members in her building, Ms. Oliver has successfully garnered support from the District Office to provide targeted programs for both novice and veteran teachers. Several seminar and workshop sessions have included training about: having difficult conversations with family members; using mindfulness in classrooms; launching project based learning activities in the local community; fostering a trauma sensitive learning environment; implementing restorative practices; and reducing implicit/explicit bias both inside and outside the school building walls. A majority of the staff members employed in this school report enjoying these trainings, and being highly satisfied with the quality of their work lives.

The incidents in this story actually occurred over two years, and primarily involved two male students, both of whom are high academic achievers, and quite talented athletes. Zach Bell had been a student in Ms. Oliver's school since the Kindergarten, was in 4th grade when this story began, and has two older siblings. Harrison Cleever's family moved into the district when he was entering the 4th grade. Harrison has three older siblings, two of whom are already in college. Zach and Harrison were assigned to the same 4th grade classroom, and it didn't take long for them to recognize each other's athletic abilities during recess. Each tried to outshine the other on the playground, and they also became quite competitive for their teacher's attention during classroom Q&A sessions.

Away from school, both boys played on teams within the local community's intramural soccer league. It was during one of those games in early October that Zach's parents witnessed Harrison's aggressive, somewhat domineering behaviors toward their own son, and toward his other teammates. Harrison acted like he had all the answers, and wanted the others to take direction from him. The coach fortunately intervened, and the game proceeded without incident; even still, the Bells made a mental note about the Cleever boy's forceful nature.

During the same time period, Harrison's teachers had reprimanded him more than once for being overtly intimidating toward his classmates. Zach Bell was a popular young man, and well-liked by nearly all of his male and female classmates. Harrison, who was quite probably jealous of these natural friendships, occasionally made derogatory comments about Zach being a nerd. On the playground, Harrison challenged Zach to silly competitions, hoping to embarrass him in front of the other students. In these situations, the teachers and staff members repeatedly reminded Harrison, together with all other students, about the importance of civility, kindness, compromise, and making wise choices.

For whatever reason, it was sometime in late November when Harrison's insults finally got the better of Zach, and the two boys ended up in a shoving match in the hall, on the way to their lunch period. One of the teachers brought the boys to see Ms. Oliver, who prior to this time, had not been asked to intervene. The principal met briefly with the two boys individually, to gather each one's side of the story as to why the altercation had occurred. Harrison reported that "Zach grabbed the hood of my sweatshirt, so I swatted him back." Conversely, Zach informed the principal that "Harrison insulted me saying 'you're such a mama's boy, no wonder you wear that silly-looking shirt to school,' so I told him to shut up and mind his own business." Principal Oliver sent both boys back to their lunch period after reminding them to act maturely, treat others with respect, and follow the school's Code of Conduct.

Judith confirmed which of the two boys was most likely telling the truth as she reviewed the video-recording of the hallway episode. She next checked in with the boys' teachers, and learned they had already resolved a few non-serious spats between Harrison and Zach. The principal therefore decided to be proactive, and arrange times to meet with the Bells, and the Cleevers, before too much more time passed.

Principal Oliver had her first meeting with Harrison's mom and dad. As she described the most recent incident where their son had instigated an argument with another of his classmates, Mr. Cleever promptly defended Harrison. The boy's father said

> Our child is new to this school, and you are already singling him out as the bad guy. I'm guessing the other boy you are talking about is Zach Bell – and we've heard all about Mr. Popularity, who thinks he's better than everyone else. Whatever Harrison said to this other kid was totally harmless – ALL BOYS TALK THAT WAY.

Ms. Oliver cordially responded by describing several of the interventions Harrison's teachers had used to help him become acclimated to the new school, and the district's expectations regarding the students' emotional well-being, and requisite social skills. She described a "what-if" coaching intervention the teachers used periodically with the students just before they went outside for recess. In this exercise, the teachers depicted "what-if scenarios" that inspired the students to explain how they would make good choices on the playground. The Cleevers seemed less than impressed with the principal's explanation of her teachers' perspectives on student discipline. They ended the meeting insisting it was the other kid who needed to be reprimanded, and requesting that Zach Bell be moved to another classroom, or at least to a different recess period.

A few days passed before Ms. and Mr. Bell had time to come in and meet with the principal. In that brief time span, Harrison was heard being verbally abusive toward Zach, while the two boys were walking into the building from the bus zone. When Principal Oliver finally met with Zach's parents to discuss the earlier hallway incident, she was delighted when they took the high road, and agreed to support her teachers' and staff members' classroom management strategies. That said, while they expressed a willingness to assist their youngest son to make wise choices, and handle difficult issues more calmly, Zach's parents voiced their ongoing concerns about Harrison Cleever's heavy-handed mannerisms. It was apparent to Ms. Oliver the Bells remained apprehensive about their child's safety.

Over the next several weeks, Principal Oliver made drop-in visits to the boys' classes on an almost daily basis. She continually checked in with their teachers and the playground paraprofessionals in an effort to keep close tabs on Harrison and Zach. Judith was pleased to observe both boys doing well academically, but dismayed to learn about the tension that seemingly filled the space whenever they were near each other. In early March, Harrison threw his baseball bat at Zach during a quick game while at recess. Zach was the pitcher and had struck Harrison out to end the game, which caused him to react in an objectionable manner. The bat did not hit Zach, but the playground monitor found it necessary within the Code of Conduct to report the incident to Ms. Oliver.

The principal subsequently followed policy and issued Harrison a week-long recess detention for being physically abusive toward another person during school hours. In a decisive effort to avoid the need to eventually issue an out-of-school suspension to either Harrison or Zach, Judith next determined it would be best to separate the two boys during the recess period. And, while Harrison subsequently remained in the same 4th grade classroom, the principal switched him to a different recess period when he completed his detention.

4.2   Questions to Ponder

1. Did Principal Judith Oliver make the correct ethical decision by moving Harrison to a different recess period? Explain your reasoning.
2. What additional actions should she take moving forward?
3. Can you identify any ethical considerations she should be taking into account while attempting to resolve this case?
4. How will her decisions impact the persons involved (e.g. Harrison, Zach, family members, teachers, students, other school employees)?

4.3   What Actually Occurred?

When Principal Oliver informed Harrison about her decision to move him to a different recess period for the remainder of the year, he angrily responded "So that's it! Zach wins and I lose!" Mr. and Ms. Cleever went to the Assistant Superintendent to complain about Ms. Oliver's unfair treatment of their son, noting that she "always showed favoritism to the more popular kids in the school." Mr. Bell called the principal to express the lingering concerns he and his wife had regarding their son's safety during school hours. Judith did what she could to assuage his fears by reminding him that the two boys rarely had physical or verbal altercations during class times, and their disagreements had typically occurred on the playground during their recess activities.

Moving forward, Principal Oliver provided Harrison's teachers with ideas regarding new ways they might be able to ensure the young man would be accepted by his classmates. For example, Judith knew Harrison enjoyed science, and suggested he be given leadership responsibilities within the school's Makerspace™ facility. Teachers were encouraged to continually remind all students that derogatory statements and insults were not acceptable, and would not be tolerated. She provided a list of community resources to the Cleevers, encouraging them to find additional ways beyond the soccer league for Harrison to meet and interact with other children his age. Ms. Oliver scheduled Harrison to have a few meetings with the school social worker, wherein they set goals in preparation for him to enter the 5th grade.

Ironically, during the summer following 4th grade, Zach Bell joined a Junior Golf League and found himself teamed up with Harrison Cleever for several matches. Harrison was a slightly better golfer, and actually enjoyed teaching Zach some new techniques on the course. Even still, Harrison's domineering behaviors did not go unnoticed by the more gregarious Zach – he simply tolerated his teammate's bossy instructions to keep the peace.

Zach and Harrison were placed in different 5th grade homerooms, but did end up having the same recess period together. The playground paraprofessionals anticipated they'd see more of the same competitive/aggressive behaviors when the two boys were engaged in the same game or activity during recess. For the most part though, Zach skillfully found ways to manage and even diffuse Harrison's offensive statements. Along the way, Harrison eventually became more reflective as he realized Zach didn't really pose a threat to him, either socially or academically.

Principal Oliver credits the teachers and professional staff members for their creative and collaborative strategies that led to these generally positive outcomes. The Cleevers and the Bells remained fully engaged in their sons' educational programming, and their extracurricular activities throughout the year. It never became necessary to suspend either of the boys, and Judith believed both were well prepared to move on, and be successful in middle school. No, the two boys did not become friends per se, but each matured, and developed his own brand of adaptive social skills.

4.4   Follow-up Questions

1.   To what extent did Principal Judith Oliver demonstrate (or fail to demonstrate) the selected leadership competencies identified above for PSEL #7 – *Professional Community for Teachers and Staff*?
2.   2. How do you think Ms. Oliver's leadership approach may have changed if the teachers were not able (or willing) to implement the classroom management strategies she proposed?

Notes

1   Contributing author: Frederik Ahlgrimm, Ph.D.
2   EDTC is also a pseudonym.

Meaningful Engagement of Families and Community

1   I Love My Kids

PSEL – Standard 8: Effective educational leaders engage families and the community in meaningful, reciprocal, and mutually beneficial ways to promote each student's academic success and well-being.

Selected Elements:
8b – Create and sustain positive, collaborative, and productive relationships with families and the community for the benefit of students.
8c – Engage in regular and open two-way communication with families and the community about the school, students, needs, problems and accomplishments.
8e – Create means for the school community to partner with families to support student learning in and out of school.
8h – Advocate for the school and district, and for the importance of education and student needs and priorities to families and the community.

1.1   *The Story*

Principal Noelle Hartwick was a few months into her sixth year at a suburban elementary school, when a series of events occurred that required her to make a critical decision on behalf of two students in her building who she had come to know quite well. Mrs. Hartwick's K–6 school is located in a suburban district, enrolls approximately 445 students, and employs 38 teachers. When Noelle was first appointed as the building principal, Justin Tellior was in 1st grade and his sister Julia was in Kindergarten. Both children were fairly quiet, seemed well-adjusted, and attended school regularly. While both students had already begun to establish friendships, Julia's social network was a bit broader than her brother's. As Mrs. Hartwick actively engaged with families and community members throughout her first couple of years, she noted both the children's parents regularly attended school functions, and participated fully in teacher conferences. Through ongoing two-way communication, the principal

© KONINKLIJKE BRILL NV, LEIDEN, 2020 | DOI: 10.1163/9789004436862_009

eventually learned that the family lived within a few blocks of the school, and the children's maternal grandmother shared their residence.

It was during the year Justin had entered the 3rd grade Principal Hartwick began to notice significant changes in the dynamics of his family and home environment. While his sister Julia, now in 2nd grade, continued to enjoy coming to school each day, Justin's attendance became increasingly erratic. Justin regularly missed school for several days at a time prompting Mrs. Hartwick to contact family members to determine the reasons for his many absences. Both the mother, and occasionally the grandmother offered tenable explanations – he has allergies, not sleeping well, feeling sick to his stomach – as to why Justin was missing school.

The principal next learned that a neighbor had contacted Child Protective Services (CPS) to report he suspected Mr. Tellior had begun to treat his son "quite roughly, and a bit too often." A local CPS caseworker visited the Telliors' residence and determined there was no immediate threat to the son's life or health. This was to become the first of several visits a representative from the CPS unit would make to the home of Justin and Julia Tellior, more than one of which was necessitated by reports filed by members of Mrs. Hartwick's professional staff.

Justin and Julia's father moved out of their home and took up residence in a nearby town outside the school district the following year. It was unclear if their parents had filed for and obtained a legal separation agreement. Throughout his 4th grade, the school psychologist and school counselor met with Justin on a regular basis. While he never displayed any noticeable trauma behaviors, they noted his general disinterest in his class work, and the pattern of missing school had not subsided. They also learned he disliked going to visit his father on weekends. Julia continued to be engaged with her classmates and rarely, if ever, missed school. Principal Hartwick monitored Mrs. Tellior's participation in school functions, during which she observed her to be a mom who loved her kids, and wanted the best for them in spite of the unstable home environment.

During Justin's 5th grade year, his mother started to exhibit very obvious signs of addiction. Office personnel noticed the smell of alcohol on her breath several times when she dropped her children off at school. A CPS caseworker became involved again when Justin's lack of attendance worsened. Principal Hartwick routinely noticed Mrs. Tellior showing up at the school with very suspicious characters in unknown vehicles; on several occasions the mother could barely walk straight as she entered the building to pick up her children. The principal contacted Mr. Tellior to encourage him to become more directly involved in the care of his son and daughter. By this time Justin was regularly seeing his father on weekends, but Julia refused to visit him. This apparently was not an issue since the parents still had not obtained and legal paperwork for custody, or visitation rights. The children's grandmother repeatedly covered for Mrs. Tellior when she was contacted by the school regarding Justin's lack of attendance.

Early in the fall of the next year (Justin is in 6th grade, Julia is in 5th grade), Principal Hartwick assembled a meeting with Mrs. Tellior and included both the school psychologist and school counselor. The purpose of the discussion was to collaboratively establish a plan to ensure Justin would start attending school all the time. It quickly became apparent Mrs. Tellior was very high on some form of narcotic – Noelle suspected heroin. The mother displayed very erratic behavior, fell off her chair, and attempted to use her cigarette case as a telephone. When pressed for an explanation, Mrs. Tellior insisted she was fine and demanded to take her daughter home at that time. The entire team watched her and Julia walk down the sidewalk toward their home. Up until this point CPS reported they did not have reason to remove the children from the home, nor could they force their mother to seek help for her addiction.

Shortly thereafter, the CPS caseworker followed up on another neighbor's report, gained access to their home, and discovered there were multiple drug users on the premises. The local police were called and the grandmother answered the door when they arrived. A couple arrests were made, but neither Mrs. Tellior nor her children were at home during this incident. Within a few days however, Mrs. Tellior was arrested for stealing cigarettes from a local convenience store.

By this time, and in the absence of any formal directives from CPS, Noelle and her team had ceased being neutral in the case, and repeatedly contacted Mr. Tellior urging him to take responsibility for his children's welfare and safety. Shortly thereafter, the children's dad called Principal Hartwick to say he was coming to pick up his son and daughter that day. Near the time of dismissal, the principal brought Justin and Julia to her conference room where Mr. Tellior was waiting for them. Together with the school psychologist, she explained to them their mom was very sick, and they would be going home with their dad. Justin agreed, but Julia immediately started crying insisting she wanted to stay with her mom, and refusing to leave with her father.

During this emotional outburst, an unknown vehicle swerved dangerously into her school's parking lot. It was driven by an individual who appeared to be under the influence of some type of drug or alcohol. Within seconds, Noelle saw Mrs. Tellior dash out of the car.

1.2   *Questions to Ponder*

1. What action(s) should Mrs. Hartwick take at this time?
2. Are there any legal issues she should be considering?
3. How will her decisions impact the persons involved (e.g. Justin & Julia, father, mother, grandmother, staff members, etc.)?

1.3   *What Actually Occurred?*

Principal Hartwick briefly left the conference room and quickly called one of her district's School Resource Officers (SRO) to come to her building and assist with an emergency. Fortuitously, the officer was nearby and arrived on the scene within minutes. Mrs. Hartwick returned to the conference room to find Julia still having a tantrum, refusing to leave with her father. She stated "I just want to go home to be with my grandma. My mom gets sick a lot, but I know she still loves me!" At this point in time, since there had been no legal agreements regarding the children's custody, the principal felt sincerely it was in their best interest to go home with their father; at the same time her heart ached for Julia who loved her mother unconditionally.

The SRO arrived and spoke directly with Mrs. Tellior in the Main Office, who kept stating over and over "I LOVE MY KIDS, and I came to bring them home with me. You have no right to prevent me from doing so!" In the midst of this commotion, Principal Hartwick and her school psychologist slipped the two children out the back door of the building, and brought them safely to their father's vehicle. Shortly thereafter, having been repeatedly coached by Mrs. Hartwick and her leadership team, Mr. Tellior filed for legal/physical custody of his son and daughter.

For the remainder of that school year the father drove Justin and Julia to school each day. Guidelines within this State's Education Law allowed Justin to finish 6th grade and attend his elementary school's graduation ceremony. Both children transferred to the school district where their father resided the following year. The mother stopped fighting for custody. She showed up at the school briefly to watch her son graduate from 6th grade. Knowing there had been additional arrest warrants out for Mrs. Tellior, Principal Hartwick made sure the SRO was present for the graduation ceremony. When the children's mother took note of the SRO's presence, she quietly left the building.

Both Julia and Justin continued to visit their grandmother. Julia maintained several of her friendships, and was therefore able to attend some of the ongoing after-school activities with her girlfriends when she visited the neighborhood. Noelle Hartwick felt confident she made the correct decision to support Justin and Julia's learning both in and out of school.

1.4   *Follow-up Questions*

1.   To what extent did Principal Noelle Hartwick demonstrate (or fail to demonstrate) the selected leadership competencies identified above for PSEL #8 – *Meaningful Engagement of Families and Community?*
2.   How might Mrs. Hartwick have handled Justin and Julia's case differently?
3.   Can you identify any ethical considerations she should be taking into account while attempting to resolve this case?

2   Don't Make Me Get on the Bus

PSEL – **Standard 8:** Effective educational leaders engage families and the community in meaningful, reciprocal, and mutually beneficial ways to promote each student's academic success and well-being.

Selected Elements:

8a – Be approachable, accessible and welcoming to families and members of the community.

8b – Create and sustain positive, collaborative, and productive relationships with families and the community for the benefit of students.

8c – Engage in regular and open two-way communication with families and the community about the school, students, needs, problems and accomplishments.

8d – Maintain a presence in the community to understand its strengths and needs, develop productive relationships, and engage its resources for the school.

8h – Advocate for the school and district, and for the importance of education and student needs and priorities to families and the community.

8j – Build and sustain productive partnerships with public and private sectors to promote school improvement and student learning.

2.1   *The Story*

When 2nd grade student Evette was placed in this urban elementary school, Dr. Florence Saunders was in her third year as principal. Principal Saunders' K–5 school enrolls approximately 346 students and employs 30 teachers. The building is located in a neighborhood where many of the children walk to school and/or are escorted by members of their family. Approximately 40% of the students take a bus to and from school each day.

As she started 2nd grade, Evette was living in a foster home located a distance from the school (approximately 10 miles) where she was required to ride the bus to and from the building. Dr. Saunders learned Evette had been recently separated from her mother, sister, brother, and grandfather. The mother had been known to cause harm to Evette, and reportedly allowed others to cause her harm. Shortly after the school year had begun, the principal became aware of Evette's emotional outbursts many of which had to do with her mother. In her seven-year old mind, Evette believed if she acted up during school, she would be allowed to see (or be with) her mother. There were a few occasions when Evette expected her mom to visit her at the school, which Dr. Saunders permitted, only to have her not show up as planned. In these instances, Evette's tantrums were the most agitated.

Dr. Saunders continually sought ways to engage in open communication with families and the community about the individualized needs of all students in her building. In so doing, she made it possible for Evette to receive visits from her grandfather at the school, and these seemed to go well for the most part. However, as the principal learned from the social worker who had been assigned to Evette's case, there were apparently a number reasons he had not been identified as an appropriate legal guardian for his granddaughter, which was why she was living in a foster home.

One of the most difficult episodes came each day when it was time for Evette to get on the bus to go home in the afternoon. Dr. Saunders noted her persistent unwillingness to board the bus, and began to wonder if the foster home environment was either unsafe or possibly causing Evette to feel traumatized while she was there. Things came to a head one chilly afternoon in November when Evette screamed over and over "DON'T MAKE ME GET ON THE BUS!!" She was eventually escorted into a seat on the bus by a member of the teaching staff, and the bus departed. Her tantrums continued to accelerate which caused the bus driver to pull over and call the police. The officers arrived and took Evette to a respite care/group home facility at a nearby Children's Hospital. In less than one day, the little second grader managed to escape from this center. She ran down the street in the freezing cold weather, and ended up at a convenience store/gas station where police officers subsequently found her. This time, concluding she was not safe at the respite care facility, they took her back to her foster care home from where she had been missing since the previous afternoon.

During the regular school day, Evette spent most of her time in the general education classroom with her 2nd grade classmates. Her teachers reported she seemed genuinely engaged in the assignments, exercises and activities, and got along well with the other students. Evette had therefore not been identified as having a learning disability. However, since her life away from this educational setting was filled with significant trauma, Evette was also assigned to spend a portion of her time each day in a self-contained K–2 classroom for children who had been identified as having emotional disabilities. This split schedule represented an ethical dilemma for Dr. Saunders – she remained unconvinced this was the most beneficial learning environment for this young girl. To confound matters more, Evette's social worker asked for the child to be reassigned stating "she'd be better served by someone younger than me, who is also African American."

2.2   *Questions to Ponder*

1.   How should Dr. Saunders proceed to address Evette's special needs?
2.   Can you identify any ethical considerations she should be taking into account while attempting to resolve this case?
3.   With whom should she consult to take actions regarding Evette's future in this school?
4.   How might her ultimate decisions impact the persons involved (e.g. Evette, her siblings, mother, grandfather, foster family, staff members, etc.)?

2.3   *What Actually Occurred?*

Principal Saunders believed it was imperative to address Evette's educational requirements as well as her social and emotional needs – both inside and outside of her school building. She knew the living situation would remain complicated for Evette, but remained determined to spearhead a multi-faceted collaborative process to do all she could to advocate for this child.

Florence's first step was to bring all of Evette's teachers together for a meeting with her and the school psychologist to identify her academic strengths, as well as those curricular areas where she may need more specialized attention. The general education classroom teachers reported Evette thrived in her art/music activities, and stated she truly enjoyed the applied math and science assignments included in the 2nd grade curricula. They noted she occasionally seemed distracted during ELA lessons, and the special education instructor who taught in the self-contained classroom made a similar observation when asked to assess Evette's reading ability and writing skills.

Dr. Saunders next contacted the Child/Family Services Association (CFSA) to have Evette's foster home reviewed. She urged persons in this office to locate Evette's younger brother Derrick, and asked them to investigate potential opportunities to bring the two children back together. Florence invited Evette's new social worker and case manager to meet with her so she could provide them with a clearer understanding of the child's academic strengths, and her needs for consistent social and emotional supports.

Within a few weeks, the CFSA secured the required paperwork to remove Evette from the current foster home, and was able to reunite her with her brother in the foster home to which he had been assigned. Ultimately this new environment proved to be far less distressing for Evette, and her slightly shorter bus rides to and from school no longer caused her intense anxiety.

Dr. Saunders structured Evette's school days for the remaining half of the year such that she had time to meet regularly with the school psychologist who was able to guide her through the transition to the new foster home environment. He also provided strategies for Evette to make the necessary social adjustments that would gradually allow her to spend her entire day in the general education classroom with her 2nd grade classmates. By the time the school year ended, Evette had achieved this goal.

Principal Saunders stayed in contact with Evette's foster family on a weekly basis throughout the summer. She provided them with a series of educational activities they could facilitate and monitor for Evette and her brother Dwight. Unfortunately, the two siblings had no further contact with their older sister or their mother during the time these events took place. Evette's case manager ensured that her new social worker was also assigned to meet regularly with her brother. When it came time for the next school year to begin, Dwight was allowed to transfer to attend 1st grade with his 3rd grade sister Evette at Dr. Saunders' school.

2.4   *Follow-up Questions*

1. To what extent did Principal Florence Saunders demonstrate (or fail to demonstrate) the selected leadership competencies identified above for PSEL #8 – *Meaningful Engagement of Families and Community?*
2. Can you describe possible interventions Dr. Saunders might have considered to improve the environment on Evette's school bus?

3   Our Son Must Have Mr. Thorwall

PSEL – **Standard 8:** Effective educational leaders engage families and the community in meaningful, reciprocal, and mutually beneficial ways to promote each student's academic success and well-being.

Selected Elements:
8a – Be approachable, accessible and welcoming to families and members of the community.

8b – Create and sustain positive, collaborative, and productive relationships with families and the community for the benefit of students.

8c – Engage in regular and open two-way communication with families and the community about the school, students, needs, problems and accomplishments.

8e – Create means for the school community to partner with families to support student learning in and out of school.

8f – Understand, value, and employ the community's cultural, social, intellectual, and political resources to promote student learning and school improvement.

8i – Advocate publicly for the needs and priorities of students, families, and the community.

3.1   *The Story*

Mr. Eric Larson has enjoyed a long tenure as principal of this suburban elementary school located in a relatively well established neighborhood, within a large school district. Having served in this capacity for seventeen years, Principal Larson has hired many of the school's 30 teachers within the last seven years, and a dozen are non-tenured. The school enrolls 400 students in grades K–4.

During the first couple years as the school's novice principal, Eric quickly learned that one of his most challenging tasks was interwoven in the annual master scheduling process. While he had learned about how master schedules were assembled during his graduate degree program in Educational Leadership, he had no idea teachers could become so confrontational and competitive when they assisted the principal with assigning students to specific classrooms as they advanced to the next grade level.

Principal Larson discovered a few scheduling traditions had evolved over the years in this seemingly quiet elementary school. First, the veteran teachers generally "claimed" the students who excelled academically, and presented few if any behavior management concerns. Conversely, the newly hired teachers were assigned to work with a disproportionately higher number of students with special needs, and those who may have demonstrated disruptive behaviors in the classroom. Third, parents or family members who served on the Parent Teacher Organization (PTO) could pretty much ask for whichever teachers they wanted, and their children would then be assigned to those classrooms. Similarly, Board of Education members also expected to have their sons and daughters placed in the classrooms with the "best" teachers.

By the end of his second year as principal, Eric knew things had to change. The teachers and staff members had become comfortable with these scheduling procedures, but in no way did they represent best practice. Intrinsically, he felt a moral sense of obligation to advocate publicly for the social/emotional needs and learning priorities of the young students in his building.

Coincidentally, at about the same time, the school district's Assistant Superintendent for Elementary Curriculum & Instruction (ASECI) issued a new policy instructing her twelve elementary school principals to gradually begin implementing a new blind grouping system for assigning students to their new classrooms each year. Principal Larson immediately jumped on board, and enthusiastically introduced the proposed plan to his teachers and staff members, and informed them it would be used to create the next master schedule for their building.

Needless to say, not everyone was delighted with this significant organizational change. Some staff members were more vocal than others about all the reasons the new system would never work. On the other hand, and perhaps surprisingly, several members of the silent majority quietly expressed their support to Mr. Larson. They embraced the rationale for the new system which purported to create heterogeneous groups of students within each grade level. Whenever he was questioned about the changes, Principal Larson consistently defined three major points: (1) This approach is truly better and more equitable for all kids; (2) We are a public school where every child has an equal right to work with every teacher; and (3) All teachers are certified, and should be fully prepared to teach all students assigned to them.

During the early weeks of April in the first year implementing the new student grouping process, Mr. Larson provided guidance on an individual basis with the teams of teachers at each grade level. Given the size of this elementary school, there were generally four homeroom classes assembled per grade. Teacher teams were instructed to work collaboratively to place students into groups using the following four categories: Gender; Academic Ability (i.e., below, at, or above current grade level); Special Services Needed (e.g., ENL, AIS, Speech); and Behavior Management (i.e., concerns ranged from minimal to moderate to serious, and focused on the extent to which students were disruptive in class, and/or required additional, more intensive monitoring of their class work and assignments). After the students were sorted into these four groups, the names of the next year's teachers were randomly drawn, and then randomly assigned students until similar-size classes were created.

Interestingly, during their first time using this new system, teachers were not willing to pull the names of their other teaching colleagues out of the "hat." They expected Principal Larson to "own" the resultant assignments, and observed him draw the names and assemble the teachers' classes.

It didn't take long for parents and family members to begin calling teachers and Mr. Larson himself to request favors. In one such instance, a 4th grade teacher in a neighboring district (Pamela) called one of Mr. Larson's 2nd grade teachers (Gerard) to ask him to do what he could to ensure her daughter would be placed with a specific 3rd grade teacher the following year. As it turned out, Pamela was then teaching Gerard's twin boys and offered to return the favor by placing them with a "great" 5th grade teacher in her building. She made this request under the guise that her daughter needed a more structured classroom environment.

Mr. Larson received word through various channels that his teachers, by name, were being labeled with one or more of these descriptors: creative, strict, highly structured, competent, caring, fair, child-centered, and accessible. On a sadder note, he also heard speculations about a few teachers, also by name, who had a tendency to be: disorganized, lazy, boring, incompetent, and non-communicative. Family members and teachers alike used the more positive set of adjectives to justify reasons why they were calling to request a specific teacher for their sons or daughters. Similarly, family members were quite vocal about not wanting their children placed with those teachers who were allegedly deemed less than competent.

While Principal Larson had made it very clear that he maintained the oversight to make final changes to the class lists created via the blind grouping process, he knew it was critically important to maintain open and regular two-way communication with families, especially with regard to their children's individual learning needs. Eric also valued the collaborative and productive relationships he had begun to establish with the parents and family members during his brief tenure at this school.

One evening, a few days after the letters to parents/guardians were sent out informing them about their child's room number and teacher, Eric received a phone call from a belligerent parent who seemed quite upset about the teacher with whom his son had been placed for the following year. The parent stated with much conviction

> OUR SON MUST HAVE MR. THORWALL for 2nd grade next year! My wife and I are friends with his family, and our son plays soccer with Gerard's twin boys. We know Thorwall is the best second grade teacher in your school, and we want our son to be taught by him.

Before the principal could respond, the angry parent insisted he'd call the superintendent if his request was not honored, and abruptly ended the call.

3.2   *Questions to Ponder*

1. How should Principal Eric Larson respond to this parent's special request?
2. Can you identify any ethical considerations he should be taking into account while attempting to resolve this case?
3. With whom should he consult prior to taking actions regarding the master schedule?
4. How might his ultimate decisions impact the persons involved (e.g. students, first grade teacher team, second grade teacher team which includes Gerard Thorwall, staff members, family members, Eric himself, etc.)?

3.3   *What Actually Occurred?*

Many thoughts and ethical questions flooded through Eric Larson's mind as he sat in his family room staring at the receiver of the telephone following his brief one-way conversation with the father of one of his school's first grade students. While not a current member of the PTO, this particular parent was active in the community and owned a local pharmacy; he seemed somewhat accustomed to having decisions made in his favor. Eric knew other family members who happily volunteered their time for school functions, participated in fund raising events, and served actively in the PTO. If the occasion arose, how might he deal with their requests for specific teachers? In a different but related vein, should he feel compelled to reward his star teachers who always pulled more than their equitable share of the weight whenever he called on them to assist with special projects?

The principal also knew family members spoke to one another about the school's various teachers and staff members. The rumor mill was abundant with commentaries about which teachers were great, as well as those to be avoided. On any number of occasions Eric learned about teachers who undermined the system by telling the family members of their current students which teachers they should request for the following year. And, in those instances where his teachers enrolled their own children in his school, Eric allowed them to choose specific teachers for their sons or daughter – was this actually best for the students?

If Eric Larson moved one dissatisfied parent's child at his/her request, he'd be setting a precedent and could easily expect to receive dozens more demands from parents in the coming weeks. He decided to call the ASECI to apprise her of the situation, and let her know he'd be sending a follow-up letter to the parent. All these years ago at the end of his second year as principal, Mr. Larson held his ground and did not move the pharmacist's son into Gerard Thorwall's class.

During that year's summer professional development days, Principal Larson spent additional time with all teachers and staff members in an effort to rectify some of the issues that had plagued the implementation of the blind grouping system. He reiterated the rationale many times over, stating "it is always our goal to create heterogeneous classes that are well-balanced to benefit *both* students and staff members."

Fast forward a dozen or more years, and all stakeholders have now become more comfortable with and accustomed to using the school's grouping process. And, in the age of social media, it has become quite evident that nothing remains off the record for very long, if at all.

Principal Larson has created a Scheduling Committee consisting of teachers, special educators, and the school counselor to assist him with the process of assigning students to classes for the following academic year. With their input, very specific criteria have been established within each of the aforementioned grouping criteria (Gender, Academic Ability, Special Services, and Behavior Management). The members of this committee generally meet with the principal once or twice during the summer as last minute changes are often necessary since new students may not register until July or August.

Mr. Larson also crafted an explicit letter to parents and family members to explain the grouping process to them. The letter states very clearly that requests for specific teachers will not be accepted. However, the correspondence also encourages family members to share their concerns in writing with him, with specific reference to: (1) Their son's or daughter's learning style denoting strengths and/or limitations; (2) Essential information about their son or daughter to which teachers may not have access; and (3) A request to not place their child with a specific teacher because one of his/her siblings has already been instructed by that person. Principal Larson documents all of these concerns and shares them with the Scheduling Committee as the final assignments are made.

Now a veteran school building leader, Eric Larson continually reflects on how to maintain the sanctity of this grouping process to ensure the overall classroom experience across sections within each grade level is of consistent high quality. While there may be times when he feels strongly about placing a student with one teacher vs. another after the assignments have been completed, he makes these decisions judiciously and infrequently. The ethical questions that guide Eric in every one of these cases are these: First, who actually knows what is truly best for these kids – me or their teachers? And, perhaps more importantly, is it fair for me to expect every teacher to be competent to have any student, or are there actually situations where one match might be better or worse than another from time to time?

3.4   *Follow-up Questions*

1. To what extent did Principal Eric Larson demonstrate (or fail to demonstrate) the selected leadership competencies identified above for PSEL #8 – *Meaningful Engagement of Families and Community?*

2. As a future or practicing school leader, how might you answer the ethical questions Eric Larson has pensively posed for himself?

4   Mom Wants the Checkbook

PSEL – **Standard 8:** Effective educational leaders engage families and the community in meaningful, reciprocal, and mutually beneficial ways to promote each student's academic success and well-being.

Selected Elements:
8a – Be approachable, accessible and welcoming to families and members of the community.
8b – Create and sustain positive, collaborative, and productive relationships with families and the community for the benefit of students.
8c – Engage in regular and open two-way communication with families and the community about the school, students, needs, problems and accomplishments.
8d – Maintain a presence in the community to understand its strengths and needs, develop productive relationships, and engage its resources for the school.
8g – Develop and provide the school as a resource for families and the community.
8j – Build and sustain productive partnerships with public and private sectors to promote school improvement and student learning.

4.1   *The Story*

Although the incidents in this story occurred some time ago, the issues remain incredibly significant in the current age of unrestrained social media. Suffice to say, no school principal wants to be slandered in any public forum, especially those readily available to students, families, and community members. Dr. Bridget Estabrook had been principal of this suburban elementary school for just under two years when the members of the Parent Club came to her with an intriguing proposal. Her school, located adjacent to the District Office, enrolled approximately 600 students in grades K–5, and employed 30 teachers. A majority of the school's teaching staff was tenured, only five of whom had been hired by Bridget since her initial appointment.

The school's Parent Club (PC) had been in existence for a number of years prior to Dr. Estabrook's arrival, and it seemed to be functioning well. The group's members met on a monthly basis, and were usually joined by the principal, and two or three teachers for each session. Each meeting's agenda allowed time for the principal to give a formal report, followed by a Q&A period. These interactive sessions allowed Bridget to engage with, and be accessible to her students' family members.

The PC's primary function involved fundraising activities that would enable them to facilitate a variety of mission/vision-focused events for the school's students, families and other interested stakeholders in the district. A few examples at the time included: Wildlife & Nature Walk, Halloween Parade, Trivia Night, Holiday Toy Workshop, and Spring Community Clean-Up.

Parent members who were interested in becoming a PC Officer submitted their names to Principal Estabrook prior to their April meeting, and her administrative assistant created a ballot to be distributed for the annual election. Using a typical governance model, PC members elected their officers for staggered two-year terms each spring – the officers included president, vice president, secretary and treasurer.

At some point near the middle of Dr. Estabrook's second year, all four officers requested to meet with her to propose a new governance structure. The principal agreed to meet to hear their ideas. For a wide range of whys and wherefores, each of the PC's current officers wanted to step down. It seemed that no one wanted to serve in any position by him/herself. They subsequently proposed to allow each officer's position to be split resulting in co-presidents, co-vice presidents, and so forth. Bridget didn't see a problem with this structure, and actually thought it might work to get an even larger number of parents or family members engaged with the PC's activities. The new slate of eight officers was elected in April. Dr. Estabrook congratulated those who won, and they were inducted into their positions at the PC's final meeting in May.

During the summer, Bridget hosted these persons for an informal BBQ at her home. She wanted them to get to know her, and each other better. The principal also expected she would learn more about their personal interests and talents as well. Two of the newly elected officers had served the PC previously, but the other six individuals had never held any significant leadership roles. Over the years, all eight persons had met one another at PC events or other school functions. As it turned out, the two women who had been elected to be Co-Presidents were close friends who had lived in the same Cul de sac for eight years. Both had school-aged children – Sylvia's daughter was in 3rd grade, and Randy had twin boys who were in the 10th grade.

It was on a Monday night at the end of a three-day weekend in October that Dr. Estabrook received a frantic telephone call from Marc, one of the PC's co-treasurers. She listened as he informed her about an altercation that had occurred over the weekend between Sylvia and Randy, their husbands, and a couple of other neighbors. Marc didn't have many specific details, but he had heard through his own kids that the police had been called, and the argument had something to do with the PC's checkbook. Bridget thanked him for getting this incident on her radar, and spent the remainder of her evening reflecting on the conversations she would likely be having very soon with the PC's co-presidents.

Early the next morning (7:30 AM on Tuesday), Sylvia showed up in Principal Estabrook's office demanding to speak with her. Bridget invited her in and listened calmly as she recounted her side of the story. Sylvia wanted to do some shopping in preparation for the Halloween Parade, and apparently needed the PC's checkbook in order to do so. Randy had the checkbook, so Sylvia sent her daughter across the street to retrieve it. When Randy opened the door, Sylvia's daughter politely stated "my **MOM WANTS THE CHECKBOOK**." The young girl returned home to say Mrs. "G" had been mean to her, and told her to have your mother come over and get the checkbook herself! Feeling slightly dismayed, Sylvia went over to see Randy, and was accused of improperly using the PC's funds – and Randy therefore refused to hand the checkbook over to her!

Dr. Estabrook responded by asking Sylvia a few more clarifying questions. She then learned, in the midst of the two women's heated discussion, Randy's husband returned from his golf outing. Upon hearing their raised voices, but without even knowing the context for the disagreement, he ordered Sylvia to go home and cool off. Sylvia responded by asking him to mind his own business, and within minutes her own husband showed up in the driveway to find out what was going on. All four adults became embroiled in a heated argument over a seemingly harmless incident. Another neighbor called the local police department; two officers arrived on the scene to take a report – no arrests were made, but Sylvia's young daughter and a few of her friends witnessed the whole embarrassing event. Sylvia was visibly shaken as she concluded her story by stating "I've always been fully compliant with all of the PC's rules and procedures that govern our treasury, and it sickens me to be accused of mishandling our funds!"

Principal Estabrook thanked Sylvia for coming it to see her so promptly, and promised her she would further investigate the issue immediately. Bridget asked her administrative assistant to contact Randy Green to see if she had time to meet with her that afternoon, and to bring the PC checkbook along as well.

Randy, eager to tell her side of the story to the principal, happily agreed to re-arrange her schedule in order to come in at 2:30 PM as requested. And, for the second time that day, Dr. Estabrook listened to the other PC co-president report the weekend's unfortunate events. Randy admitted to being upset when Sylvia's daughter unexpectedly showed up at her front door on Saturday morning asking for the PC's checkbook. She stated

> I'm not handing an official document over to a child, and I'm not even sure Sylvia can be trusted to use the checkbook properly. The last time we let her purchase snacks for Trivia Night, she neglected to keep any of the receipts, so we had no record of what she actually spent!

Principal Estabrook acknowledged Randy's observations and inquired as to whether or not she, or any of the other PC officers, had discussed these concerns with Sylvia. Randy's response was a bit evasive, and Bridget inferred she had simply avoided having that difficult conversation with her close personal friend. Randy reluctantly handed the checkbook over to Dr. Estabrook and demanded to know what she was going to do next. The principal assured her she would think seriously about the best way forward, and also somewhat subtly implied the "co-president model" might not be working as well as she'd expected it would back in April.

4.2   *Questions to Ponder*
1.   What actions should Principal Bridget Estabrook take at this point?
2.   Can you identify any ethical considerations she should be taking into account while attempting to resolve this case?
3.   With whom should she consult prior to taking actions regarding the future governance for the Parent Club?
4.   How might her ultimate decisions impact the persons involved (e.g. Sylvia, Randy, PC officers, PC members, students, staff members, community agencies, Bridget herself, etc.)?

4.3   *What Actually Occurred?*
Bridget stared at the telephone on her desk as she reflected on the two emotional conversations she had encountered with the Parent Club's co-presidents. She decided to contact a couple of the other PC officers individually to determine how much they knew, or did not know, about the whole checkbook debacle. She started with Marc, the co-treasurer who had contacted her the

previous evening. He explained his reason for giving Sylvia/Randy the check-book at the start of the school year was primarily one of convenience. He requested they each inform him with specific details whenever a purchase was going to be made, and he then authorized one or the other to move forward.

Marc was one of the two "new" PC co-officers who had served in the trea-surer's role previously, and he privately shared his feelings with Dr. Estabrook about the new governance model stating, "I really had no clue as to how well this co-presidency thing was going to work!" He routinely monitored and reconciled the PC's bank account which generally had a balance of between $5,000 and $6,000, and had no reason to believe anyone had misused their funds.

Principal Estabrook next contacted Rita, one of the PC's co-vice presidents to get her perspective on this issues at hand. Rita was the other "new" PC offi-cer who had served as its president in the past. She admitted to not knowing Sylvia or Randy very well, and had remained optimistic the new slate of offi-cers would be successful in its new format. She hadn't heard about the check-book incident, but recalled the many times when she had been responsible for making PC purchases. In the past, she had spent her own money and then submitted her receipts for reimbursement by the PC's treasurer. During this conversation with Rita, Dr. Estabrook expressed her emerging reservations about having so many PC officers in place at the same time. Bridget also took the opportunity to ask Rita "off the record" if she'd be willing to step in to serve out the year as the PC's president if necessary.

That evening Bridget decided to check in with a few of her colleagues in the region to seek their advice regarding the current state of disputation in her school's Parent Club. She also consulted with the person who was Chair of the School Site Council (SSC) to determine the extent to which the PC's issues were on that group's radar. The SSC was an elected body composed of 50% teachers and 50% family members. They served as an advisory group to the principal with regard to the policies and procedures for expending funds provided to the school by the State.

By the end of the night Dr. Estabrook determined she needed to take actions that would most likely cause some hurt feelings. On Wednesday morning she contacted Sylvia directly and asked her to come in for a brief meeting. She respectfully explained her reasoning, and asked Sylvia to step down as the PC's co-president. Without hesitation, Sylvia easily agreed to Bridget's request, and stated she knew it would be in the best interest of the students and the entire school to get the PC's officers' roles back on track. When Principal Estabrook called Randy later that same morning, her response was more skeptical, but she agreed to come in that afternoon. Unfortunately, she was less amenable to

Bridget's request, but left stating "I'm reluctant to do so since I was elected to be one of the PC's co-presidents, but I will step down to make you happy."

By this time some of the students had apparently heard that a couple of parents were fighting, and several of the teachers reported hearing some "name-calling" on the playground that day. Principal Estabrook convened a special staff meeting the following morning (Thursday), and explained her reasons for asking the two women to relinquish their positions as PC co-presidents. No one seemed the least upset or worried by her decision, and everyone agreed to let the whole incident blow over.

Dr. Estabrook asked her administrative assistant to organize a meeting for her with the Parent Club's remaining six co-officers. At that point she planned to work with them to amicably re-organize the governance structure for the group. Her draft proposal entailed asking: Rita (one of the co-vice presidents) to serve out the rest of the year as president; the other co-vice president to remain as vice president; Marc (one of the co-treasurers) to serve out the year as treasurer; the other co-treasurer to step out for this year to become treasurer the following year; and the co-secretaries to determine which of them would serve out the year, and who would become secretary the following year. In Bridget's mind, these resolutions would eventually work out fine.

Unbeknownst to Dr. Estabrook, Randy and Sylvia were no longer speaking to one another; and Randy had called her husband to report "the principal had fired her as the PC's president!" Mr. Green immediately got in touch with a Board of Education member and learned they were (coincidentally) having their second October meeting that evening. Mr. Green attended that meeting and demanded time to speak out about the unfair way his wife had been mistreated by Dr. Estabrook, who by the way was not present at that meeting. On Friday morning the Superintendent appeared in Bridget's office to ask her if she'd seen the local newspaper. Her photo was featured on the front page alongside a headline that read "Principal of ABC School Fires Parent Club's President!"

Another two months passed, during which time Bridget endured several additional newspaper articles, more than one of which quoted family members who demanded she be fired. Throughout this difficult period, the Superintendent's entire administrative team and all members of the SSC stood behind her, and expressed their complete support of Dr. Estabrook's leadership decisions. Toward that end, at the first BOE meeting in November, the Superintendent had delivered the following public statement on Dr. Estabrook's behalf:

> Any time there are extra-curricular activities that impact the ongoing operation of the school, the building principal has full authority to make

decisions she/he believes are in the best interest of ALL stakeholders, especially the students.

With resilience, and always thinking the incident had been put behind her, Dr. Bridget Estabrook weathered this extended media storm. She successfully led her elementary school for another few years, at which point the Superintendent asked her to consider becoming the district's Director of Curriculum, Instruction & Innovation. She effectively took on this districtwide leadership role prior to becoming the principal of an elementary school in another school district. As Bridget reflected on this incident years later, she acknowledged to herself she may have acted too swiftly in an autocratic manner when she asked Sylvia and Randy to step down from positions they quite possibly enjoyed having. In retrospect, she realized their egos and self-esteem were damaged as a result of her somewhat impulsive decision. In fact, neither of these two parents ever spoke to her again.

If she had it to do over again, after hearing the women's stories, Dr. Estabrook would have first spoken with her superintendent for his insights and advice. She would have taken a few more days to give the Parent Club's officers time to meet with her as an entire group. Collaboratively, she would have solicited their input with regard to how well, or not well, they thought the PC was functioning at that point. Most importantly, Bridget would have given each member the opportunity to express her/his perspectives on how to make the newly devised governance model work effectively.

4.4   *Follow-up Questions*

1.   To what extent did Principal Bridget Estabrook demonstrate (or fail to demonstrate) the selected leadership competencies identified above for PSEL #8 – *Meaningful Engagement of Families and Community?*
2.   How do you think Dr. Estabrook's story may have played out differently today, within a variety of social media platforms?

Operations and Management

1 We Are Not Welcome

PSEL – Standard 9: Effective educational leaders manage school operations and resources to promote each student's academic success and well-being.

Selected Elements:
9a – Institute, manage, and monitor operations and administrative systems that promote the mission and vision of the school.
9c – Seek, acquire, and manage fiscal, physical, and other resources to support curriculum, instruction, and assessment; student learning community; professional capacity and community; and family and community engagement.
9e – Protect teachers' and other staff members' work and learning from disruption.
9f – Employ technology to improve the quality and efficiency of operations and management.
9k – Develop and administer systems for fair and equitable management of conflict among students, faculty and staff, leaders, families, and community.

1.1 *The Story*

Mr. Joaquin Norwell was in his third year as principal of a rural elementary school when the tragic mass shooting occurred at Marjory Stoneman Douglas High School in Parkland, Florida. His PK–5 school enrolls 619 students and employs 39 teachers. In the aftermath of this horrific event where 17 persons lost their lives, the superintendent of Principal Norwell's school district procured the services of a school security company that has studied the history of attacks on schools, and now provides training, preparedness plans and assessments to help school administrators be proactive against threats and attacks. Over several months, the consulting firm conducted an audit and provided a series of recommendations, several of which were quickly implemented.

It was during this consulting phase Mr. Norwell learned that his elementary school was deemed the most vulnerable building in terms of its security features. This reality was partially due to the age of the building, but mostly owing to the many traditions the elementary students' parents and family members had become accustomed to honoring over many years. For the most part, moms and dads had free access to their sons' and daughters' classrooms. They walked the school building's hallways without restrictions, and dropped in to have lunch with their kids any time they felt the need to do so. In 1st grade, the students made gingerbread houses during the month of December, and parents loved being a part of that activity. Weather permitting, Kindergarten students built snowmen, and family members eagerly participated in this outdoor event. This list of other classroom activities went on and on. Perhaps one of the greatest annual traditions was the district's Halloween parade, which ultimately became a pivotal component of this story.

During the late spring and summer, the superintendent hired two new School Resource Officers (SRO), bringing the total number to three district-wide. Funds were also allocated for a substitute SRO to be hired in the event one of the full-time staff members was absent during regular school hours. A capital project referendum was developed – it focused primarily on including more secure entrances for each of three school buildings, and making it impossible for outside visitors to reach student areas without encountering additional security. Additionally, the district proposed making it possible for classroom teachers to be able to initiate a school lockdown if necessary through using a code on an app installed on their phones.

At the start of the school year following the Parkland, Florida tragedy, the superintendent, together with her leadership team, held a community forum to discuss these changes, and the critical need to strengthen and increase security in all school buildings. New procedures for school visitors were described in great detail. She also reminded family members about a policy the Board of Education approved during the previous school year regarding the process whereby they could become approved volunteers in school buildings. Finally, she highlighted the details of the pending capital project that would come up for a vote in October.

Community members who attended were allowed to ask questions, and express any concerns they had regarding the new security policies and procedures. Many of the persons present asked questions and made statements like: "Can I still bring cupcakes in to celebrate my son's birthday with him?" And "Are we still going to have the annual Halloween parade?" And "We all want what is best for our children, but we don't want them to feel like they are entering a prison every time they come to school." And "I moved my family to this school district because I knew we'd always have access to our kids' activities both inside and outside of the classroom walls!"

During his school's professional development day for teachers in August, Principal Norwell informed his teachers and staff members about the new security procedures they would be expected to follow when the school year began. He reviewed the district's current policy regarding the background checks required for all persons who expressed an interest in being volunteers in the school. He reminded them this policy had been in place for a year, but not all families were aware of it. Joaquin also described some of the changes that would be made to the building itself after the capital project was approved; in the interim however, procedural changes were required to increase security overall. [Note: the capital project was approved by an overwhelming majority of the district's taxpayers who voted in October.]

Most teachers seemed amendable to the new practices, and many actually expressed distaste with having family members drop in to classes whenever they felt the urge. One stated "it's difficult for us to do our teaching jobs well during the school day when the kids expect their family members to join them on a regular basis!" On the flip side however, a few teachers noted they would miss having an extra set of hands in the classroom during various project-based learning activities, and a few reported "we are able to make lasting connections with those family members who spend time with their children in our classrooms."

During the first few weeks of the school year, Mr. Norwell's office staff members strictly adhered to the new security procedures, and noted several parents seemed disgruntled when they were told they couldn't escort their kids to their classrooms. They also distributed quite a few application packets to family members who expressed an interest in becoming approved volunteers. When he received a bill from the district office for the background checks that had been completed, Joaquin decided to revise the process – he instructed his office personnel to have family members schedule meetings with him to describe the reason they wanted to be approved as volunteers in his school building. This change was not received well by family members. Regardless, Principal Norwell believed they would gradually become accustomed to the new protocol.

The elementary school's Halloween parade was an event many community members looked forward to attending each year. They lined up along the village streets and watched all the young students walk the route (which spanned approximately half a mile) with their teachers, and dressed in their Halloween costumes. Prior to the year this story took place, parents often went to their children's classrooms to help them with their costumes; this practice was no longer allowed which angered some family members. On the day of the parade, the weather was quite severe and Principal Norwell made the difficult decision to move the event inside his building – doing this however made it necessary to "suspend" the new security procedures allowing hundreds of extra persons into the building to watch the children parade up and down the hallways in their costumes. This temporary return to the "way things used to be" was just enough nostalgia to rile up some of the more vocal parents.

One mother (Candace Porter) wrote a scornful letter to the superintendent and school board president stating that

> parents are very upset about the way the elementary school is being run – the principal is changing things left and right, such that we can no longer help the teachers during school functions or pass out cupcakes for our kids' birthdays!

She also expressed disgust with having to be "pre-screened by Joaquin before being able to fill out the necessary paperwork to pass the background check and be approved as a school volunteer." After sending the correspondence electronically to its addressees, Mrs. Porter posted the letter in its entirety on her public Facebook page. Within hours many other parents, alumni and community members rallied around her. They chimed in offering lots of additional criticisms of and insults directed at Joaquin Norwell. The resounding tone to the entire thread was "WE ARE NOT WELCOME, and it's time to have our voices heard!"

1.2   *Questions to Ponder*
1. What actions should Principal Norwell take at this time?
2. Can you identify any ethical considerations he should be taking into account while attempting to resolve this case?
3. How will his decisions impact the persons involved (e.g. students, family members, office personnel, teachers, Candace Porter, himself)?

1.3   *What Actually Occurred?*
Joaquin Norwell is himself an alum of the school district. His two children attend school there, and he owns a working farm with his wife who is employed as a teacher in another nearby school district. He empathized with the family members who wanted to participate in traditional school functions as they had always done, and also knew how important it was to ensure the safety and security of all individuals in his building. In his brief period in school leadership, Mr. Norwell had developed thick skin and didn't allow the

verbal attacks being posted on social media to bother him. He was however a bit frustrated by the fact Candace Porter had not taken the time to speak with him personally about her disagreement with the newly established building security protocol.

Mr. Norwell believed he had worked hard to establish positive relationships with many family members and caregivers, fully acknowledging the importance of parent and family engagement with the students' educational activities. He recognized the critical need to maintain open communication channels with all stakeholders, and sent out monthly newsletters to all of his students' families. Shortly after the Facebook incident, Joaquin called Candace Porter and invited her to meet with him. During this meeting he allowed Mrs. Porter to vent and get all of her frustrations out on the table. He patiently responded to each of her concerns and convinced her to join the building's Parent Teacher Organization. Both of them benefitted by having this discussion, and each learned a lot. For example, Candace informed him that parents rarely read his wordy newsletters, and he needed to find a better way to communicate with them. Joaquin explained the school volunteer protocol to her, and she ultimately used her Facebook page to clarify misunderstandings others had about the new procedures, and why they were necessary.

The principal decided to use the district's website to create a Facebook Live TV Show that aired on the first Friday of every month at 4:30 PM. He used the "Remind" smart phone app to invite parents and family members to send in their inquiries ahead of time about the topics he would be discussing for each show (e.g., transportation, playground structures, curricular changes, volunteer protocol). Stakeholders were also encouraged to make suggestions about issues they wanted him to discuss. Once aired, the programs were archived and indexed making it easy for families and community members to view, or review them in their entirety or one segment at a time. Essentially, Principal Norwell found a way to make far-reaching and inclusive connections with all district stakeholders on the platform they were already using and felt comfortable with.

1.4   Follow-up Questions

1.   To what extent did Principal Joaquin Norwell demonstrate (or fail to demonstrate) the selected leadership competencies identified above for PSEL #9 – *Operations and Management?*

2.   Can you think of any other resources Joaquin Norwell might have acquired to support and make positive connections with family members and community residents?

2   Standards Uphold the Status Quo

PSEL – Standard 9: Effective educational leaders manage school operations and resources to promote each student's academic success and well-being.

Selected Elements:
9a – Institute, manage, and monitor operations and administrative systems that promote the mission and vision of the school.
9b – Strategically manage staff resources, assigning and scheduling teachers and staff to roles and responsibilities that optimize their professional capacity to address each student's learning needs.
9g – Develop and maintain data and communication systems to deliver actionable information for classroom and school improvement.
9i – Develop and manage relationships with feeder and connecting schools for enrollment management and curricular and instructional articulation.
9l – Manage governance processes and internal and external politics toward achieving the school's mission and vision.

2.1   *The Story*
While the incidents in this story occurred quite some time ago, the issues remain astoundingly relevant across today's competitive and often inequitable educational landscape. Dr. Lauren Bargetto was the Founding Principal for a small magnet school in a large metropolitan center. The junior high school's mission and vision highlighted an "Arts & Academics" theme across the entire curriculum. During her tenure as the school's leader, this junior high enrolled 230 students in grades 7–8 and employed 15 teachers, all of whom were hired by Dr. Bargetto when the school first opened.

The new school was located in a neighborhood whose residents were primarily Latino and African American. The district had a junior high school choice process, wherein all elementary school students completed an application for admission. The application form allowed families to indicate their junior high school(s) of choice in rank order. Students who resided in neighboring districts could also apply for admission to these same junior high schools.

The application process for admission to Dr. Bargetto's school required parents of interested candidates to visit the school for an orientation, during which they completed an application form. The students themselves were required to spend a full day at the school, and were escorted by a current 7th or 8th grade student. During one portion of the day, students were required to take a teacher-made mathematics test, which was subsequently used for placement purposes once they were accepted. Students were also interviewed by a staff member at some point during their visit. Admission was based on the candidates' diversity in race, ethnicity and socioeconomic level, and on their expressed interest in attending the school which featured specialties in studio art, writing and mathematics.

Within a few years of opening its doors, Lauren Bargetto was proud of the diversity of her school's student body where 60% identified as persons of color, and 40% reported being Caucasian, non-Hispanic. Approximately 27% of the students' families identified as being eligible for free and/or reduced cost lunch. Additionally, more than two-thirds of all students proved to be high academic achievers as demonstrated by their outstanding performance on statewide assessments in Mathematics and ELA.

Unfortunately, the data were not as impressive for the school's African American and Latino 8th graders who opted to take a state-required standardized entrance exam for the city's prestigious, specialized academic high schools. It was known as the *Entrance Exam for Specialized Secondary Schools* (EESSS).[1]

Dr. Bargetto had actually been a student in this city's school system when the EESSS was initially approved and adopted. She then later taught English and Reading at the junior high school level for ten years, and served as a vice principal for three years prior to becoming principal of this new magnet school. Lauren was therefore well aware of the fact the EESSS was being used as a screening tool, but she did not know the extent to which affluent white students generally scored higher on this admission test than their non-white peers.

Lauren Bargetto and her teachers believed the EESSS was an inaccurate measure of their school's Latino and African American students' competencies, since many of them who did not make the cut-off scores on this test were actually quite competitive with their white peers in ELA and mathematics. In fact, they took the same classes, and scored equally well on the assignments and assessments administered within them. Knowing this, Principal Bargetto surmised the EESSS must be discriminatory. While nearly 70% of all 8th graders in this magnet school, regardless of race or socioeconomic background, scored very high on the statewide assessments, their pass rate on the EESSS ranged from about 2% for students of color, to 50% for white students. Dr. Bargetto was infuriated by these results.

Having taken her share of applied research courses and graduate level statistics classes, Dr. Bargetto knew that the same groups of test completers must score both high and low in order for standardized norm referenced tests to be considered reliable. Therefore, the consequence of reliability standards is to "UPHOLD THE STATUS QUO," which Lauren felt was also the primary purpose of these tests. As both a former English/Reading teacher and a school administrator, she had become an opponent of these types of assessments because of their inherent flaws that systematically harmed particular populations of students, especially when they were used as single gate keepers. Nonetheless, the school offered after school test preparation sessions for these exams to all students who wanted to attend. And because many students paid for test prep from a private provider, Bargetto was able to procure scholarships for some students whose families could not afford this fee.

Principal Bargetto, together with all other junior high school principals, received an official memorandum from the district office that described how students who did not score high enough on the EESSS might be able to attend a summer program to be admitted to one of the city's specialized high schools.

Junior High School principals could recommend students who scored below the cut score on the EESSS for a six-week summer program provided by each of the three specialized academic high schools. Students had to meet certain eligibility requirements to be recommended, and if they successfully completed the summer program, they were offered admission to that specific high school.

Dr. Bargetto felt she had an ethical obligation to her students to help them navigate what she and her colleagues believed to be a blatantly unethical, and socially unjust policy being used to identify students for admission to specialized high schools. Especially because these students of color demonstrated the same or better proficiency in mathematics and ELA as their white peers who consistently made the cut scores for the city's three specialized academic high schools. In essence, she felt obligated to redress the unfair, exclusionary policy that routinely denied them equitable access.

2.2   *Questions to Ponder*
1.   What actions might you take if you were Principal Lauren Bargetto?
2.   Describe additional information you might want to obtain before changing anything?
3.   What legal issues should she be considering?
4.   How do you think her decisions can impact the status quo for persons involved (e.g. students, family members, teachers, external agencies, herself)?

2.3   *What Actually Occurred?*
Lauren's school partnered with a few well known organizations that matched students to both local and out-of-state boarding schools where they received scholarships. So, while they may not have been admitted to one of the city's specialized high schools by virtue of their EESSS scores, they received access

to an education equivalent to or better than the specialized high schools for which they did not make the cut scores. Dr. Bargetto later learned several of these students ultimately earned scholarships to attend Ivy League Colleges.

Principal Bargetto met individually with those students who scored within the acceptable range below the EESSS's cut score to inform them about the six-week summer program that would enable them to become eligible for admission to a specialized high school. She asked them if they were interested in attending. If they said yes, and nearly all did, she next had to determine if they met the "disadvantaged" criteria established by the program's providers. The criterion regarding "free and/or reduced lunch" was the only one that might apply. As noted above, many of the school's families did not qualify for this service. In these cases, Dr. Bargetto advised the student's parents:

> If they completed the Title One form indicating an income level required for free or reduced lunch, she could submit a corresponding application for their child to attend the specialized high school's summer program.

This practice continued for nearly four years during which dozens of well qualified students of color were admitted to and graduated from specialized high schools. Lauren Bargetto felt obligated to follow her moral compass to help her students gain access to something, that in her view they had demonstrated capacity for, but due to an unfair and erroneously enforced policy had systematically been denied. While she might not be able to truly level the playing field for all junior high school students, she did what she could to at least give those students in her care a fair shake. Dr. Bargetto is disgusted to see the same erroneous and discriminatory policy of using a single test score to make a high stakes decision still in effect three decades later, but remains cautiously optimistic there will be ongoing public discourse about it, and intentional discussion about change in the near future.

2.4   Follow-up Questions

1. To what extent did Principal Lauren Bargetto demonstrate (or fail to demonstrate) the selected leadership competencies identified above for PSEL #9 – *Operations and Management?*
2. Describe ways you believe, or do not believe, standards have proven to uphold the status quo during your own experiences in leadership and/ or teaching.

3. Can you identify any ethical considerations she should be taking into account while attempting to resolve this case?

4. What more could Dr. Bargetto have done to take on an advocacy role beyond her building, especially at the state level, to provide more equitable access to specialized programs?

3   Mathematically Speaking, It Was Beautiful

PSEL – Standard 9: Effective educational leaders manage school operations and resources to promote each student's academic success and well-being.

Selected Elements:

9b – Strategically manage staff resources, assigning and scheduling teachers and staff to roles and responsibilities that optimize their professional capacity to address each student's learning needs.

9d – Are responsible, ethical, and accountable stewards of the school's monetary and non-monetary resources, engaging in effective budgeting and accounting practices.

9f – Employ technology to improve the quality and efficiency of operations and management.

9 g – Develop and maintain data and communication systems to deliver actionable information for classroom and school improvement.

9h – Know, comply with, and help the school community understand local, state, and federal laws, rights, policies, and regulations so as to promote student success.

9i – Develop and manage relationships with feeder and connecting schools for enrollment management and curricular and instructional articulation.

9j – Develop and manage productive relationships with the central office and school board.

3.1   *The Story*

Dr. Marisol Sastre was appointed to be the Mathematics Department Chair of a large suburban high school when it was first opened nearly twenty years ago. She served in that role for seven years before being appointed as one of the schools four Assistant Principals (AP), a position she has now held for ten years. The high school enrolls approximately 4800 students in grades 9–12. The four APs report to Kris Lindeman, Executive Principal, who has held this position since the school opened. Dr. Sastre enjoys Mr. Lindeman's distributive leadership style, as he empowers all members of his leadership team to bring new ideas to the table, and trusts them to carry out tasks he assigns to them with skill and fidelity.

When the high school opened, the leadership team designed and implemented a master schedule where students completed four courses in the fall, and then completed four new courses in the spring. Final exams and Advanced Placement (AP) exams were all administered at the end of the school year. Therefore, in cases where students might require continuity of exposure to the content (especially mathematics), alternative schedules were devised so students could take two classes in sequence, such as Honors Math in the fall and AP Math in the spring.

This basic 4 × 4 schedule was fiscally sound, and had been working well for nearly fifteen years. Further, in an environment where physical space was limited, the school was still able to accommodate a huge testing schedule that began in May and ran through the end of the school year. A complex combination of locally designed, course-embedded final exams, State Assessments, Advanced Placement, and Cambridge (AICE – Advanced International Certificate of Education) Exams were administered in this location annually. In other words, Dr. Sastre had been influential in creating an efficient schedule where secondary students from across the county sat for approximately 20,000 exams over a three-week period near the end of each academic year.

At some point in late April that year, Principal Lindeman informed his leadership team that the District Office (DO) had enacted a new policy requiring all of its high schools to implement a new master schedule where all students would complete seven courses that spanned the entire school year. The new district-wide schedule was slated to go into effect at the start of the next school year, at which point each class was required to be 50 minutes in duration, and students needed at least 30 minutes for lunch each day.

Given the size of this high school, four lunch periods were required to feed the students in a safe and efficient manner. Knowing the shift from a "4 × 4 block" schedule to a "straight 7 period" schedule would be a challenge on many fronts, Kris Lindeman authorized Dr. Sastre to lead this master scheduling transition effort.

Marisol was a true problem solver, and had easily worked with various stakeholders over the years to ensure all voices were heard before a resolution to any problem was reached. She recognized her colleagues were counting on her to propose a scheduling solution that would bring their high school into compliance with the DO's directive within a matter of weeks before everyone departed for the summer break. And, to make matters more provocative, the mammoth testing schedule was just around the corner.

Dr. Sastre sat in the conference room, and stared at the partially completed 4 x 4 block schedule displayed on the wall – the one she and others had already been working on for next year, and one all teachers and staff members had grown accustomed to over many years. The Assistant Principal opened her laptop computer, and examined a few scheduling algorithms as she pondered the leadership challenge Principal Lindeman had handed to her.

3.2   *Questions to Ponder*

1.   What course of action should Assistant Principal Sastre take to get this mandated initiative underway?
2.   With whom does she need to consult as she outlines the new master schedule?
3.   What sorts of budgeting or resource allocation policies should she should be considering?
4.   How will her proposed actions impact the persons involved (e.g. students, teachers, staff members, family members, office personnel, leadership team)?

3.3   *What Actually Occurred?*

Since she had worked with a majority of the high school teachers and school counselors for many years, Dr. Sastre knew which persons most needed to be included in these initial discussions about the imminent shift to the new class schedule. She also recognized the group would need to work efficiently given the constraints of the upcoming testing schedule, combined with the normal end-of-year duties to which everyone had to attend.

Marisol met first (in person) with the members of the School Counseling staff to alert them about the DO's expectations regarding a revised master schedule, and asked them to make room in their schedules to be able to participate in a series of discussions about proposed solutions over the next two weeks. Dr. Sastre then contacted the heads of all academic departments (via electronic mail) to essentially inform them about the forthcoming shift away from the 4 × 4 block schedule, and invited all to select one or two teachers from their departments to join her and provide input to the team's dialog as time permitted. She prompted them to be certain to include perspectives from those who regularly taught Honors or AP courses, as well as other specialized elective offerings.

Other operational considerations came to mind as Assistant Principal Sastre moved through the planning phase for this significant organizational change for her high school. The Director of Food Service had to be consulted since the lunch periods would likely be impacted by the revised schedule. The DO's new mandate would only fit two 30-minute lunch periods and seven 50-minute classes in the daily schedule. Dr. Sastre knew it would be impossible for the cafeteria to safely handle feeding 2400 students during each lunch.

The high school also had a Junior/Senior Privilege Option which allowed upper classmen who had maintained high GPAs to come in later or depart earlier each day. On an annual basis, 550 or more students were generally eligible to take advantage of this opportunity for increased flexibility in their class schedules.

Following a series of productive discussions with key stakeholders, Dr. Sastre ultimately employed a statistical model that proved it possible to "post" class schedules to a variation of the DO's proposed seven period schedule. She created eight equal 50-minute periods each day – a simulation which demanded a slightly shorter passing time between periods for students to change classes. Periods 3, 4, 5 and 6 were designated to be the four lunch sessions, and each ran for 50 minutes, as opposed to the four 30-minute blocks in the previous 4 × 4 schedule. Members of the School Counseling staff concurred with Marisol, acknowledging that students might make use of the extra time during "lunch" to make appointments to meet with them as necessary.

MATHEMATICALLY SPEAKING, IT WAS BEAUTIFUL, and Dr. Sastre presented the proposal to Principal Lindeman. He endorsed it and submitted it to the DO for review well in advance of the Superintendent's requested due date. It was ultimately approved by the Board of Education, and received a decent level of community support as well. Teachers and staff members were given professional development hours over the summer to revise their curricula and instructional strategies as required to deliver course content within the newly designed schedule.

While the schedule met the DO's mandated criteria, and may have been "mathematically beautiful," it was "operationally unappealing."

Students had gotten comfortable with taking four different courses each term. Many therefore found it a struggle to keep up with attending, and completing assignments/homework for seven different courses each day, every day. Teachers complained about feeling stretched to the max as they regularly ran short of time to teach lessons, introduce project-based assignments, or facilitate small group activities within the shorter class periods. Teachers and support staff members found themselves with modified, somewhat shorter, planning periods in order to accommodate the lengthier lunch sessions in the middle of the day, every day. Students on the other hand appreciated the longer, more leisurely lunch sessions, and there were no significant changes in disciplinary problems while students were eating. Nevertheless, everyone grew tired of hearing bells ringing every 50 minutes!

This eight-period master schedule remained in place in Marisol's school for three years, while the DO's seven-period schedule was employed in the other secondary buildings. All stakeholder groups managed to move forward; students graduated, assessments were administered, teachers survived, and the building's leadership team largely remained intact. Regardless, the teachers' union consistently advocated for a return to the 4 × 4 block schedule.

Eventually, the District Office heard feedback from its stakeholders, and coordinated a three-day Summer Leadership Retreat. All building principals, assistant principals, and union representatives were invited to participate. While the primary focus of this conference was "Experimentation & Innovation to Promote Comprehensive School Improvement," one full day was devoted to master scheduling challenges and opportunities. To nearly everyone's satisfaction, Dr. Sastre's high school, and most of the other high schools on the DO's "straight 7 schedule," were subsequently sanctioned to transition to a "modified A/B 4 × 4 block schedule" the following school year, and it remains that way today.

3.4   *Follow-up Questions*

1.   To what extent did Vice Principal Marisol Sastre demonstrate (or fail to demonstrate) the selected leadership competencies identified above for PSEL #9 – *Operations and Management?*

2.   Give other examples of school-based organizational changes that were initially defined to be economically practical, and then later proved to be operationally unsuccessful.

Note

1   EESSS is also a pseudonym.

CHAPTER 11

School Improvement

1   Is This a Credible Threat?

PSEL – Standard 10: Effective educational leaders act as agents of continuous improvement to promote each student's academic success and well-being.

Selected Elements:
10c – Prepare the school and the community for improvement, promoting readiness, an imperative for improvement, instilling mutual commitment and accountability, and developing the knowledge, skills and motivation to succeed in improvement.

10f – Assess and develop the capacity of staff to assess the value and applicability of emerging educational trends, and the findings of research for the school and its improvement.

10g – Develop technically appropriate systems of data collection, management, analysis, and use, connecting as needed to the district office and external partners for support in planning, implementation, monitoring, feedback, and evaluation.

10i – Manage uncertainty, risk, competing initiatives, and politics of change with courage and perseverance, providing support and encouragement, and openly communicating the need for, process for, and outcomes of improvement efforts.

10j – Develop and promote leadership among teachers and staff for inquiry, experimentation and innovation, and initiating and implementing improvement.

1.1   *The Story*

Dr. Victor Lancaster had been principal of a suburban high school for nine years when the following events occurred. Prior to this appointment, Dr. Lancaster had served as an assistant principal in the same building. The school enrolls approximately 1400 students in grades 9–12, and employs 70 teachers, many of whom were hired by Principal Lancaster. An athletic director, two assistant principals, dean of students, two school psychologists, and four school counselors report to Dr. Lancaster. It was early one Wednesday morning in February when the principal, assistant principal, dean of students, and

© KONINKLIJKE BRILL NV, LEIDEN, 2020 | DOI: 10.1163/9789004436862_011

the principal's administrative assistant received a extremely disturbing email message.

For this secondary building, the school day begins at 8:10 AM, and teachers report at 7:50 AM. Principal Lancaster is typically in his office by 7:00 AM each day, and his administrative assistant likes to be at her desk not later than 7:30 AM. While Dr. Lancaster was out of the office making drop-in visits to those teachers who had arrived early to get their classrooms organized, he received an urgent text message from his administrative assistant at 7:32 AM. She informed him that she, and three others, had received an email message from someone threatening to "shoot up the entire (expletive!!) high school."

Dr. Lancaster immediately accessed his email account on his mobile phone, and read the ominous message as he raced back to the Main Office complex. While reading the threatening language, he called to mind the school district's crisis management plan that had been in place for the past five years. He knew the members of his leadership team were familiar with the actions to be taken should a crisis occur. Additionally, all teachers had received authentic training with regard to their duties and responsibilities in the midst of unforeseen, dangerous events that might occur during the school day.

The sender had used a non-recognizable email address, and the subject line read *Geeks Will Die Today*. The offender's statement mentioned the 1999 Columbine High School massacre, noting "If you think that shooting was bad, you haven't seen nothing. There will be much blood on the floors of your (expletive!!) building, and many more kids will die violently. Call the police all you want, but you cannot stop these killings from happening today."

By the time Victor returned to the office (7:35 AM), members of his leadership team had also read the email message, and were prepared to follow his lead to set the crisis management plan in motion. While each person, in her or his own way was wondering, **IS THIS A CREDIBLE THREAT?**, they collectively knew time was of the essence given the severity of the sender's message.

Per the district's plan, at 7:37 AM, Principal Lancaster contacted the local police department to inform them about the impending situation. Simultaneously, the assistant principal contacted the superintendent's office to apprise its staff members of the events that were about to unfold in the high school. The superintendent had begun her third term in the district at that point, and fully trusted all of the school building leaders to follow the crisis management plan with fidelity.

At 7:40 AM, Dr. Lancaster's administrative assistant sent a text message to all staff members informing them to shelter in place as the building was in a lock-down. Other members of the principal's leadership team dispersed to their assigned locations in the building to ensure teachers and any students who had already arrived were following the shelter in place directive. The team estimated there to be 20 or so teachers inside, along with perhaps 125–150 students gathered in classrooms, and the library. All had been trained to barricade themselves away from any potential intruders. Those teachers who were still en route, and had not yet entered the building, received the warning message, and followed the district's plan to move to the pre-designated safe location in the vicinity.

While waiting for the law enforcement team to arrive, and knowing some parents were dropping off students, at 7:42 AM Principal Lancaster was stationed at the main entrance where he calmly welcomed the newly arriving students, and then quickly instructed them where to go for the lock-down. Since the parking lot had not yet been barricaded, the principal determined it was not practical, and quite possibly unsafe, to send students back out to their parents' departing vehicles.

A staff member in the District Office remained in constant contact with the high school's assistant principal. By 7:45 AM, the Director of Public Relations (DPR) had handled the transportation logistics, and efficiently diverted the school buses to the pre-determined location in the district, thus allowing most students to wait securely in another building, located a good distance away from the high school. The DPR also sent a text message to all upperclassmen who drove themselves to school, instructing them to convene at the same location, to wait with the students who rode the bus each day.

At 7:46 AM, the team of police officers arrived on the scene. The parking lot was barricaded, and other measures were taken to secure the high school campus' perimeter. At 7:57 AM, the law enforcement team began its methodical search (internal and external) of the entire building.

By this time however, many nervous students had already used their mobile phones to contact their parents, and it didn't take long for these family members to return to the high school thinking they could somehow retrieve their sons and daughters. A huge number of cars parked along the roadway bordering the high school's grounds, and, despite the cold weather, several adults began clamoring for their students to be released.

Inside the building, the classroom teachers did their best to keep students calm, but tensions were mounting. Being isolated in these rooms without knowing if there was an armed intruder in the building was cause for great anxiety. Staff members and students alike also worried there might be some type of explosive device in the facility. No one knew how long the lock-down would remain in effect, and they hated not having access to information.

At 8:02 AM, news reporters from the local television station joined the large cluster of family members just outside the high school campus. Mixed messages about the offender's threatening email communication were already circulating throughout various social media channels.

1.2 *Questions to Ponder*

1. What further actions might you take if you were Principal Victor Lancaster?
2. To whom do you believe Dr. Lancaster is primarily accountable at this point?
3. What legal issues should he be considering?
4. How do you think his decisions might impact the various stakeholders (e.g. students, family members, teachers, staff members, administration, community at large, etc.)?

1.3 *What Actually Occurred?*

Dr. Lancaster knew he was responsible for the safety and well-being of all persons who were in the school building, and his unflappable demeanor camouflaged his inner fears as he remained in contact with the leader of the law enforcement team who was directing the search. Per the district's plan, the dean of students had contacted the local hospital alerting them of potential injuries. The assistant principal continued to provide updates to the superintendent and her staff members as the search continued. Approximately every fifteen minutes, the principal's administrative assistant continued to send group text messages to the custodians, cafeteria workers, librarians, and classroom teachers, keeping them updated about the progress of the police team's search – and the lock-down continued.

At about 8:10 AM the DPR communicated with parents and family members via social media, email, text and automated voice messages. To the extent possible at that time, the District Office provided information about the police-led search underway, assured family members that all precautions for their children's safety were being taken, and instructed them to stay away from the building until which time it was declared to be clear of any danger. These communications also requested family members to refrain from making repeated telephone calls to the Main Office as it was essential to keep these lines open during the emergency.

Still in crisis plan management mode, and uncertain about how long the search would take, at 9:15 AM Dr. Lancaster determined it was necessary to cancel the high school's classes for that day. He informed the superintendent, and she supported his decision. Buses were sent back to the location where most of the high school students were being retained, and those individuals were transported home.

The law enforcement team worked for more than three hours, fastidiously moving from room to room, and ultimately declared the building to be "all clear" just after 11:30 AM. Regardless of the fact no suspect(s) had been found in or near the high school, the police officers determined the threat was not imminent. Buses were directed back to the high school, family members were allowed to follow protocol to pick up their sons/daughters, and upperclassmen were given permission to drive themselves home. Teachers and staff members were sent home at 12:15 PM, and Dr. Lancaster's administrative team remained in the office to debrief with one another about the morning's difficult events.

Several topics were placed on the table as Victor facilitated the discussion; these four items were among others on the list: (1) Should the varsity basketball game scheduled for that evening go on as planned? (2) How should they prepare for the possibility of copy-cat threats in the days ahead? (3) Should classes be canceled on the following days? And (4) What additional precautions should be put in place to address students' and staff members' anxieties in the days and weeks ahead?

In consultation with the superintendent, Dr. Lancaster concluded it was important to send a message of unity and resilience to the community, and they decided to allow the varsity basketball game to be played as scheduled. Additional law enforcement personnel were called in to monitor the evening's sporting event. Classes were not canceled for the remainder of the week, but a number of families did not send their students to school – attendance was down by approximately 10–15% on Thursday and Friday. Principal Lancaster reached out to several community wellness clinics, and they provided mental health counselors to be available for students to speak with during school hours.

Victor devoted many hours to communicating personally with parents and family members throughout the days immediately following the crisis. He remained accountable to all stakeholders, responded to each and every request for information, and agreed to meet with all family members who asked to see him in person.

The local law enforcement agency collaborated with the FBI over the next few days, and the alleged suspect who made this serious threat was ultimately found, and taken into custody by the end of the weekend. The person who was eventually found guilty of this serious crime, was actually one of the high school's own 11th grade students. The district's Legal Counsel guided the superintendent's actions to provide confidentiality and due process for the juvenile offender who gravely violated the school's Code of Conduct.

The student received the maximum consequence for these egregious actions, and was summarily expelled from the high school. The district's administrative team deemed it essential to send this decisive message to the community, indicating its cohesive desire to act as agents of continuous improvement to promote academic success and well-being for all students.

1.4   *Follow-up Questions*

1.   To what extent did Principal Victor Lancaster demonstrate (or fail to demonstrate) the selected leadership competencies identified above for PSEL #10 – *School Improvement?*
2.   Which, if any, of the actions taken by Dr. Lancaster during this crisis did you question? And why were these decisions of concern to you?

2   It's Always about the Money

PSEL – Standard 10: Effective educational leaders act as agents of continuous improvement to promote each student's academic success and well-being.

Selected Elements:
10a – Seek to make school more effective for each student, teachers and staff, families, and the community.
10b – Use methods of continuous improvement to achieve the vision, fulfill the mission, and promote the core values of the school.
10d – Engage others in an ongoing process of evidence-based inquiry, learning, strategic goal setting, planning, implementation, and evaluation for continuous school and classroom improvement.
10e – Employ situationally-appropriate strategies for improvement, including transformational and incremental, adaptive approaches and attention to different phases of implementation.
10h – Adopt a systems perspective and promote coherence among improvement efforts and all aspects of school organization, programs, and services.
10i – Manage uncertainty, risk, competing initiatives, and politics of change with courage and perseverance, providing support and encouragement, and openly communicating the need for, process for, and outcomes of improvement efforts.
10j – Develop and promote leadership among teachers and staff for inquiry, experimentation and innovation, and initiating and implementing improvement.

2.1   *The Story*

While the nature of this final story is slightly different from others recounted in this collection, it truly highlights the many challenges educational leaders confront on a daily basis in their efforts to initiate positive change for continuous improvement in their schools. Similar to others presented thus far however, this school leader did recount a serious dilemma she confronted – one that potentially threatened the financial stability of her school. Dr. Regina Angelis was the Founding Principal for a small international school located in the capital city of a small island country. She oversaw the school for nearly three decades, and described her leadership journey as a consummate, unmitigated labor of love.

At its inception, the school enrolled students in the primary grades (K–6), and also included a pre-school program for 2- and 3-year old children. Approximately ten years into her tenure as the building's leader, Dr. Angelis' school expanded to include the secondary grades 7 through 13. Students in the highest grades were given an opportunity to complete the International General Certificate of Secondary Education. At its largest, the school enrolled 250 students and employed 45 teachers and professional staff members, all of whom were recruited and hired by Regina Angelis and her Director of Operations.

The school's mission statement highlights the importance of understanding the relationships between happiness, confidence and learning for all students, through the delivery of an international, culturally rich and diverse curriculum. At all grade levels, students are encouraged to undertake their own journeys of personal growth, creativity, discovery, and innovative thinking.

Principal Angelis is extremely proud of the highly supportive culture, and the multi-cultural, multi-lingual learning environment she and her team of dedicated staff members have fostered in the school over the years. In addition to its comprehensive array of academic offerings based on the British National Curriculum, the school's staff members also provide extensive pastoral care for their students. All teachers and support staff members have open, developmentally appropriate dialogue with their students to educate them about what is right, and what is wrong. As often as possible, students are given opportunities to reflect on what it means to act maturely in a responsible and mutually respectful manner.

Dr. Angelis knew her staff members felt ownership in the mission, vision and core values of their school, and truly believed they all loved coming to work each day. While she couldn't always afford to raise their salaries at the same rate as other schools in the region, Regina did what she could to keep the size of their classes relatively low (i.e., maximum of 12 in the pre-school classes, and 15–18 in the primary and secondary grades). Teachers have always been given a high degree of autonomy to experiment with pedagogical strategies, and encouraged to investigate alternative ways of covering curricular content. They reportedly felt a strong sense of "familial-like" togetherness, and therefore the school's retention rate for its employees remained quite high.

The principal's aforementioned "labor of love" refers to her inability to remember even one year when she and her Director of Operations did not have to worry about making ends meet. Regina constantly found herself balancing her intense love for educating children, with the never-ending demands of running the international school as a business. Year after year Dr. Angelis found it necessary to seek additional external funds to maintain the high quality teaching and learning facilities her school had become noted for providing. Simply stated, regardless of the topic being considered – infrastructure, curricula, faculty qualifications, or compliance with regulations – Dr. Regina Angelis will tell you "IT'S ALWAYS ABOUT THE MONEY."

In the midst of one of many budgetary-focused sessions, and during which an ongoing dispute with the school building's landlord was under review, Dr. Angelis received a bit of disturbing news from her administrative assistant. The parents of a 2nd grade male student had just submitted an official statement accusing one of her teachers of sexual misconduct. They demanded the teacher be fired, and threatened to file a lawsuit against the school if their terms were not met immediately.

2.2   Questions to Ponder

1.   What actions might you take if you were Principal Regina Angelis?
2.   Describe the additional information you might want to obtain before contacting the parents who have made these serious allegations?
3.   What legal issues should she be considering?
4.   Can you identify any ethical considerations she should be taking into account while attempting to resolve this case?
5.   How do you think her decisive actions might impact the future reputation of her school and its stakeholders (e.g. students, family members, teachers, external agencies, alumni, herself)?

2.3   What Actually Occurred?

Dr. Angelis knew this allegation against one of the school's veteran teachers demanded her immediate attention. Regina also felt she could not afford to walk away from the meeting she was having with the school's attorney, who had been arguing their long-term case against the educational facility's landlord.

Approximately a decade earlier, after investing over a million Euros to renovate and update an abandoned office building, Dr. Angelis had moved her school to its existing location. Their international school thrived here for a couple years, at which time Regina received a notice from their landlord. He informed her that his personal circumstances had changed, and demanded they vacate their current location at the end of the following year. The school's attorney subsequently determined they were legally entitled to six more years (vs. one) to find an alternative location – one that would be suitable and still convenient for the nearly 250 families whose children were enrolled in the school. It was during the current meeting Principal Angelis' lawyer explained it was doubtful their request for an additional year on their soon to expire lease would be granted.

Later in the day, with this disappointing news weighing on her mind, Regina found time to reflect privately on the story one of her 2nd grade boys had apparently revealed to his parents. Over the years, Dr. Angelis had found that most children told her the truth about their experiences, both inside and outside of the classrooms in her school. Still, there were those occasions when students exaggerated their recollections of events, and in a few others the kids ultimately admitted to having told a lie. In all cases, the principal fully investigated the reported incidents before taking any action.

The first call Regina made was to Saul Barton, the teacher who had been accused of mistreating the young boy. He had been a primary grade teacher in her school for more than fifteen years, and she had always known him to be a dedicated and compassionate educator. Dr. Angelis invited Mr. Barton to come in for a meeting, and, despite her request being made during his summer holiday, Saul happily agreed to see her. When he arrived in the principal's office and learned the purpose of the discussion, Mr. Barton respectfully denied the student's allegation. He went on to fully explain the harmless event the student most likely recounted to his mom and dad, who then misinterpreted the young boy's story. He suggested Dr. Angelis contact the school's physical education instructor who could corroborate his statement, which she did after Saul had left her office.

What she discovered during both of these conversations was this – the 2nd grade students had completed their swimming activity, and, while in the locker room, a few of the young boys were having difficulty removing their bathing trunks; Mr. Barton and the physical education teacher simply assisted these individuals, enabling them to more efficiently and easily change back into their school uniforms and return to their classroom.

Soon thereafter, Principal Angelis contacted the young boy's parents to schedule a meeting with them. Both the mother and father showed up to speak with her and the Director of Operations the following morning. The boy's mom informed them that Mr. Barton had "pulled their son's pants down." Dr. Angelis listened to their story and followed up with her own questions, all the while reassuring them their child was safe and protected in the school. She asked the boy's parents if their son was experiencing any other anxieties at home, and/or if he had reported feeling uncomfortable in school prior to his describing this particular incident. Regina then respectfully described the clothing incident to them, as told from the two teachers' perspectives. The parents ultimately sent a written apology to both teachers, acknowledging their son's accusations had been an unfortunate misunderstanding.

This seemingly innocuous episode, though quickly resolved, is representative of the normal routine for a school building administrator. Dr. Angelis therefore never shied away from difficult conversations with her school's stakeholders, and constantly found new ways to fulfill the mission and promote the core values of this unique school. For most of her professional career, Regina Angelis had confronted the politics of change with courage and resolve. She had worked tirelessly with her staff members to manage uncertainty in order to finance competing initiatives that ultimately resulted in significant school improvements. Over the years, hundreds of alumni had written to her, and applauded the exceptional education they had received while in her care.

It was therefore with a very heavy heart that Dr. Regina Angelis informed her school's Board of Trustees that she had determined the time had come for the school to be closed. It was no longer feasible to invest millions of Euros to build a brand new campus, and new licensing would take at least two years, if not longer, to obtain from the Ministry of Education. She and her Director of Operations worked tirelessly to ensure all of the students could be faultlessly relocated to other schools in order to begin their next grade year on schedule. They also assisted all of their teachers to find positions in other schools in the region.

And, just shy of the school's 30th year of operation, its doors were closed. Dr. Angelis is now a highly sought after educational consultant who provides guidance regarding situationally-appropriate strategies for school improvement.

2.4   Follow-up Questions

1.   To what extent did Principal Regina Angelis demonstrate (or fail to demonstrate) the selected leadership competencies identified above for PSEL #10 – *School Improvement?*
2.   Describe some of the leadership traits Regina Angelis possesses that enabled her to champion the mission and vision of her school for nearly three decades.

Final Reflections

> There is no check-box for ethical leadership. It is an ongoing individual and organizational journey. Ethics in leadership is about how we hold ourselves accountable for thinking beyond our own interests.
>
> THORNTON (2013, p. 7)

∴

1　Ethical School Leadership

The American Association of School Administrators' Code of Ethics promotes twelve tenets to which all school leaders must be faithful (AASA, 2019). Primary among them, which have relevance to the case studies presented in this collection, are these four:

- Makes the education and well-being of students the fundamental value of all decision-making.
- Fulfills all professional duties with honesty and integrity, and always acts in a trustworthy and responsible manner.
- Supports the principle of due process, and protects the civil and human rights of all individuals.
- Implements [with fidelity] local, state and national laws.

As affirmed by Donlevy and Walker (2011), "Ethics pervades everything we do. As educational or public leaders we are in the people business, and ethics is embedded in that" (p. 10). Add to this idea the following opinion: "Ethical decisions must be legitimate decisions ... they should aim at worthy ends, treat people fairly and respect their rights, honor evidence and argument, and be open to debate" (Strike, 2007, p. 5). And, when it comes to ethical decision-making behavior, Johnson (2018) tells us *not* to expect perfection. He suggests leaders should "make the best choice they can after thorough deliberation, but recognize that sometimes they may have to choose between two flawed alternatives" (p. 201). The bottom line is that a leader's ethical behavior in educational settings should not be reserved solely for difficult decisions, but must permeate her/his daily actions in all settings, which will ultimately command respect and trust from all stakeholders.

Ethical educational leaders possess the confidence and capability to positively impact the actions of others, as they work to achieve a common school district mission/vision, while also ensuring respect and dignity for all students. Moreover, educational leaders have both an ethical and legal obligation to provide all students with manifold and equitable opportunities to learn, and achieve their fullest potential for academic success and social/emotional well-being. It is therefore imperative for educational leaders to uphold high moral standards. They must possess and demonstrate integrity, self-awareness, objectivity, humility and fairness in their dispositions and actions.

For a majority of the educational cases recounted in the previous chapters, readers were asked to examine the ethical considerations the principal or vice principal should be taking into account while attempting to resolve specific challenges. As should be apparent by now, ethical resolutions in educational settings must be guided by morality, and the leader's commitment to making critical choices in situations where there may not be one logical, clear cut, or correct approach.

With this in mind, by way of example, and in alignment with the above named AASA Code of Ethics, here are a few of the ethical considerations the school building leaders featured in the following case studies could potentially have been taking into account as they settled on an appropriate course of action:

Case Title: Do I Blow the Whistle? (Chapter 3, Sections 1.1–1.4)

- For many years, Principal Taft has worked very purposefully to eliminate unethical practices in her own high school building. At the same time, she has actually chosen to remain silent with regard to the same unethical practices she has witnessed in other buildings across the district. What is different about this latest incident that has pushed her over the edge to action?
- There must be conflicting messages in her mind after she learns that her summative evaluation of the new assistant principal's leadership effectiveness had been altered. While she is certain about who did this (i.e., the interim superintendent), she has no specific proof.
- She nonetheless felt seriously compelled to advocate for the young assistant principal (Max Buchanan) she had mentored.
- Her leadership integrity prevents her from telling AP Buchanan the truth about the falsified document. Should she however share her candid opinions with the Assistant Superintendent for Human Resources?
- When the Interim Superintendent subsequently made defamatory remarks about Principal Taft's abilities as a school building leader, she remained resolute and insouciant. Were these behaviors ethical given the apparent culture and climate of this school district?

Case Title: I Never Thought I was Cheating (Chapter 5, Sections 1.1–1.4)
- Vice Principal Gomez must simultaneously respect the academic freedom of the two teachers who suspect a student of plagiarism, and investigate the veracity of the students' recounting of the events surrounding their completion of the course assignment.
- Who ultimately has the authority to determine a student's grade on an assignment?
- Are the instructors themselves taking time to see alternative sides of this scenario? They both believe their assignment parameters are concise, and their grading criteria are fair.
- Although the student who was accused of plagiarizing her paper did not think she had done anything wrong, the technological evidence (e.g., time-stamp on the uploaded work) suggests otherwise. The VP therefore has an obligation to provide guidance to both her and her classmate so they will not make similar mistakes in the future.

Case Title: Do Summative Reviews Ever Make a Difference? (Chapter 7, Sections 4.1–4.4)
- Academic Assistant Principal Lenkiewicz is seemingly trying to do an honest job of completing her evaluations of the faculty members for whom she is responsible. She notes however that her reviews are somewhat more critical than those of her colleague who is also her supervisor (i.e., the Executive Principal). Should she be bringing this to his attention?
- To what extent is it ethical to connect bonus pay to the results of a teacher's evaluation report?
- Did it make logical sense for the AAP to suddenly begin making unannounced visits to Candace Turner's classroom? What message did this change in the administrator's behavior potentially send to the teacher?
- Ethically speaking, the reasons we do summative evaluations of employees include the following: provide actionable feedback; make employment decisions; improve teacher or staff member performance; document problems; comply with mandates; and, in the most serious cases, remove substandard teachers or staff members.

2   Essential Legal Guidelines

As school leaders strive to be ethical, they must also ensure their proposed resolutions are legally sound. While the purpose of this book is not to provide an overview of education law, it is essential for both prospective and practicing educational leaders to be knowledgeable of current legislative mandates and regulations that guide/direct their actions, and to which they will be held accountable.

In the United States, the Constitution's Tenth Amendment declares that most education policy is made at state and regional levels. At the federal level however, there are a few enduring education laws that define the due process rights of P–12 students. These include:

– IDEA – Individuals with Disabilities Education Act
– ADA – Americans with Disabilities Act
– Title IX of the Education Amendments of 1972
– Civil Rights Act of 1964
– FERPA – Family Educational Rights and Privacy Act

At the state level, an important piece of legislation that has prompted much attention among school leaders, along with a variety of new clauses in school districts' Codes of Conduct is:

– DASA – Dignity for All Students Act

First passed in New York State in 2012, this measure was designed to provide students with a safe and supportive environment free from discrimination, intimidation, taunting, harassment, and bullying on school property, while riding a school bus, and/or while attending a school function. There are eleven protected categories specified in this law including: race, color, weight, national origin, ethnic group, religion, religious practice, disability, sexual orientation, gender, and sex. At the time of this writing, fifteen other States and the District of Columbia had also passed legislative measures that explicitly prohibit harassment and bullying on the basis of these categories.

At both the federal and state levels, laws are revised/updated regularly, and new interpretive court decisions are decreed on a continual basis. It is therefore imperative for school districts to employ educational attorneys (either on their own, or through shared cooperative services) to assist in instances where building and/or central office administrators need accurate answers to specific legal questions.

One of the "questions to ponder" listed for a dozen of the cases presented in the previous chapters asked readers to consider the legal issues the principal or vice principal should be addressing as s/he crafted a plan of action to resolve the dilemma(s) at hand. With this in mind, by way of example, and in alignment with the above named AASA Code of Ethics, here are a few of the legal issues the school building leaders featured in the following case studies could potentially have been exploring as they devised an appropriate course of action:

Case Title: Where Have You Been? (Chapter 3, Sections 3.1–3.4)
– Principal Delgado could have provided the vice principal with a counseling memo after his first offense (i.e, unexcused absence from his work duties)?

- The counseling memo might serve a variety of purposes. It can: call the employee's attention to a breach of school policy or work performance; encourage compliance in the future; provide instruction regarding compliance; offer resources for improvement; issue a warning regarding future consequences; inform the employee that the memorandum will be placed in her/his personnel file; and alert the employee that disciplinary charges are not ruled out.
- Legally speaking, Principal Delgado's counseling memo should include this language: "Let me reiterate that the purpose of this memo is to warn you of the serious consequences of any future incident, and to instruct you as to how to avoid such problems in the future. This memo should not be construed as a formal accusation, charge, or formal disciplinary action. Neither is it intended to rule out formal disciplinary action for this incident, prior incidents, or future incidents of this nature" (Budmen, personal communication, 7 November 2019).
- Did the principal effectively engage in progressive discipline? Her supervisory efforts were not well-documented for a lengthy period of time.
- Perhaps Principal Delgado could have provided re-training opportunities or a formalized Employee Assistance Program (EAP).
- Did the principal unintentionally create a potential liability for the school district by writing him an unqualified letter of reference for a teaching position?

Case Title: We Can't Find the Error (Chapter 3, Sections 4.1–4.4)
- Principal Quincy seemed to suspect there may have been criminal conduct prior to her appointment as the building's leader. She therefore could have taken steps to contact law enforcement and follow their lead on the resultant investigation.
- While the principal believed it was unlikely, either one of the two administrative assistants could have taken the missing funds. Interestingly, one of the two women (Felicity) decided to resign from her position unexpectedly.
- The principal could have also contacted the Business Manager immediately to ask his office to conduct a background/forensic investigation in a discrete manner.
- Was the principal's assumption of ethical behavior on the part of those directly involved (i.e., the two administrative assistants) truly justified? Where does one draw the line – specifically, since only $2,500 was missing from the fundraising account, the principal believed she could make things right? Would she have felt differently if she had discovered a $5,000 or $10,000 discrepancy?

– Lydia's refusal to accompany the principal to her meeting with the Business Manager may be construed as insubordination within her role as the principal's Administrative Assistant.

Case Title: I Never Said Any of Those Things (Chapter 4, Sections 2.1–2.4)
– The health and safety of all students must be first and foremost in Principal Barnes' mind. She found Tomas in the nurse's office and spoke with him at length. Regardless of his insistence he later felt fine, sending the boy home on the bus might have created a potential liability for the school district.
– Did Principal Barnes do a thorough investigation prior to making a determination of what consequences any of the students should have received?
– The DASA legislation needs to be consulted in this case since Alex bullied Tomas.
– While Alex honestly admitted to assaulting Tomas, his consequence was not in alignment with the Code of Conduct (i.e., he received a one-day vs. the prescribed five-day suspension). The principal morally believed there were important mitigating circumstances – Alex was standing up for decency and protected another student (Garret) who was being bullied repeatedly by Tomas.
– Did the principal ensure the due process rights were afforded to all three boys?

Case Title: Not Mine, Smoking Stinks (Chapter 6, Sections 1.1–1.4)
– Principal McIntyre correctly notified the Assistant Superintendent when she first learned about the law guardian's breach of confidentiality. This unethical behavior could lead to a complaint being issued against the law guardian to the Bar Association or to the court itself.
– It's important to know that law guardians are appointed by the court, and are instructed to intervene when necessary to protect the safety and well-being of the children to whom they are assigned.
– Schools may allow them to meet with the students for whom they are responsible. Education attorneys generally advise schools to encourage the law guardians to have their meetings in their own offices, as opposed to on school property. As one might imagine, this approach may not be practical, and it may seem overly intimidating to young persons who are expected to have difficult conversations with their law guardians.
– Principal McIntyre's follow-up plan, which provides a protocol for law guardians who visit her school, may have unintentionally created an unsafe situation for students in the future. The plan prescribes a secure room with the door closed; perhaps they might consider providing a room with a window, so the law guardian is not totally alone with the student during the scheduled meeting.

In summation, my final reflections are in no way meant to suggest or imply that any one of these seven building leaders acted either unethically or illegally as they resolved serious problems in their schools. On the contrary, each one of them conscientiously followed her/his personal moral compass, which provided an avenue for advocacy on behalf of students, employees, or family members. As we have noted several times in this narrative, school leaders routinely find themselves called upon to resolve problematic situations where more than one "right" course of action seems evident. And, when all options appear to be flawed in one way or another, these educational leaders must: critically examine all pertinent data, be decisive in their actions, and above all, hold themselves accountable for the outcomes – both those anticipated and those that might be unintended. That said, I am deeply indebted to the thirty-five school leaders who came forward, and took time out of their busy schedules to share their stories with me! Absent their commitment to excellence in educational leadership, this book would not have come to fruition.

References

AASA. (2019). *Code of ethics: AASA's statement of ethics for educational leaders.* Retrieved from https://www.aasa.org/pages/templates/gsesearch.aspx?q= code%20of%20ethics

Donlevy, J. K., & Walker, K. D. (2011). *Working through ethics in education and leadership: Theory, analysis, plays, cases, poems, prose, and speeches.* Rotterdam, The Netherlands: Sense Publishers.

Johnson, C. E. (2018). *Meeting the ethical challenges of leadership: Casting light or shadow* (6th ed.). Thousand Oaks, CA: Sage Publications, Inc.

Strike, K. A. (2007). *Ethical leadership in schools: Creating community in an environment of accountability.* Thousand Oaks, CA: Corwin Press.

Thornton, L. F. (2013). *7 Lenses: Learning the principles and practices of ethical leadership.* Richmond, VA: Leading in Context LLC.

Index

Printed in the United States
By Bookmasters